30p

When the Bough Breaks

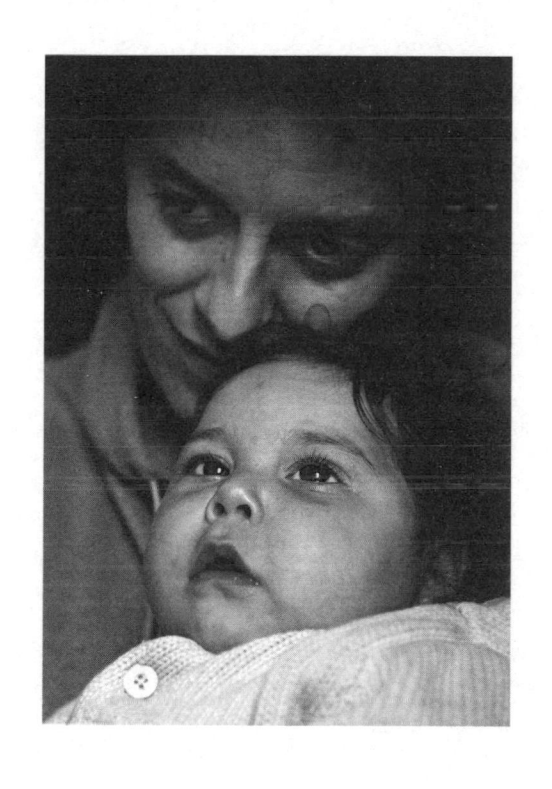

When the Bough Breaks

A Mother's Story

JULIA HOLLANDER

JOHN MURRAY

First published in Great Britain in 2008 by John Murray (Publishers)
An Hachette Livre UK company

I

© Julia Hollander 2008

The right of Julia Hollander to be identified as the Author of the Work has been asserted by her in accordance with the Copyright, Designs and Patents Act 1988.

Frontispiece photograph © David Mansell 2003

A CIP catalogue record for this title is available from the British Library

Hardback ISBN 978-0-7195-6457-4

Typeset in 10.75/13 Monotype Bembo by Servis Filmsetting Ltd, Manchester

Printed and bound by
Clays Ltd, St Ives plc

John Murray policy is to use papers that are natural, renewable and recyclable products and made from wood grown in sustainable forests. The logging and manufacturing processes are expected to conform to the environmental regulations of the country of origin.

John Murray (Publishers)
338 Euston Road
London NW1 3BH

www.johnmurray.co.uk

For my family

This is a true story, although some identities have been disguised.

And a woman who held a babe against her bosom said,
Speak to us of Children.

And he said:

Your children are not your children.
They are the sons and daughters of Life's longing for itself.
They come through you but not from you.
And though they are with you yet they belong not to you.

Khalil Gibran, *The Prophet*

Introduction

I BEGAN WRITING this story three years after it had taken place. With enough distance to make it bearable, I felt compelled to go back over what had happened. I wanted to do it for myself, for my family and for families with similar stories, now and in the future. I wanted to break some taboos.

From that period of my life, I possessed photo albums, appointment diaries, official documents and letters, and also my 'emotions journal'. I have kept such a journal at intervals since I was a teenager. Whenever important and confusing things are happening to me, the process of putting them down on the page drives me closer towards understanding them.

On opening my journal (filling three large notebooks), I was struck by the detail. My descriptions seemed amazingly vivid, many of them (in retrospect) strangely portentous. I very much wanted to use these as the basis for my memoir, but realised they would need a lot of reworking. Often the prose was fragmented, repetitive, so intimate that there was little likelihood of an outsider comprehending it. Despite the journal's length, there seemed to be huge parts of the story missing.

The more I thought about it, the more I was convinced that real life, especially one lived in extremity as mine had been at that time, was just too huge and too chaotic to be contained in a book. How then to give a true picture of what I had experienced? Clearly I would have to leave a lot out, but in doing so would I not be skewing my reality? I would have to simplify things, and yet I needed the reader to know how complicated they had been.

I do not think I have entirely solved these problems, but, in the process of writing, I have found ways round them. I have also accepted that my words and their structuring can give only a limited sense of the truth. I have come to see this memoir as one version of what happened, recalled at one particular time. Quite possibly I will read it in the future and be surprised by what I have written. I may remember things quite differently by then. For now, the writing process has fed back into my real life in surprising ways. Feelings that I had been frightened to revive have become more manageable; events that I had thought irrelevant have proved to be extremely significant.

After three years waiting for expression, many of my memories were still on the surface of my mind, easy to access. Others lay deeper, buried safely away in forgetfulness. These especially I wanted to resurrect. Convinced that they would eventually find their way out, I knew it was better to face them now rather than wait for their destructive power to jolt me. And I was not simply facing them; I was sending them out into the world in this new form of a book.

But what about the other people involved in my story, especially my daughter, Elinor? She might not feel the same about my digging up memories and placing them in the public domain. I worried that, years down the line, she could be deeply disturbed by what I had written; I didn't want to give her any more pain.

I think this dilemma is the main reason so many parents choose not to tell their stories. Mothers like me feel ashamed, frightened of repercussions, and most of all we want to protect our children. The trouble is that, in protecting them, we are concealing a fundamental part of ourselves, and our children sense it. In my experience, a family's efforts at concealment can create layers of mystery and evasion that prove more disturbing than the truth itself. So I opted to present Elinor with my version of our life in 2002–03. When she is old enough, if she likes, she can read it. By investigating our story as openly as I can, I hope I am demonstrating to her that painful experiences need not remain fixed. Like the rest of life, always evolving and changing, they have the potential to become something other than themselves.

Though seldom told, I was well aware that my story was not unique. In the process of creating the memoir, I decided to get in touch with mothers who had had similar experiences – people I would never otherwise have met. I discovered that, though our present situations might differ, our memories were uncannily alike. There was relief on both sides, I think, to share the darkest and most shameful areas of our common past. We laughed a lot. When I went back to my computer, I found my words given extra significance by the knowledge that they belonged not only to me but to them too.

Julia Hollander

August 2007

I had a little nut tree,
Nothing would it bear,
But a silver nutmeg
And a golden pear

Wednesday, 19 June 2002

THE PAIN IN my gut wakes me soon after three in the morning, and I am glad. Two weeks earlier than her due date, this baby (my second) should be a nice comfortable size. I am quite looking forward to the massages and homeopathic oils on offer at the midwifery unit.

By the time I have made myself a cup of tea the pain is already intense. I had better get things rolling: wake Jay, ask him to make the phone calls – first the midwife, then our neighbour Nadine, so she can come and look after Elinor.

When I get upstairs again, I can't stop moving. Distracted, fretful, I lean over the bed and sigh. I go carefully down the steep cottage stairs, out of earshot of my sleeping two-and-a-half-year-old. This doesn't feel like last time; the ache is too low, too heavy. Jay reports that there is only an auxiliary nurse running the unit – the midwife is forty minutes away; she will ring back. By the time the call comes I am on all fours in the living room and can't get up. Jay holds the phone to my ear. 'What's this pain?' I plead.

'Why doesn't it stop?' The midwife tells me to go to the John Radcliffe Hospital in Oxford and hangs up.

Now what? This was not what I planned. Somehow I am meant to call the JR hospital (do we have the number?) and survive a twenty-mile drive through the middle of nowhere (will the baby arrive on the way?). I feel as though a sword is slowly being inserted into my gut.

Jay has got through to the JR. I should go there – it's the big hospital. They want to speak to me. I adjust my weight so I can take the receiver. The voice at the end is reeling off a string of questions that seem completely irrelevant. How many children have I had? Why can't the local place take me? Why is the midwife forty minutes away? I am finding it difficult to concentrate. I need all my faculties to cope with the blade slicing through my abdomen and my mounting panic – does nobody want to help me? Maybe I sound like a hoaxer, an hysteric. The term 'Munchausen's by Proxy' leaps madly into my head.

Then a rush of liquid between my legs. I kneel to watch the juices sinking into the carpet and sigh, as somehow the pressure has been released. The voice interrupts.

'What's happened?'

'My waters have broken.'

'I think you should go to the local centre. Immediately.'

At last, some sort of decision, a concern even. The expert's opinion is that I should go to the midwifery unit after all – the place I have been imagining having this baby for the past scores of weeks. I lunge towards the doorway and shout to Jay to get my black dress from our room, the one I wore so recently for Ellie's birth. It will bring me luck.

Nadine is here. 'I went back to sleep after you rang,' she confesses.

It doesn't matter. Nothing matters except this pain, so different from my last labour. Then, I remember giving myself to each contraction, riding the wave that surged inside me. But now there is nothing to follow, no natural arc, just a solid steel line. I'm back on the floor – 'Massage my back, massage my stomach, try and push out the . . . oh my God . . .' Jay's gestures are useless; I am moving about too much for him to assert any real pressure and my stomach is rock hard. Why? I'm sure it wasn't like that last time. I swing my hips back and forth, round and round, trying to escape the blade.

Someone has spread a waterproof sheet on the back seat of the car. This is what we did when Ellie was born – the same piece of spotted white plastic. It was the same time of night too, but then it was the winter solstice and dark (if the glow of London's street-lamps can ever be called dark). Now it is midsummer in the Cotswolds and already light. I clamber into the car and, as the engine starts, I vomit. I watch the liquid trickle through the folds of plastic, glittering in the rosy dawn. I look up and see the same vivid light on the hedgerows – from the speeding car I can see the perfect pink heart shapes of dog-rose petals. The pain stabs me again and I am head down, eyes tight shut, trying to concentrate on the patch between them, which throbs gold. But I can't keep mind or body still; they writhe against the constant onslaught. I can hear the soft babble of a baby – 'Bu bu bu, mu mu mu.' I look up to see where it is coming from and realise it is me.

We are in the midwifery unit car park. Here is the midwife's shiny little car rushing up behind us. Thank God, she has come after all. She bustles past me and up the stairs: no lift – it is being mended, we have to walk. I remember flashes of that clamber up to the first-storey delivery suite, leaning on the walls, easing myself up one step at a time. Onto the bed, black skirts held high.

'You're not going to strap me down with monitors, are you?' I plead.

'We don't have those here.' Her probe is out and she is search-ing across the right side of my belly for the baby's heartbeat. 'Please keep still.' I breathe in deeply, trying to control my body. She can't find the heartbeat. Don't panic. I am still in control of my mind, still in control – yes, I remember a midwife examining me yesterday, and the heartbeat was on the left.

'Here,' I indicate, and she shifts the probe. The beat is strong. 'That's me,' I manage.

'No, it's the baby.'

My mind is clearer than ever. 'Half the speed it should be,' I say. 'Yes.'

The auxiliary hurries off – she must be calling an ambulance. The midwife again: 'I need to examine you. Please try and open your legs, and keep still.' I try. 'Three centimetres dilated.' Oh no, not even halfway there. The nurse is back and talking to Jay. There is some issue about where the ambulance should take us – he must insist on the JR, that's the centre of excellence. She goes off to make another call. All I can think is that this baby should be born as soon as possible. How can she get out if I am only three centimetres dilated?

'Will they give me a general anaesthetic?' I ask.

'Yes.' I imagine the surgeons cutting me open and rescuing the baby. I must face the fact that I will not be conscious for her birth. She will enter the world in someone else's gaze – dead or alive. These are my preoccupations as I writhe, the precious minutes ticking by.

Then I remember my friend Nerys's story of her labour here a couple of weeks ago. When they called an ambulance, it took nearly an hour to arrive. They told her that there is only one serving an area of twenty miles' radius and that it is always out on a cardiac arrest. Meanwhile, my baby is struggling with a heartbeat of sixty and going down.

'Why don't we drive?' I say. The midwife is uncertain.

'I can do it,' says Jay.

She nods in agreement and, under her breath to Jay, adds, 'As fast as you can.'

I stumble back down the stairs and out to the car, leaning on the arm of the auxiliary who is trying to reassure me.

'You'll be OK, love.'

'It's not *me*,' I shout, 'it's my fucking baby!'

I crawl like a wounded beast, back into my slippery den. Where is the midwife? Surely the paperwork can wait. I must concentrate on getting this baby out. I can hear the screech of gears as Jay negotiates a sharp bend in the road. Oh God, it's the road to Banbury. They're not taking me to the best hospital, instead to the closest. That's the rule in an emergency.

On top of the constant knifing pain, furious contractions now begin their assault. As another one rises, my arms are flung across the width of the car and I grab hold of the coat handles above the windows, wrenching my poor body upwards and the baby down. Thank God for these sturdy handles, thank God for the roaring engine.

Bright sunshine pours in – the day is trying to cast its blessing over us. I look up and see the sheer walls of Cotswold stone that frame the road at South Newington. This was the horror version of the birth I had imagined: speeding towards the rural hospital along impossibly winding roads. As my eyes focus on the slope ahead, to get my balance, I see the dinosaur head of a juggernaut bearing down on us. 'Oh God, oh God. Save this baby. God, please look after us. Ave Maria. Ave Maria.' I have never been a Catholic, but now I'm chanting with the conviction of a lifelong devotee. Car gears scream again and the pain pulls me back down onto the seat.

We are nearing the hospital.

'Left?' I hear Jay ask.

'No, right.'

The midwife is guiding him towards the entrance. The engine stops. The door is opening and I am tumbling out. I sense people supporting my arms; someone is saying, 'Sit down, love.'

I can't, I can't. I need to shit. My vertical position in the car has thrown the baby down. She is coming out. Again they are urging me to sit in the wheelchair; it is moving along but I am standing up in it somehow, my feet on the steps, my hands on the arms, holding my body weight in the air. We are hurtling down the corridor towards double doors – the operating theatre. But, at the last minute, the chair takes a sharp right into another room with sunlight streaming in through a high window and the branches of a tree knocking at the glass. As we pass the open door I see its number – thirteen.

I am shitting. I am shitting. I can smell it and feel it inside my dress as I scramble out of the chair and onto the bed.

And then she comes. This miraculous little body that I have kept safe for thirty-eight weeks. I can feel it: one push – her head ('Pant, pant,' I hear someone say); two pushes – shoulders; third push and she slides out.

'Beautiful, beautiful,' I hear.

Then silence. Horrible silence. My screams have stopped, but nothing has taken their place.

'Have you given me syntometrine?' I call out, anxious that I had not felt the injection to stop me haemorrhaging.

I hear a faint 'Yes'.

I open my eyes and look over to the group of nurses gathered around the resuscitation table. Jay is sitting beside me; we are holding onto each other; now we are praying – 'Please God, save our child. Please God, save our child. God have mercy.' I look over to the table again. Someone is holding a little blue balloon in the air and squeezing it at regular intervals. Perhaps they are punching her chest, I don't know. I can see pink skin in the gaps between the nurses' backs. Pink skin is good.

From the group I hear my midwife call out, 'Did you know what sex your baby was?'

Why is she using the past tense?

'Was!' I shout. 'What do you mean, fucking "was"!'

'Is,' she hurriedly corrects herself.

'Yes,' I say, flatly, 'it's a girl.'

Later she comes over, clutching her handbag, and lets us know she is going home. She has been up since six o'clock yesterday morning, twelve hours working at the maternity unit and then twelve hours on call. She had just got in from delivering another baby when I rang. I say nothing.

My placenta slithers out, a big red jelly. The gaggle of midwives carries it away for inspection and a woman in a dark blue uniform comes forward.

'They've taken your baby upstairs. Don't you worry – she's a fighter. The girls usually are.' I feel sure she is right.

A cup of tea is held out to me on a saucer. My hand is shaking as I lift it to my lips and swallow – warm rather than hot, it is thick with sugar, just what I need.

'And you,' says the senior midwife, 'you're in much better shape than lots of mums I've seen.'

'What do you mean?'

'They found a clot on your placenta — you were bleeding inside. You're OK now though.' She beckons her young assistant over and they lift up the bloody sheet to inspect me. 'What do you think? A couple of stitches?'

I ask for a local anaesthetic — no more pain, please, ever. The older woman returns with her kit and starts preparing the syringe. We are chatting now.

'At least you're sewing me up,' I tease. 'Last time they forgot, and the cut never sealed — I've had a split down there ever since!' She does a double take.

'That's what I was about to repair!' We laugh, a near miss! The other midwives gather round to investigate my private parts.

'Ooh yes,' they giggle. 'You have got funny flaps!'

I feel quite light-headed as I get down from the bed, refusing the nurses' offer of a wheelchair to get me over to the shower cubicle. Last time, after twenty-four hours of contractions, I hobbled and groaned, but this second labour has left me feeling strangely euphoric. As I wash, I shout over the noise of the water, telling Jay that, after such a heroic drive, he could qualify as a paramedic.

In the lift they get me into the wheelchair and push me into a bright room like a small kitchen. Jay has gone home to look after Ellie. The young paediatrician is standing at the sideboard, busy with some intricate work. 'What a dramatic job you have!' I say, but she does not reply. Her tiny patient is splayed out on the table in the centre of the room, wires attached with suckers to her chest, a huge splint with plastic tubes coming off it taped to her left hand. Around her right wrist is a plastic label that must have my name on it, though I am finding it hard to associate this clapped-out body with the energetic one that so recently danced inside me. An X-ray nurse arrives with her equipment, and I am wheeled out into the corridor to wait, reading the flyers on the noticeboard.

When I am allowed in again, the baby lies in the same position: on her back, hands up by her head, knees bent outwards against the hospital towel. Like a frog squashed on the road. The young nurse who has replaced the paediatrician explains that she is monitoring her for seizures.

''Course, fitting's not the worst thing that can happen to a person,' she muses. 'If you're epileptic, you can still lead a perfectly normal life.'

'Insurance companies might not agree,' I counter, swinging along with her theme, not for a moment considering that it is to do with my child and her future.

'Well, it's amazing what people get used to. I mean – if you can't drive a car, it's not going to spoil everything, is it?'

With the nurse out of the room I dare to manoeuvre myself a little closer, though not enough to touch the frail creature lying there. Her dark hair, tousled with vernix and blood, frames a heart-shaped face. The eyes are squeezed shut against my uninviting world. A tube from one nostril is taped hard across her cheek, beneath which hangs a huge red mouth, lips slightly parted. Her limbs, her long fingers and toes, seem to open up to Heaven as if she is offering herself to God. Maybe she is God's, not mine at all.

When the nurse returns, she says the baby is stabilising; soon she will go to SCBU – the Special Care Baby Unit. I am taken to a small ward where a mother is propped up in bed, her newborn at her breast. The curtains are closed around me and I lie in their shrouds, feeling absolutely nothing. I'm not fearful, nor angry; I am simply a neutral vessel emptied of its charge. After the vivid pain of the labour there is nothing inside me, nothing at all. The responsibility and companionship of my baby have been replaced by hollow emptiness. I wonder if this is how it is going to be. Perhaps no milk will arrive in my breasts this time. Perhaps I will never feel anything for the splayed-out creature they have labelled mine. The other woman's baby is crying. I ask to be taken to a private room.

Through my new window overlooking the car park, sunshine

flashes off the cars. I don't want to see that life, moving and breathing, so I lower the blinds and lie down to wait for my parents' arrival. They enter quietly, my mother in front holding a bunch of roses – I recognise them from our childhood garden; 'New Dawn' is their name. She stands there in the half-light, poised and upright as ever, but silent. The bouquet is drooping.

Thirty-nine years ago, fifteen months before I was born, Mum lay in a darkened maternity room like this, alone. Her absent firstborn (a boy) had been taken straight to the mortuary, buried without ceremony. Is that what she is remembering now? The thought awakens an old urge in me, probably the oldest one I have: I need to show my mother that tragedy doesn't repeat itself, that this baby is not going to die. A feisty girl, she is warm and safe in SCBU. 'Scu-boo' – that playful, babyish name they use for the place our modern newborns are nursed. It is full of optimism. SCBU will bring her back to life.

I lead them down the corridor to a ward where baby Hollander is the solitary resident, lying in a big shiny tank in the corner. The nurse draws up a chair for me, unhinges the side of the tank and wraps my baby's naked limbs in layers of cotton blanket before passing her to me 'for a cuddle'. I have to be careful not to move, or I might unplug the wires emerging from the bottom of my little package. Like a new umbilical cord, they link her to the machines that now guard her life. I pull the folds of cloth from around her chin and lay her lips on my right nipple (the one that I remembered producing the most milk last time). Her tongue flickers across my skin; her dark eyes flash open for a moment. We are playing our roles pretty well. My parents smile.

That night I ask for a sleeping tablet. Free of the responsibility of contaminating my foetus, I need to block out my babylessness.

I am woken by a nurse shaking me hard. 'We need you in SCBU.' I pad after her obediently, taking up my position by the incubator. 'She seems to be distressed – you might be able to calm her down.' I unbutton my nightdress and take the bundle in my arms. The nurse leans over me, trying to direct the baby's head towards my bosom. As I lean forward to help her, I feel myself lolling asleep. Someone says I should go back to bed and I retreat, relieved.

I sleep fitfully, drifting in and out of my empty feeling. It is as if I have gone back in time to the person I was before I was pregnant. Not just before this pregnancy, but the me of three years ago, before I ever created a baby. Come to think of it, babyless me is the one I know best.

I vaguely remember my baby brother, two and a half years younger than me, suckling at my mother's breast; I remember nursing my dolls in the cradle I was given for my third birthday. But these encounters had more to do with growing out of infancy than growing towards motherhood. For more than thirty years, my life contained people of my own age and older, never babies.

Between the ages of nine and eighteen, I attended an academic girls' school in Oxford. Childbearing was low on our list of ambitions; in fact, anyone who admitted to such an aspiration was considered to be letting the side down. We were taught to take advantage of our generation's privileges, the battles fought and won for us by our mothers.

When *The Female Eunuch* had hit the shelves, Mum was the same age as its author, but already shackled with babies. 'I could have done so much if I hadn't had children . . .' she used to say. Lots of my friends' mothers said that sort of thing.

So we daughters tried to make up for it. We worked hard. I got a scholarship to university. Then, at the end of the 1980s, I got a good job in London. My ambition was set: I loved music and theatre, and I wanted to excel in an area previously closed to women – opera. When I agreed to direct a show in English National Opera's West End theatre, I was the first woman ever to do so. Women played fabulous, powerful roles on stage, but everywhere else in the industry the power lay with men. If any of them had babies, they never mentioned it. This world was as far from domesticity as you could get. I loved its uncompromising passion, its extravagance. I often worked far away from home and I worked hard.

On rare visits to my parents, my mother would plead, 'When am I going to be a grandmother?' and I would shrug my shoulders.

'People are asking me to stage shows and teach drama courses,' I said. 'I'm lucky to have these jobs – there isn't room for anything else.'

'But bringing up a child is the most creative thing you can do in life.'

Mum should know. Not only had she brought up my brother and me, but (like her mother before her) she was a primary-school teacher for thirty years, helping to bring up other people's children.

'Look, most women get to be mothers,' I said, 'but not everyone can be this creative in the way they earn money. You used to say interesting work was the most important thing for a woman to have.'

Now that she was feeling broody for grandchildren, she had forgotten all those years of 'if I hadn't had children'. Or maybe she secretly wanted me to suffer the same restrictions that she had – parenting as payback time.

Mum got her way with the birth of my first daughter, two weeks short of my thirty-fifth birthday. I was ready for a different kind of life. Along with the glamour and the excitement of the opera world had come loneliness and instability. Until Jay came along, that is. We loved one another; we made each other laugh; his warmth and understanding grounded me, making me feel happy in myself. I knew he would be a good dad. Some of my friends had started having babies or trying for them; our biological clocks were ticking. After three years together, Jay and I weren't married, but we saw no reason to go through that convention. We were ready to take the baby plunge. 'You're a champion!' the midwife cried as I staggered from delivery suite to birthing pool and back. 'You're a real champion!' And when we got home we sent her flowers and champagne to celebrate our triumph.

Thursday, 20 June

My second baby was already a day old. I went early to SCBU and sat beside the incubator whilst a new nurse fiddled with the microtechnology. Baby Hollander was clearly awake, as she was stretching her legs. It was good to see this sign of life and I put my hand through the porthole in the side of her box, laying it gently on the limbs.

'Oh no, you can't touch her, I'm afraid,' the nurse tutted.

'But yesterday I held her!'

'Yesterday she wasn't fitting!'

So it had begun. That must have been why they summoned me in the middle of the night. Drowsy from the tablets, I had been oblivious. Wide awake now, I chastised myself for having been so out of touch with my own baby.

'There, cycling movements!' declared the nurse, as the legs kicked one by one into the warm air, toes flexing. It still looked like simple baby exuberance to me. Could I really have forgotten the way newborns behaved?

'If you watch her eyelids you will see them flicker!' I couldn't help feeling there was a note of satisfaction in her voice, as though, by her very vigilance, the child had obliged.

'If I put my hand on her she'll calm down!' I insisted.

'No, love, wait for the doctor to come and he'll explain. How would you like it if you had the worst headache in the world and a clumsy great hand came down on you?'

Candice Walker (her name tag was dangling in my face) smiled her professional smile. I hated her for defending her charge against me, for preventing me from applying my healing hand of love, my mother-love. Rather than sit around feeling useless, I retreated down the corridor to the breast-pump room. There I fished a plastic funnel from the bucket of sterilising fluid, attached it with plastic tubing to the pump, pressed it to my breast and turned the dial to maximum. The machine began pulling at my nipple, sucking it, grossly elongated, into the neck of the funnel. As the pressure released, the nipple relaxed back to its normal shape, then stretched again. My breasts did not feel swollen at all. There was every possibility that the glands had shut down.

In – out, in – out, the rhythmic slurp of a milking parlour. And gradually the first golden droplets of colostrum gathered in the funnel, eventually sliding down into the little medical bottle below. There, at last: a thimbleful of evidence that yesterday my body had produced a baby.

When Jay arrived we walked together to the neonatal ward. More urgent than anything, we agreed, was the need to grant our child a name. Before our first daughter's birth, we had spent a long time going over well-loved family names, considering their meanings. We had created a shortlist, uncertain of how to make the final choice. But when her forceful body arrived, shouting its triumphant song, and when we saw the flash of her eyes, drank in her sweet, seductive smell, we knew immediately which names were hers. There, on the bed where she had landed, she became Elinor Eve.

In contrast, this baby had been more than a day in the world and yet was still anonymous. I had no idea what we should call her. Jay's suggestion was Imogen. It had not been on our list, he had plucked it from nowhere, but it sounded right. Perhaps the name suggested 'image'. We'd had so little intimacy with her, preserved there in her plastic case, that our only sense of Imogen was a visual one. By the time we reached the incubator, the decision was made – Imogen Cecile. Cecile had been Granny's second name: my mother's mother, who had lived in the Cotswolds and died in this same hospital ten years earlier.

Cecile also came from St Cecilia, the patron saint of music. It was music that had brought Jay and me together. We first met in London at an opera production I was directing. I spotted him across the auditorium, his shock of curly black hair, his burly, sensitive look. I remember the way he offered to buy me a drink, a mixture of charm and thoughtfulness that struck me as full of integrity. I remember the extra beat he took to hand me the glass, expectation in hand and eye. A composer and teacher, he shared my enthusiasm for theatre and music, and was unashamedly passionate about both.

From that evening on, music was something that linked us in work and play. During our pre-baby partnership we collaborated on new opera productions – colourful shows, full of wildness, eclectic and uncompromising. I used to say he had found the perfect manager in me, someone who could bring his vision to life. But he, in turn, encouraged my artistic expression, giving me confidence. At home there was always music – music to cook to, to dance to, to make love to. We played the piano together and he would accompany my singing. As I was surrounded by professional singers by day, my great pleasure was to sing for my man when I got home.

Around ten o'clock, the doctors came on call. First a tall, bearded man with a flock of assistants, wheeling their brand-new sonic scanning device. 'She's like a cherub,' the doctor complimented me. His probe floated around her head, the screen behind him projecting blurry blackness. He declared what he could see as 'normal' and departed.

Next, Candice escorted the paediatrician to our corner. He explained that the baby was having epileptic seizures. 'Think of this as a temporary blip,' he reassured us, 'a common reaction to a difficult birth. She'll be fine.' I trusted this must be so, blind as I was to the minuscule signals the experts were picking up. The doctor explained that they had started administering anticonvulsants (phenobarbital, the oldest one in the book; I thought I remembered it as Marilyn Monroe's drug of choice). They were unfamiliar with the treatment and so they were phoning the neonatal unit in Oxford for advice. The only problem might be if her condition worsened (which was very unlikely, he insisted), as this hospital did not have intensive care facilities. He therefore thought it best for her to be transferred to a bigger unit as soon as a bed became available.

Left alone again, I remember moving away from the incubator, trying to compute what was happening and how I was meant to behave. Surely I should be anxious about the move and distressed about my baby, but I wasn't. Instead, those feelings were transferred to my other child. I thought how Elinor must be missing me, how, for more than two years, I had been a constant part of her lively, laughing life and now suddenly I wasn't.

Candice bustled in to say the doctor had been phoning around and had managed to secure a place in Northampton. Northampton – more than an hour's drive further from home. An hour and a half from Ellie.

'Unfortunately, the hospital only has room for baby; you won't be able to stay.'

I left the ward and walked towards the consultant's office. The door was open and, as I entered, the paediatrician put down the phone. Very calmly, I said, 'I'm sorry. I can't let you take my baby to a hospital without me. Northampton is too far. What about the JR in Oxford? If things had been handled properly we would be there anyway.'

He picked up the receiver again, gesturing to me to leave. I hovered out of sight behind the door.

'Look,' I heard him say, 'I really think this one's yours. I'll tell you what – we'll take *two*.' The deal was struck. I went back in and thanked him, expressing surprise at the bartering system. 'It happens all the time, I'm afraid,' he confided.

That same afternoon I stood in the car park whilst what looked like a baby's white coffin was wheeled up a ramp into the ambulance, guardian angel Candice and her paperwork close behind. We had been asked to follow them, just like a funeral cortège. When I turned to get into our car, I spotted the doors of the maternity unit – the ones I must have plunged through in the wheelchair, Imogen's head already forcing its way between my legs. And then I began to cry, tears I had not shed since the labour began, only yesterday morning but now an age away.

At last, the white fortress of the John Radcliffe Hospital. Entering its concourse I had the sudden realisation that I was going in the wrong direction. Last time I'd had a baby I had walked out of hospital with her in my arms on the very same day. That was what I had expected to do this time. I was a capable, gutsy woman; I should be stepping out into the next stage of my life, not creeping back into hospital.

'Can I open the window?' I asked, when I got to my new room. 'It's very hot in here.'

'Oh, you like it cool, do you? Me, I like my bedroom nice and warm.'

The midwife pulled the sides of her cardigan together against the June breeze as I swung the window outwards. From here on the seventh floor I could see the vertical tower of the hospital incinerator and behind it the dark lines of hedgerows forming lozenge shapes around pale fields. It was a landscape I knew well, where I had spent much of my childhood, cycling and swimming and riding ponies. I could still feel its contours, its hidden bogs and ditches. Summer after summer I galloped bareback through those cornfields, kicking at the heads of wild poppies where they nodded above the crop.

These memories were not new ones; I had rehearsed them only a few months earlier whilst staying in a hospital room with an identical view. Back in January, eighteen weeks pregnant, I had come in for tests after I found I was bleeding slightly, and a registrar thought I might miscarry. Back then, in anticipation of imminent disaster, my midwives all had that stooping demeanour with which people show respect for suffering. 'If there's anything I can do . . . a little chat, just press the buzzer, even if it's the middle of the night . . .' I hated this business of strangers feeling sorry for me. It was the first time I had spent a full night in hospital, and I was convinced the place made healthy people like me sick. Already I could feel the baby fluttering about and my instinct was to protect it from their scary care. The winter wind whistled spookily through the windows; clouds shifted across a clay-coloured sky. Looking out at the fields reminded me of my plucky young rider-self, of the country air where I wanted my children to grow, even whilst they were still inside me. Next day, I discharged myself.

Now that I had returned for a longer stint, I noticed the midwives still wore their respectful look, not just for me but for everyone along the corridor. Perhaps all the rooms on this floor contained some sort of tragedy or potential tragedy – mothers mourning their stillborns, their late miscarriages and abortions, their sick and dying progeny. I dumped my bag and descended to the ground floor again in search of my baby.

There, Jay and I were initiated into the neonatal etiquette that would become so familiar over the coming weeks. The first thing was to ring the doorbell and wait at the wooden half-door until a nurse came to receive us. We were then escorted down a corridor past photos of all the dear children who had been through this process: their stories and messages of thanks; relief at having survived traumatic birth; or birth at record prematurity – twenty-five, twenty-four, twenty-three weeks. We were ushered past the blue room on the left where those tiny tots lay under UV light, tended by masked and hooded figures. At the end of the corridor we washed at a huge stainless-steel sink with long-handled taps, manoeuvred with our forearms. We were shown how to soap our hands correctly, rubbing the backs and the palms and up the wrist for several minutes. I liked this cleansing ritual – washing away dangerous grime from outside the haven we were entering. By the time I reached my baby, I would be as pure as she was.

The incubator had been labelled 'Imogen Hollander' and left in a windowless side room whilst they cleared a place on the ward. Perhaps the two sick babies due for transfer to Banbury were being discreetly removed. I wondered how far their parents would have to travel and whether they would be offered somewhere to stay. A young man showed us our baby sleeping soundly and reassured us that the fitting was a passing phase. He explained that my placental bleed had caused oxygen deprivation, an 'insult', during Imogen's birth and she would take time to recover. I wanted to know whether she was receiving my healing colostrum through the tube in her nostril, but was told that all her digestive system could take was dextrose. Thin and colourless, hardly a food at all, I thought.

They wheeled her into the ward, a long narrow space with

eight identical containers against the wall, facing a row of windows. At the far end was a door into the recovery area where babies went when they neared the time to go home. Perhaps this place had originally been a corridor, linking the sci-fi blue room at one end and home comforts at the other. It seemed like a no man's land. Limbo. In Limbo the babies have died and now float between life and the afterlife. These ones had been born but had not yet entered life. Fragile beings, they lay suspended between pre-life and whatever was to come.

Midsummer's Day

At 6 a.m. sharp a spectre appeared, haloed in the bright light of my bedroom doorway. 'What would you like for breakfast?'

A rectangular packet of cereal arrived on the table above me, lined up alongside a bowl of milk and one of sugar. Their whiteness and strict arrangement struck me as a clinical parody of a real meal, like Imogen's dextrose. I lay there on my back with my palms against the mattress, trying to send healing vibes down to my child, seven floors below. Later I rang Jay and asked him to bring me a large bag of French pastries and a flask of strong coffee. This gesture of independence made me feel better. I was not going to be made an invalid by this institution's food.

Into my room I wheeled the elegant chrome breast-pump (which some wag had labelled 'Ermintrude') and began the comforting process of expressing my milk. Prolific amounts of custard-coloured goodness spurted from my breast, striking the side of the bottle with a defiant hiss. Once labelled with my name, the bottle must be placed in the fridge near the lifts, ready to be taken down to the SCBU freezers. I lined it up next to the others, noting how small and pale those specimens were in comparison to mine. I could feed the whole neonatal ward if they wanted.

Before I went to see Imogen I decided to make the phone call I had been delaying – to tell Elinor about her sister's arrival. I remembered this experience so clearly from my own childhood: when I was exactly the same age of two and a half, I heard my mother's voice on the phone proclaiming, 'You have a little brother.' I wanted to sound just as joyful and, after a good night's sleep, I thought I could do it. There was my toddler squeaking, 'Hello, Mummy.'

'Do you know,' I forced an upbeat tone with a smile, 'you have a little sister!' Silence.

'Mummy, I need a climbing frame.'

The neonatal paediatrician was downstairs, ready to talk to us. Neat and smiling in a pretty summer skirt, Virginia Nicholas was now Imogen's doctor. And as far as she was concerned, Imogen was *her* baby. 'My babies', she kept on saying as she ushered us into the 'family room' with its bamboo furniture and pastel prints. 'My babies are carefully monitored' . . . 'My babies need time; you are going to have to be patient.'

'How long is she going to sleep like this?'

'Only Imogen knows the answer to that, I'm afraid.'

This 'only Imogen knows' was to become her mantra as the days went by and the unanswerable questions kept coming.

'When will she be able to have my milk? When can we start lowering the phenobarbital? When can she come out of the incubator? When will her body temperature stabilise?'

'Only Imogen knows.'

My questions were tempered by a sense of pride that made me try to emulate the doctor's style, assuming what I hoped was a coolly professional stance. Nonchalantly (I thought) I asked about her patient's condition, when and why the seizures might have begun. I remember suggesting (like an eager junior doctor) that perhaps the epilepsy had started *in vitro*. As I said it I realised I meant *in utero*, but Dr Nicholas did not flinch. She was used to terrified parents like me trying to pretend I was not. I let the mistake pass. If I were to admit it, then my brave front might crumble altogether.

In the corridor ward Imogen lay just as before, wired up and breathing but oblivious to anything around her. Dr Nicholas thought she was calm enough now for me to hold, so the nurse lifted her swiftly out of her plastic womb and I stuffed her under my shirt where she would be warm, still attached to the bleeping monitors. She smelt of sickly-sweet washing powder. I sat for an age, silently, trying to feel her shallow breaths against my skin. 'It's almost as good as pregnancy,' I said, and the nurse looked away, confused.

I had loved being pregnant. Both times, I felt fit and lithe; my skin glowed, my hair became thick and glossy. I loved feeling my babies' bodies growing inside me. They were separate beings but also a part of me, and I found that intimacy incredibly satisfying. Now, with this baby held tight against me, I felt whole in a way that I realised I had missed during the past couple of days. I had been busy being one kind of mother, producing milk, seeing doctors and nurses, but here was my true mother-self – this pure link between my body and hers.

She was safely put away when Elinor arrived. The pregnancy books warn that an older sibling can feel jealous if Mum is holding the new baby at their first meeting. Much of what was in the books seemed absurdly idealised in the face of my recent experiences, but I still wanted things to be exactly right for my daughters. Sisters, companions: this was the beginning of a precious relationship. For weeks Elinor's boast had been, 'I am going to be a sister!' and now here her sibling was, wired up and sleeping, but here. I led my toddler into the ward and lifted her onto a stool to look into the incubator. If I could keep strong and confident, then she wouldn't be afraid.

'This is your sister,' I said, opening the porthole. 'What shall we sing to her?'

Without prompting, in her breathy voice, she began, '*I had a little nut tree, nothing would it bear . . .*' I hummed along, following the upward arc of the melody and twice back down again, in charmingly awkward symmetry.

I knew exactly why she had chosen this rhyme out of all the ones we sang together. In our nursery rhyme book it was illustrated with two girls, one tall and one small. They were dancing under a glowing tree on a lawn full of yellow flowers like the buttercups and daisies at home, birds and butterflies fluttering all around. In Ellie's mind these were two sisters, laughing together with their pretty curls and flowing dresses. And I supposed I was the tree, for whose sake they danced. *Nothing would it bear.* The tree (me) was barren but for them – silver and gold, pear and nutmeg. I had created this lovely pair, one fleshy and sweet, the other small and hard and yet to release its fragrance.

When Elinor had left, the nurse came up to me. 'Don't compare this child with your first,' she warned. I was nowhere near it. Not for one moment could I afford to remember the joy of my first baby. I was head down, here, focused on drugs and machines and doctor-speak.

Lunchtime. Back in my eyrie, unwrapping my luxury pastries, I had no appetite for them. They seemed just too rich, too extravagant. On the bed someone had left a list of institutional fare on offer for supper. I got out a pen and, without hesitation, ticked the boxes next to shepherd's pie and rhubarb crumble.

My obstetric consultant visited during the afternoon with a posse of students, their eyelines low. There was none of the gung-ho charm he had shown at my antenatal check-ups; instead he had assumed gravitas. I wanted to know whether my small bleed at eighteen weeks had been a warning of what was to come.

'Perhaps,' he said. 'But then many, many women have a bleed or two during their pregnancy without anything more serious happening.'

Then how did the bleed during the birth happen? Could it have been my yoga exercises the afternoon before?

He said, 'These things happen out of the blue . . . One in a hundred pregnancies end with internal bleeding – abruption. There is nothing you could have done. Don't blame yourself – the worst thing you can do is blame yourself.'

It occurred to me that maternal guilt must be seeping out of every room here on the tragedy floor. By concentrating on what we had done wrong, we could feel like mothers again, responsible for our babies' lives rather than separated from them. At the same time, blaming ourselves might well be a slippery slope towards despair. My consultant must be trying to save me from that.

All right, I was not to blame, but others might be. Why had no one asked me about my symptoms when I was at home on the phone? One of the midwives here at the JR had said a rock-hard stomach was a sign of abruption, yet at the time no one had even enquired. Now I was angry. I ranted about the shortcomings of the rural midwifery unit that he had recommended, the lack of ambulances, the inadequacy of the Banbury SCBU. . . He mumbled about statistics and risk factors. He asked how Imogen and I were doing. I said she was unconscious and I was in agony.

'The word "agony" was invented for this situation,' I said, looking him straight in the eye. I wanted him to enter my reality, to drop his professional front and acknowledge that the midwifery unit had been the wrong place for me to have the baby. I boasted that I knew good lawyers. If Imogen had suffered permanent damage, then I would sue the Trust for any incompetence that could be proved. The consultant picked up on this new theme, explaining that there was a complaints system and he would send along someone to help me fill in the forms. With that, the coterie retreated.

Grandparents, uncles and aunts all arrived that afternoon, and I took them to the neonatal ward to gaze into the cabinet. There wasn't much to say — a bit of 'She looks just like you!' celebration, but how could they tell? She was just another wizened newborn. They must have been shocked by the wires and machines. Upstairs, they all squeezed into my room as I sat high on my bed, hooked up to Ermintrude. Jay fetched teacups and we filled them with sweet elderflower cordial that I had made from our garden blooms just a few innocent weeks ago. 'Here's to Imogen!' we chorused. I think it was mainly for Elinor we were doing this — to give her confidence that the situation was not going to last, that the doll in the display case downstairs was a real sister. For the next year or so, any time there was a toast, Elinor would pipe up, 'Here's to Imogen!'

★

And so the days went by. The focus of my life was now a box on wheels parked in a corridor. The baby inside did not wake up. We watched and waited and nicknamed her Sleeping Beauty. Virginia Nicholas said she did not know what kept her sleeping: her drugs or her 'insult'. No one ever said she was in a coma, but perhaps she was – that would have seemed very frightening indeed. They insisted that eventually she was going to open her eyes. When? Only Imogen knew.

Often I would go down to the Limbo ward in the middle of the night and sit by her incubator, chatting to the nurses. I listened to their complaints – troubles with low pay and lack of staff and unhealthy hours – and they asked about me. In this strange, other-worldly place I found myself recalling adventures I had not shared in years, anecdotes from my travels as an opera director, far away and long ago. The nurses encouraged me; perhaps they were trying to avoid talking about the baby. I had the feeling they knew more than the doctors, because they were constantly in touch with her, and I would search for a look on their faces that signalled what they really thought. Sometimes I read pity. Was that because they knew this was a hopeless situation?

In the morning the other mothers turned up. On one side of us a woman described her daughter's encroaching surgery, her shoulders curling forward with the burden of it all. The doctors had discovered a blocked oesophagus whilst the baby was still in the womb and had been able to treat her after an elective Caesarian. But the big operation at the ear, nose and throat hospital was yet to come. On the other side was a young couple whose swollen-headed little boy had been here since I was last upstairs, having survived birth at twenty-four weeks. He lay propped up on his back, gazing at a yellow mobile that played the tune of John Lennon's 'Imagine'. The nurses were fond of the boy, who had been with them for so long. When the ward was peaceful, they wound up his toy and sang along.

We parents tended to sit quietly with our children, attempting to obey the ward rule and not get involved with other families, despite their proximity. One mother who broke down in tears when she visited her incubator was tactfully removed. Another who kept loudly quizzing the nurses about treatments for her daughter's spina bifida was given a place in the side room. Only one child had no mother come and visit him. That boy lay in an open cot with cuts and bruises all over his body like a car-crash victim. He was big and healthy, apart from the shocking wounds, and devoured bottles of hospital milk. A passing nurse came and leant over him. 'Oh dear,' she said to the baby, 'nasty forceps delivery, little chap.' I imagined his mother somewhere in intensive care, maybe on the edge of life after some terrible blood loss. Meanwhile, here was I, not even anaemic, with my unblemished Sleeping Beauty hidden under my shirt.

Hour after hour I sat pretending I was pregnant again with the tell-tale wires poking out. My only other physical contact with Imogen was during routine nappy-changing and 'top and tailing'. At the appointed hour, I was allowed to open up the side of the incubator; unsealing pots of sterilised water and little packages of cotton wool, I wiped her body clean. Her skin was wrinkled and red – a loose hide, ready to grow into. The only sign of her traumatic birth was her left hand, which had become swollen, blotched black and blue from the hurried insertion of the first drip and then all its successors. This part I avoided as I washed her, lifting her limbs upwards to stretch out every fold. And sometimes she would move about, as if objecting to my interference.

As I worked, I chattered away in my sing-song voice for babies. Though her eyes were tight shut and her mouth too, Immie's ears must be open. I could connect with her through them. Once she was clean, I closed the incubator and squeezed my face against the open porthole, my cheeks blocking out the harsh bleeping of monitors. And then I began to sing – streams of lullabies, hardly a beat between them, filling the air around my baby.

Exactly a week after we arrived at the JR, Immie opened her eyes. Nothing very dramatic, just a squint of a look as I topped and tailed her. Her legs and arms seemed more animated in their response to the water – maybe things were developing? I reported my news to the nurses, who smiled and nodded. I shouldn't expect it again immediately, they warned. But if I concentrated on her clinical state, it was evident that things were advancing. The drugs, for example. Gradually the anticonvulsant levels were stabilised so that the seizures would not resume, and then lowered very slowly, excruciatingly slowly, without the fits starting up again. She was transferred to an open cot for increasing amounts of time until she was able to remain there without her body temperature dropping, wrapped in layers of woollen clothes and a charming bonnet knitted for freezing climes, not this 30-degree heat.

The most significant change was in her feeding. Instead of dextrose, tiny amounts of my colostrum were unfrozen and dripped into her stomach through the nasal tube. It gave me great satisfaction to witness this process at last. The next stage would be to get her to suck, just lying there without opening her eyes. There was no way she would be strong enough to find my breast, but at least I could offer her the taste of me from a bottle, in drops of defrosted colostrum.

I took her out of the cot and cradled her carefully in my arms; then I tilted the hospital bottle, stroking its pink rubber teat across her lips. Often there was no response. But sometimes the dry little mouth would part and a yellow drip would roll inside, dissolving away without any perceptible swallowing. On the most satisfying occasions, as I forced the teat between her gums, her eyes opened wide and the lips latched on. Then she would suck, perhaps two or three times, before dropping away, exhausted. That was enough – it was the first sign of normal babydom, of a life beyond the Limbo.

Of course, that life would eventually be away from this place. What would happen when at last we were able to go home? What might be the long-term consequences of all this? The effect of the 'insult' could not be fathomed, they said. Babies can survive a huge level of oxygen deprivation; that's why they can swim underwater; that's why they are good at being born, they said. Dr Nicholas needed to do a CT scan of Imogen's head, but whatever the results, we wouldn't know for certain what state her brain was in. Newborns' brains were very hard to read and could often look scrambled and abnormal just because they were newborn. There was no way the doctor could give a prognosis.

On Virginia Nicholas's day off, I quizzed her replacement about what my baby's likelihood of a full recovery might be. The paediatrician was calm – she said Imogen had started feeding within two weeks of the fitting (thirteen days, to be precise); that made the odds roughly fifty-fifty that there might be long-term brain damage. She pointed out that the spectrum of symptoms was enormous, and that it took several months, often years, to discover them.

I was not perturbed by her statistic; maybe I had expected something much worse, or maybe I was simply relieved to have a figure, any figure. I was a pretty optimistic person – life had never given me a reason not to be. Fifty-fifty seemed neutral, non-committal, nothing to get worked up about. I could live with fifty-fifty; in fact, I could put it to the back of my mind.

Dr Nicholas had a different way of presenting the odds: 'More of the babies upstairs on the general ward will end up with problems than mine down here,' she said. As if 'special care' ensured that her patients would be healthier than those given just the standard welcome. The trouble with this 'special care' was that the longer it went on, the less competent I felt in delivering any sort of care myself. Had Imogen been on the general ward, I would have taken her home soon after the birth and got on with things, just like last time. But the SCBU experience had changed me. Now I questioned how I would manage away from her professional parents, the nurses and doctors. I trusted their routines and protocol; I trusted their bleeping boxes, the definitive information they imparted – they were so much more reliable than I could ever be.

*

Jay persuaded me I should try an afternoon away from the hospital. Dr Nicholas looked intrigued when I said I was going out for some 'garden therapy'. Our cottage garden had been a big project during my pregnancy and I wanted to see what had happened to it during my absence. On the way, we stopped to pick up Elinor from nursery school. As I stood waiting at the gate, for the first time I noticed that my pre-pregnancy jeans were hanging off skinny hips. I had never lost weight like that before – without trying. My wrist was bound with the plastic tag labelling me as a hospital inmate. To the bunch of kids filing towards me I must have looked quite frightening. As Ellie approached, she held tightly on to her teacher's hand. I crouched down and opened my arms to her, and stiffly, shyly, she entered them.

Back home, I sat outside on the lawn, surrounded by the lushness of summer. A brand-new climbing frame stood alongside the lime trees, its double swing waiting for a pair of sisters to play. There were musky nicotiana plants tumbling from pots around the front door, but I found it hard to connect them with the minuscule shoots I had patiently tweezered from their seed trays. I marvelled at sweet peas clambering high up the sunny wall, foxglove spires in the shade on the other side. On the terrace stood pots radiant with colour: orange and brown marigolds, blood-red nasturtiums, magenta verbenas and the little multicoloured clown faces of heart's ease. Whilst I had been locked away in SCBU, this glorious show had arrived without me.

In the car on the way back to hospital, Jay wept. He pulled onto the side of the road and I hugged him, drawing his sobs into me. The past few weeks must have been horribly stressful for him – the endless waiting, the uncertainty. Whilst my life had been suspended along with Imogen's, his had continued in real time, trying to keep things together for Elinor. I wished I could have been there for them. Now I realised that I had to end my hospital incarceration. And my baby's? I had created the garden for her whilst I was pregnant; all those months I had imagined nursing her in it. The garden was the place she would be truly healed.

As if to prove the power of positive thinking, when we got back to the ward Imogen's nurse was celebrating: 'I got her to take the bottle! A whole thirty minutes! You'll be out of here soon enough.' From that day on I was allowed to unhook her from the monitors and take her to a private feeding room. This act of independence strengthened my confidence – of course I could care for my child; I had done it with Ellie. The room, which had a low sofa and carpet tiles, was clearly meant to feel homely, despite its lack of windows and the resuscitation equipment in the corner. I would place my baby on a V-shaped cushion in my lap and wait to see whether her rooting reflex compelled her towards my nipple. Holding her head in one hand and my breast (bigger than the head) in the other, I brushed my nipple against her lips, tempting her to suck. When this awkward manoeuvre yielded no response, I resorted to the bottle, jamming it between her gums and jiggling it around until she began to feed.

It was on one of these occasions, hands full and breasts bared, that I looked up to see a tall woman in a suit hovering apologetically by the door. I knew I recognised her from somewhere. Then it came to me – she was my games teacher from secondary school. 'Hello, Mrs Langridge!' I said. She and I had spent so many hours running up and down hockey pitches together that I remembered her name straight off. Little had altered in twenty years: her muddy tracksuit and hockey stick had simply been traded in for management gear. Mrs Langridge ('Call me Clare' – I couldn't) was now 'Comments and Complaints Manager' at the hospital and was here to help me file my complaint against the midwifery unit. She voiced her sympathy and enquired whether I felt our previous acquaintance might compromise me. I said I thought not, although, secretly, I hoped our bygone teacher/pupil relationship might weigh in my favour. She sat down and began filling in forms for me, writing down a list of questions about what had happened at Imogen's birth that might form the basis of an 'internal inquiry'. It felt perverse, trying to nurse my frail offspring whilst voicing anger at what I perceived as our mistreatment. I dearly wanted to leave my angry self behind in hospital and get home to the nurturing one.

The nurses wondered whether baby Immie was well enough to go home. But she had passed her due date and the ward was overflowing again, with a sick neonate stuck in the side room.

'Fine,' smiled Virginia Nicholas, 'go home, and try to pretend the past couple of weeks never happened. Just treat her like a normal baby!'

Jack fell down and broke his crown
And Jill came tumbling after

Saturday, 6 July

TWO AND A half weeks after her birth, we brought Immie home, all bundled up and groggy. Still convinced that the garden was the best antidote for her hospital confinement, I was nevertheless nervous of taking her out there. She hadn't ever been outdoors. The only solution was to bring the garden in to her.

From the lawn Ellie gathered dandelions and buttercups and crammed them into vases, their heads drooping on weak stems. My secateurs culled stronger trophies – great fronds of philadelphus pouring out of the pitcher on the windowsill. Around it was space for the baby cards, but I felt uneasy about displaying them, especially the one showing the soles of a baby's feet, toes tensing in a way that looked horribly like a sign of fitting. Inside, it said 'Welcome the Patter of Tiny Feet'. I must have got similar messages after Elinor's birth, and we were meant to be pretending the past couple of weeks had never happened, so the cards had to go up. Within a day they were anointed with a sprinkling of yellow pollen from the flowers above.

Stiff sweet-pea stems were squeezed into pots to decorate bedside tables. This year I had grown an old-fashioned variety with uniformly small, purple-pink flowers recommended by my mother for their voluptuous perfume (she said they had been Granny's favourite). In their heady cloud my baby slumbered. I had tacked blackout material into the curtains of our room, so the summer light would not disturb her. But there was no need: she was used to sleeping under NHS strip lighting. And sleeping was her thing. In the first few days, it was broken only for feeds, which Jay and I administered every three hours, round the clock, just as the nurses had done.

My favourite feeding times were during the night. When the alarm clock whirred, I carried my Sleeping Beauty from our bedroom and laid her on the sofa on the landing. Then I lit the candle. I had read that its brightness and flickering might stimulate a baby's developing eyesight, but I also saw it as our symbol of hope as we emerged from the SCBU Limbo. Before going to bed, I had prepared a cold-bag containing a calibrated bottle with the exact measure of defrosted breast-milk from my hospital hoard. Now, by candlelight, I unscrewed the lid, replaced it with a brand-new teat and slid it between her jaws. Without opening her eyes, Immie sucked.

In those early days my sleep reserves were high, and I was happy to wake towards dawn to administer the second feed waiting there in the bag. Just outside, above the window where I sat, the house martins rustled and squeaked. They had arrived early this year, quickly re-establishing their homes under our eaves. Before I went into hospital, the first batch of fledglings had appeared, and now it sounded as though the second was hatched. How their parents toiled – even before my eyes had registered the daylight they were bringing in breakfast.

And here was I, just a few feet away, feeding my offspring. Newborn humans are strange creatures, hardly human at all. Their limbs lack all co-ordination; their eyes cannot focus; their distorted mouths open wide just like the fledglings' beaks, tongues licking the air. Flailing, they are sensual beings, totally dependent on their parents. I used to think of them as bundles of possibility, all programmed up and ready to go. These days I look at other people's tiny grubs and feel a sting of anxiety.

By day, the July heat clogged the air and a plague of thunder flies had arrived. I discovered that the insects, no bigger than a comma, had managed to squirm into the pictures on the living-room wall. Trapped beneath the glass, they created halos of dampness, permanently staining the paper with converging circles. When one crawled into Immie's eye socket I carefully teased it out with my little finger, only to discover a tiny black cousin had taken its place.

Under the living-room window was a bed covered with a soft rug on which Ellie used to lie as a newborn. I remembered undressing her on it, watching her blink and stretch. That had been in the depths of winter; in contrast, here was her sister in the height of summer wearing a woollen cardigan, borrowed bonnet and baby blanket. I unwrapped her slowly, ceremoniously. It was as if we were breaking the bonds that tied us to SCBU, taking off the swaddling bands of institutional life. My babe was in her birthday suit again – her skin mottled pink and white, much more my Irish-born mother's colouring than the olive complexion Ellie had inherited from Jay.

I picked up my camera to capture the moment, eager to make up for lost time, to have as many photos of Imogen as we had of our other child. I could not imagine having any more children – no more labours, thank you very much. From my experience with my first daughter, I now knew how fleeting babyhood was. This was my last chance to enjoy it. I had to be there for Immie's every fascinating development, to record exactly when she made eye contact, when she smiled and sat up and tried to talk.

Along with Ellie's rug, I had resurrected her first rattle. Made of intertwining glittering tubes, with brightly painted rings and balls running along them, it had proved a fascinating early toy. Now I jiggled it in front of Immie, moving it closer to her face in the hope that she might look up. But she seemed to withdraw, pulling her knees in towards her tummy, her face down into the folds of the rug. I watched her through the camera lens for a while. Her left hand (still bruised and swollen from the needles) was raised up against her ear, the right one tucked under her chin like Rodin's *Thinker*. Her hands were often round her head like this, as they had been when I first saw her on the resuscitaire in Banbury. Perhaps the nurse had been right about her having the worst headache in the world.

There is only one photo from Immie's first weeks where she is awake. I am lowering her scrawny body into a tub of water and her eyes strain open, their blackness reflecting the flash from the camera. The picture jogs my memory – the lightness of her body in my hand, the smoothness of her hair as I sweep it away from her face and, most significant of all, her voice. For, as her naked skin hit the surface of the water, she squealed like a blind kitten. At last, after those weeks of silence. I lowered her deeper into the bathtub, and the squeal broadened into something more human, more like singing. I trickled water over her head, listening to her song cascading with the liquid. It made complete sense to me that this should be her response. Ever since her amniotic fluid had flooded onto the sitting-room floor, my baby had lived in an arid world, deprived of the element that had nurtured her all those months inside me. Now, at last, she could sing as she might have done at her birth.

Or that's how I heard it the first time. Within a few days, it sounded less like singing and more like screaming, less an expression of pleasure than one of pain. Head back, eyes screwed shut, mouth stretched wide. If I try to recall it now, I remember her snorting as she voices her misery on the in-breath as well as the out. The noise is intense, forced across her vocal cords as if they, like the rest of her body, are contorted in distress. Her back arches, thighs stiffen, knees lock, sweaty. I put one hand on her back and the other against her stomach; if she has tummy ache, the pressure might ease it. I start to pat her, in the hope that some wind is trapped in her tender digestive system. But she pushes against me, flinging her head back, arms out. And she cries.

Doctors and baby books say that babies cry 'for' something – because they are hungry, or tired or distressed. It is their only way of expressing themselves, they say. Mum knows whether they have had enough to eat, or sleep or have a dirty nappy. She can find the cause of the crying and put a stop to it. But not me. Oh no, whatever I try, it makes no difference. I can't fathom anything except that, for Immie, being awake means screaming. Unable to comfort her, my impulse is to run away, but I can't do that either – I am her mum. So I wrap her fiery body against my ribs and swing back and forth. Back and forth.

When Ellie was tiny she cried, of course. I sat her on my knee and patted away, but my main response was to stop her mouth with bosom. She seemed to like it. From the very first day, I remember the way she nuzzled at my flesh, tasting me. I remember waking at night with the sting of milk surging into my nipples, even before she cried out for it.

I had to get Immie breastfeeding. I knew it was possible – I knew my own story. I'd had a difficult birth followed by ten days in hospital; by the time I came home, Mum said, I loved rubber teats and was not in the slightest bit interested in her bosom. But the midwife came every day to tutor the baby-me in its pleasures. Each time I mewled, before I was allowed my bottle I would be offered a dripping nipple. Little by little I accepted it, and, by the end of two weeks, the teats were forgotten. There is a black-and-white photo in the family album of my mother in a diaphanous gown, propped up in bed, breastfeeding her dark-haired mite. I used to pore over it when I was a child, fascinated by my tiny self. If Mum had not done this, I thought, I might never have grown up big and strong.

Now I wanted to repeat the backwards-weaning trick, but Immie showed absolutely no interest, and we lacked a midwife to bully us. I rang up a breastfeeding expert who suggested nipple shields. As a temporary measure, she advised, I could emulate a teat by wearing these silicon cones, an inch or so high, with a hole at the end for the milk to flow out. Then my bottle-addict would be sure to latch on.

Except that the shields must be held in place by the baby's mouth. This meant that dexterity and timing were crucial – at exactly the moment she latched on, with forefinger and thumb I had to slip the thing between her mouth and me. One hand around the back of her head, the other poised with my cone, I tried to guide her to her target. But I was clumsy, and so was she. Time after time, just as the operation reached its climax, her flailing hand batted the shield, sending it flying across the floor.

I was sweaty with effort, as was Immie, fretful and screaming. Perhaps she was picking up the impatience I was feeling? Only those few weeks ago she had been part of me, my every emotion feeding chemically into her. Despite our time apart in hospital, or perhaps because of it, I still thought I must be responsible for what she felt. I handed her over to Jay and he held her tight against his chest, humming a low growl that Ellie used to love. And sure enough, she started to calm down.

Maybe I had lost my technique? Next time I should do what the books advise: sit up straight, tummy to tummy, nose to nipple . . . I should use the nursing chair in the living room; it was designed for this particular travail. Taking a deep breath and seating myself firmly in the chair, I got Jay to crouch beside me, holding Immie's wild arm out of the way and helping to guide her head into place.

At last she was latched on and I clutched her against me, not daring to move for fear she might drop off again. Her suck was strong, but, with the barrier between us, the nerves in my nipple felt nothing. I just had to hope she was getting something out of her endeavour, her forehead puckered in concentration. I ran my fingers through her black locks, moistening them with the sweat of my palm. Not one strand had fallen out since her birth – rather, in just a few weeks Immie's hair had become thicker and longer. Now I could see it was beginning to curl, just like her daddy's. Her eyebrows, already defined, might well turn out as thick and dark as his.

Her outer hand was still now, stretched up on the cushion of my breast, guarding its source of sustenance. I leant forwards and drew her fingers up towards my mouth where my tongue explored the space between flimsy nail and fleshy finger. One by one, I nibbled the nails short. The next time she was thrashing at least she wouldn't scratch herself.

When eventually she was surfeited, her lips opened and her breathing settled into sleep. But a week or so after our home-coming, it was no longer Sleeping Beauty-style. More Princess and the Pea. If she sensed the slightest loosening of my hold on her, she would wake up and the mewling would begin again. So I kept holding her. At night in bed, desperate for sleep myself, I would wriggle into a lying position with both my arms still tight around her body. Often I slept all night with her bottom in my palm, her body curled in the crook of my arm, fists snuck into my side. Gently I dared to unfurl her brand-new digits and watched them close again around my forefinger. Ready-moulded for holding, that grip clung to me, even in sleep.

Just as I have fallen into a deep slumber, she bursts awake again. The scream is louder, more monotonous than ever. It takes such an effort just to lean over and check the alarm clock. She only stopped feeding an hour ago, she can't possibly be hungry. More likely she has tummy ache. I force myself out of bed and lie her across my forearm. Linking my hands together, I stand in the middle of the floor and swing the little body back and forth, shift-ing my weight from one foot to the other. The movement soon expands into broad semicircles, wide as a t'ai chi master. After ten minutes or so I abandon the tummy-ache theory. I sit on the edge of the bed, fold the baby tight into my lap and bounce up and down in the dark. It might just shake her back to sleep. Here I am at three in the morning, pounding the mattress to death.

After thirty minutes, or forty – whatever I can stand – I give up and hand her over to Jay, who is trying vainly to sleep on the other side of the bed. He has always been more patient than me. He hoicks her onto his shoulder, her tummy pressed hard against his clavicle, her sweaty head hanging down behind. Then he marches up and down the room in the dark. From my position on the bed, I can make out his bare legs under his nightshirt, the calves pumping up and down. If his regular tread doesn't immediately halt her cries, he applies a more boisterous method, taking an extra beat to thump his heel with each step. Imogen's body jolts along – she seems to like it. Amazing how boisterous you can be with a colicky baby.

Colic: that conundrum in which we parents first have to accept the strangeness of our children. Knees up, head back, mouth wide. Is it indigestion, or a more unfathomable pain of growing and being in the world at large? Or could it be some retrospective wail at the horror of birth? Ellie's colic used to erupt each evening, after a day of guzzling, when we were all exhausted. But with Immie it came at any hour of the day or night.

There are tried and tested, more or less conventional, ways to shut up colicky babies. The car, for example. They are lulled by the engine's sound and a good rollicking ride across the Cotswolds. So when I was feeling most exasperated, at three or four in the morning, I wrapped myself in a cotton dressing gown, strapped Immie into her seat and went out. Headlights up, I drove down the lane and up again, swerving round one tight corner after another, trusting that nothing was coming the other way at this hour. We thundered into town, squeezing between houses, then out again, dropping down across the river and bang! five times over the sleeping policemen, before vaulting the humpbacked bridge.

She must be well shaken up by now; she'd stopped her caterwauling. But just for good measure I charged uphill once more, further from the settlements. Taking the gear down a notch, I leant the car tight into the side of the road where the roughly patched tarmac was bumpiest. All my concentration was fixed on the solid white line on my left, to stop us careering into the hedgerow. We were close enough – maybe Immie liked the thwack of yarrow heads against her door.

I turned in at a young sycamore and parked against the gates, switching off the engine and waiting a moment in silence. When I felt sure she wasn't going to start up again, I climbed out, leaving the door ajar. Still no sound – she seemed to have settled at last. My eyes were becoming accustomed to the half-light and I could make out ridges of track ahead of me, leading down into the broad, hazy river valley. In my horse-riding days I used to love this time, neither day nor night, when I was out with the ponies before school began. It had taken me nearly a quarter of a century to find it again. I placed a foot on the cold rung of the gate, and then another. In one leap I was over on the other side, still just a few responsible metres from the car, but alone. Barefoot in the damp clover, I opened my arms a little and let the breeze eddy around me, carrying with it the scent of fresh earth and foliage.

Somewhere in the thicket close by, a blackbird started up his early morning scat. As he waited for a response, there came the crow of pheasants from the spinney on the other side of the valley. I knew where their cages were, hidden away from the footpath; only a few more months now before the shooting season began. Last summer we had passed by on regular excursions to the meadow below, where Ellie liked to observe the horses from the safety of her backpack. In September, we had discovered mushrooms in the pasture, shoving out of the turf, and we visited every few days to harvest the crop. I loved watching my toddler run about the field, uprooting plump white heads, her fear of horses forgotten. This year we would take Immie down there too.

Beyond the spinney, up the slope, I could make out the Norman church tower at the edge of our hamlet. The schoolhouse, the pub and the shop had all been sold off or destroyed, but that building was immutable. Like the church at the centre of the village where I grew up, it offered our family a place in the community. Having spent much of my early adulthood avoiding any such allegiance, I was happy to return to it. I felt at home there.

Once a month or so for the past couple of years, Jay and I had taken Elinor along to Sunday services. The old ladies who kept the place going would beam with pleasure to see the next generation join their congregation.

'Let her run about, don't worry about the disruption,' they insisted, as Ellie tottered sociably from pew to pew. Once Immie could be relied on not to scream her head off at whim, we would be back there, putting gusto into the hymns.

The church tower was framed by yew trees, masking almost fifty houses, including our own. On either side, the landscape stretched wide. To the left I could make out the domes of metal huts where the sows dozed. To the right I could see the chalk driveway up to our neighbour Anne's farm, with its huge grain silos and lambing shed. The lambs we had seen born there were now almost full-grown, ambling through the pasture at our back door. When lambing came round again, Imogen would be nine months old. She might be crawling by then, eager to explore the shed, eat every bit of dirt and straw she could find. I looked forward to all that.

Beneath the chatter of the birds, a new sound – a low throb. Into sight rolled the first train of the day, carrying early risers from further west, yellow lights in their windows. Until recently, I had done that London commute two or three days a week, leaving our rural idyll and returning to fast, worldly activities in the capital. But my freelance work had wound down; probably I hadn't made enough effort in pursuing it. I now regarded my years working in London, wearing black leather and smoking Gaulois cigarettes, as an extension of student days. I looked back on kamikaze cycle rides in the early hours, shouting at taxi drivers as I veered round Hyde Park Corner, as astounding indulgences. Now I drove a road-hugging car and went to bed early. Gradually, I had excised the expletives with which my previous self embellished conversation, packed away my glad rags.

During my pregnancy with Imogen I found it harder and harder to wrench myself away from home. This second child made my family complete. Like the families in which Jay and I had grown up, we were two adults and two children, a complete symmetry in the generations. And with that completion came commitment. Motherhood had become the only job that mattered to me.

Of course, my relinquishing my money-earning responsibilities put more pressure on Jay to pursue his. Freelance composing work had always been uncertain, so he started to focus on teaching. I knew what a good teacher he was; in our early days together I used to sneak into his lectures, giggling at the way his enthusiasm got him bouncing around in front of his audience. I was convinced he could build a career out of it to support the family.

In London we had been equal partners, financially and creatively, but now we were divided – me the stay-at-home mum, Jay commuting off to work. Our younger selves would have been appalled at the transformation.

The academic term had finished, so temporarily Jay could be at home. His main interest, just like mine, was in making up for lost time with the baby. After her disastrous birth and the weeks of Immie away in hospital, he was determined to get his cuddles.

The baby books recommend direct skin contact, especially for babies who have been in special care – 'skin to skin' they call it. The warm summer justified discarding her layers of clothing once and for all and putting her naked in the papoose. There she could snuggle up against Jay's woolly chest, smelling him and feeling him. Often she would scream and go rigid, but we forced ourselves to ignore it until she was safely strapped in, bare legs flapping out to the side. Then Jay would jig about, flexing his knees, trying to shake her to sleep. Up and down the stairs he bounced; round and round the kitchen. Bolder than me about venturing outdoors, he took off across the field at the back of the house, his wailing load startling the sheep, which bolted. When I saw him strolling home, I knew she was calm at last.

Besides his loving touch, Jay offered the healing power of music. Imogen Cecile was an excuse to get out the sheet music and sit down at the piano. He persuaded me to join him playing duets, and we revived all sorts of old favourites, with Mozart at the top of the list. If Immie's brain had been scrambled, we reasoned, this music would coax its pulses back into their natural pattern. We played boisterously, careless of wrong notes or subtle dynamics, pounding away at the keys. Surely the resonance was good for her, squeezed tight between Daddy and keyboard. Our exuberance was exactly what this sad, shaken-up little being needed.

In hospital she had listened to my nursery rhymes through the incubator window; now that we were home, she heard them all day long. From years of singing to Elinor, I had a big repertoire. With whinging babe in arms, I would begin and Jay would join me, singing the same thing over and over, often abandoning the words in order to improvise harmonies around our tune. The more strange the combination of notes, the more she seemed to like it.

And what of the older sister whist this was going on? How did Elinor get any time with both her parents so dedicated to their new baby? I confess I remember very little of her presence during those first few weeks. With the school holidays beginning, the nursery had some spaces to offer us. I knew she was happy there, and they knew what we had been through, so she started going three or four days a week. They reported that she seemed as play-ful and confident as ever. She was a charming child, whose nat-ural reserve gave her a composure beyond her years. Walking and talking had come easily to her and already she was happy in the structured environment of the nursery school, carrying out her tasks, sitting obediently in the reading corner.

At home, I tried to keep familiar routines in place. Food had always been a central part of our family life, and I was determined that mealtimes were not going to be lost in the chaos of this phase. As a result, a lot of table-laying and pot-stirring was done one-handed with screaming Immie lolling over my arm. It was through this custom that I discovered her liking for the microwave. For some reason, holding her close to it when it was buzzing always shut her up. I took to turning it on even when it was empty, just to get her reaction. But I had to watch out – the closing 'ping' of the timer always startled her and then she would roar worse than ever.

Back in March, Elinor had helped me plant potatoes on the far side of the garden. Now they were in flower, with their pretty star-shaped blooms of purple and white, she pleaded for me to unearth the treasures beneath. I said digging could not be done one-handed, and Immie's papoose would get in the way, so the potatoes would have to wait. But Ellie went on pestering until one afternoon I set myself the challenge of putting the baby down. Once she was snoring in my arms, slowly, imperceptibly, I eased myself over to the pram. I leant my upper body forward, her head still pressed to my chest, feeling her weight transfer to the mattress. I stayed there, doubled over, for several minutes before withdrawing my hold and tiptoeing away.

I had to force myself to step outside, leaving Immie alone in the house whilst I ventured over to the potato plot. Elinor was ecstatic. The garden fork slid easily into banks of soil, easing up the clods. My little girl leapt into each new crevasse crying, 'There's one . . . there's another one.' It was wonderful to feel soil beneath my fingernails again. Quickly we carried our booty back into the kitchen, and, before the baby awoke, we scrubbed the spuds, their outer surface peeling away like layers of sunburnt skin. Impatient to taste them, I flung the lot in the saucepan and turned up the gas so high that boiling froth poured down the sides. There was just time to gorge on hot, moussey flesh before the wail we'd been waiting for burst our bliss.

I had prepared myself for the hard work of having two children – this was just the beginning, as my books reminded me. But Ellie wasn't to know that.

'The baby never stops crying, Mummy. It gives me a headache,' she whined. I tried to reassure her that she had been exactly the same when she was newborn – little babies did cry, they always wanted to be held. She couldn't expect the perfect doll that she had found in the hospital cabinet to jump straight out and play. She had her new climbing frame, and a huge paddling pool out on the lawn; she just had to be patient.

There is plenty of evidence that Elinor was happy. One of my photos shows her dancing naked on the landing, swathed in strings of plastic pearls. Her dark curls are unbrushed and wild, the cheesy grin making the most of her dimples. In another picture she is sitting on an old garden chair, legs dangling, her body and the seat daubed with blue poster paint. She's definitely having fun. But where is her little sister? I search through the album; in every picture Elinor is alone – very alone. In the pad-dling pool she sits with her legs sticking straight out, hands in lap, as if she can't think what to do with all that glistening water. In a photo with Jay holding her, she is clinging on extra tight. Is she frightened she might fall?

She wanted to know what had happened to the baby, and for a while Jay and I could not think how to describe it. Eventually we told her that Immie had 'had an accident'. Ellie understood that her head might have been affected, but we could not explain how oxygen deprivation had occurred – it was hard enough for us to comprehend. So her two-and-a-half-year-old imagination formed a version of the accident where her sister had fallen sud-denly from between my legs and hit the floor head first. She had 'broken her crown'. I had no better image to replace it.

Five weeks into Immie's life and I had managed to wean her off the bottles. Which meant, of course, that I was now the only person able to feed her. A feed often took a couple of hours, and then she might sleep for anything between thirty minutes and three hours before she was awake and demanding more. There was absolutely no regularity to this feeding and sleeping; she clearly had not yet established the difference between day and night. I faced my challenge boldly – single-handedly, I was nursing the most demanding infant in the world. Like my grand-parents getting through the Blitz, I would do it with my version of back-against-the-wall resilience.

One morning, the time of day my breasts were fullest, I was sitting up in bed trying to get her latched on. Jay and Ellie were having breakfast in the kitchen below, the smell of toast and the sound of their voices percolating up through the floorboards. Spontaneously, I decided to discard the silicon shield.

I squeezed my right nipple tight and pointed it at her face, waiting for the moment to force it into her mouth. There. She grasped it with hard little gums – at last we were linked together, intimate, flesh on flesh. I leant back against the bedhead and closed my eyes so I could concentrate, burning this sensation into my every nerve. I could feel the throb of my glands, the quick energy of her tongue as it lapped at me. The milk was flowing easily, generously into my infant. I lost track of time – maybe it was half an hour, even an hour. Eventually the sucking stopped and she began to snore.

The next time she woke, I tried the same trick, but she seemed to have forgotten all about it. She screamed for the nipple shield. How I hated those bits of plastic dividing us. It wasn't purely accidental that I kept on mislaying them – if they weren't lost somewhere under the furniture, they had fallen into the washing-up, or down the sink. My great ambition was to get rid of them once and for all.

A week or so after that shield-free feed, I was sitting in bed, struggling yet again to get her latched on. For some reason, she was making more of a meal of it than ever. I could feel myself becoming increasingly irritated. Suddenly I was furious; I flung her away. 'I hate you!' I yelled. The fury startled me, but I did not lean forward to rescue my victim; instead I watched her, stranded on the white sheet like an upturned beetle. Jay came in and picked her up, his generous, gentle hands supporting head and bottom.

'It's all right, it's OK,' he murmured, as she yelled and yelled. I threw myself onto the pillow and lay there, face down, until they left the room.

Around this time, Mary the health visitor started coming to see us. A Scouse lady in her sixties with short dark hair and twinkly eyes, she had an energetic, upbeat style. She would sit there on the sofa watching Jay and me with our nipple-shield hassles, congratulating us on our teamwork. I reckoned there wasn't much Mary hadn't seen in all the decades of doing her job; I liked her.

One day she got out her post-natal depression form. She apologised for having to quiz me, but the paperwork was part of the care. Question four: *Do you feel more unhappy than you did before you had the baby? Possible answers: all of the time, some of the time or never.*

I started to blub – quietly, pathetically, like a child who has been scolded. What did she expect? I said. When I couldn't even console my own baby . . . how could I be happy? I whimpered, gazing into my lap. Nursing Ellie had been easy, I said. But this time I had messed up at the birth, and was still messing up . . .

Mary put down her form and leant towards me.

'Perhaps you could do with some help.'

Oh God, this was what I'd been dreading – the professionals pursuing me, undermining me as they had done in hospital. They're wrong to label me depressed, I thought. I've never been the depressive type. I'm reasonably on top of things still, despite my tears. It's the sleep deprivation I'm bad at.

'I want to do it on my own. I owe it to her; I'm her mother,' I explained.

'Yes, but there are some things – the feeding, for example. Why not go to a feeding clinic and get some advice about the nipple shields?'

Now that didn't seem such a bad idea: a solid, practical course of action. The fact that I would have to go back to the JR was a downer, but Mary reassured me that the breastfeeding ladies were a world unto their own. Highly respected experts, they would sort us out.

I found myself sitting opposite a woman with the hugest boobs in the world. Hers were not just bigger than her baby's head, they were simply smothering its whole body. She too was nursing her second child and this one's suck was just not right, it wasn't bothering to latch on properly. I felt better for hearing someone else's problems.

One of the experts came over and peered at Immie asleep in my lap. Behind her my new friend hoisted her bosom into view – I could see bright blue veins flowing across the skin, like rivers on a map. I released a modest mammary and offered it to my child, who eventually responded by yelling. I performed my silencing trick with the nipple shield and the expert tutted. That was good – she could help me wean her off them. She got me to insert my little finger into Immie's mouth and remove the offending article. Then, without any sign of squeamishness, she took my bare nipple, squeezed it between her fingers and fired it towards the baby. Who screamed.

We tried all sorts of strategies: I lay down on a bed, one side and then the other; I was forceful; I was passive. But Immie refused to latch on and her limbs were thrashing more than ever. My coach took the problem child and held her upright in a sitting position, her legs folded at right angles at hip and knee. With one hand under the little bottom and the other supporting her chest, she raised her up to her face and then, before Immie had time to get her bearings, back down to waist height. Her scrunched-up features suddenly relaxed, her eyes opened – she seemed intrigued by her shifting gravitational field. As long as she continued moving up and down, she was quiet. 'Never fails with newborns!' declared the expert. Forget the swing, Jay's shoulder, the jolting car rides: this was an anti-colic device like no other. It really was a definitive way forward for us. At last Jay and I had one consistent and reliable technique. And standing on one spot heaving nearly four kilos up and down was satisfyingly good for the biceps.

A couple of weeks later, Jay and I were summoned back to the JR for Virginia Nicholas to observe Imogen's progress. Posters on the waiting-room wall declared 'Give Your Baby a Head Start', 'Aqua Natal Classes' and 'Bumps to Babes'. I recognised them from when I had been here a year ago, their content as irrelevant now as it had been then.

The previous July, the patients were not babies but adults, solitary women like me. We sat silently together, avoiding eye contact, listening to the rain smash into puddles outside. One by one we entered a darkened room and lay down on the waterproof bed with its throwaway paper cover. 'It's cold,' the radiographer repeated, squirting magic gel across our bellies, spreading it with the sonic dipper. With slow circling movements, her wand could trace the tiniest flutter of life inside, inaudible sound waves bouncing off the foetus's body. Shadows were being interpreted, revealing truths about our children still hidden from us, the falsely calm patients, patiently waiting.

Back in the waiting room, back then, I wanted to break the silence with some outrageousness, some tasteless outburst that might stir everyone into life. Instead, my name rang out: it was the gynaecologist, file in hand, dressed in a baby-pink tie and baby-blue shirt. As I got up he moved towards me, disarmingly close, his head cocked to one side. 'Would you mind if a couple of my students join us?' he enquired, discreetly. Did anyone ever dare say no? I didn't really care. In coming here I had done away with privacy.

'Have you passed any fleshly morsels?' the doctor mumbled during our meeting, twice, and I shook my head. Only later did I wonder if his euphemism had actually been 'fleshy matters' – surely he couldn't have said 'morsels'.

My ten-week foetus was smaller than it should be, he said.

'Will it abort itself?' I asked. I liked using that word – abort. Right now, I imagined, in a ward across the other side of the waiting room, children far more developed than mine were being hoovered from their mothers. I knew I could not bear to have an abortion, not even if my baby were handicapped. My need to nurture a new life did not allow that I might actively destroy it. But my body's making the decision for me – that was different; that type of abortion was beyond the doctors' and my control.

The gynaecologist did not flinch at my choice of words. 'You might have your dates wrong,' he suggested.

I was unconvinced. 'I've been trying for a baby for several months; I know my dates.'

'Ah, but you can't be sure! I'm afraid you are going to have to wait a couple of weeks, to see what happens. Come back then and we'll scan you again.'

Two weeks waiting. No alcohol to raise my spirits; so careful of my charge that I would not allow myself an uphill cycle ride, or a heavy day's gardening. And all for what? The foetus was smaller than it should be, its spine and brain quite possibly deformed. My instinct told me it was not going to make it. I'd had a miscarriage before my pregnancy with Elinor; I knew that the earlier they happened, the less pain there was and the greater possibility of my trying again. When I got home I poured myself a large gin and tonic, put my toddler in her backpack and set off across the fields for a bracing walk. By the time I returned, I was bleeding hard. Already I was planning when I might get pregnant again.

Sitting here, a year later, in the same silent waiting room, I felt nostalgic for that instinctive woman I had been: the mother who dared to know better than the doctors what was going on inside her body. Since Imogen's birth I had lost that confidence; first with the invisible abruption, then with her fitting, I had learnt how ignorant I was. Despite the weeks at home, being strong for my child, coming back here reminded me how very little I knew about her.

Virginia Nicholas welcomed Jay and me into her windowless room. She carried Immie (screaming) over to the bed and undressed her with the painstaking care she doubtless took over her premature babies – those shrimps we had seen delivered to SCBU in tinfoil wrapping. I wished she would hurry so I could take my baby back and calm her.

The paediatrician levered the little head upwards, then suddenly let it fall, catching it just before it hit the bed. Immie yelled louder than ever, her hands jerking outwards. 'Good Moro reflex,' said the doctor. Then she grasped her under the arms and swung her upright so her feet were just touching the bed. Her legs trotted up and down like a hackney pony, the toes flexing prettily as they lifted off the solid surface. 'All perfectly normal!'

Dr Nicholas passed her noisy patient to the nurse, who was holding out a ragged grey blanket, and moved briskly to her desk. 'Excellent muscle tone. I wish all my babies felt so good!'

Jay and I seated ourselves side by side against the wall, ready to take in every word, every tiny signal in her body language. The doctor turned to face us.

'She's very cuddly – just what I tell my students to look for in a healthy baby. Now, how are things?'

I described the trouble I'd been having with the feeding, the constant crying . . It was all noted down.

'How are her nappies?'

'Well, they're all sorts of strange colours.' This was something that troubled Jay and me during our long night vigils. 'Her poos,' I ventured (for a moment, in junior-doctor mode, I had considered 'faeces', but the word 'poo' seemed more respectful somehow), 'can often be dark green or brown. I don't remember that with our last baby.'

Virginia Nicholas waved her pen dismissively. 'You needn't worry. They come in all sorts of colours. As long as they're regular.' She continued with her notes. 'Does she look at you?'

'I feel as though she is looking through me.'

'That's what they all do at this stage!'

'I'm sorry, we are worriers,' I apologised, 'we just need reassurance.' Dr Nicholas put down her pen and turned to face us.

'Well, what do you want to know?' The frozen smile. I couldn't think what I wanted to know. Because of these endless nights nursing Immie, I was too exhausted to use my brain.

'We'd like some reassurance about the future,' said Jay. Yes, that was it.

'There is no way we can tell at the moment. We won't have the whole picture for a couple of years.'

She must have warded off so many neurotic parents like this, reminding herself she was the baby's doctor, not ours. But Jay was determined to get something out of the meeting.

'Do you think she'll be able to go to a normal school?' he asked.

She seemed grateful for the lead. 'Oh, I'm sure she will! Though she might be a bit slow at arithmetic . . . ' Jay reflected back the smile.

'What about university?'

'Well, it's a bit soon to say, but I don't see why not!' We all smiled together.

Virginia Nicholas hopped up and took the grouchy babe. Folding the blanket tightly around her head, she clutched her close and looked intently into her face. Then, suddenly, without taking her eyes off her, she did a little pirouette in the middle of the linoleum. As they completed their spin, the doctor cupped a hand round the back of her head, calling out to the nurse, 'Sally, would you turn the lights off for us.' As the room plunged into darkness, Immie's crying halted. 'Back on again, please,' and the cries began again. 'Well, she knows the difference between light and dark!' Jay and I sat there, aware that this was meant to be a joyous moment, but unable to rise to the occasion. The doctor handed her prop to me; we gathered up our things and left.

At home we went over the details of the meeting, looking for hidden subtext and subtle clues, but we could find none. We joked about our faraway aspirations – the school, the university. Who cared whether our daughter was good at maths; all we wanted was a landmark, something in the future for us to aim towards, where things would be normal again. We just needed reassuring that she was not going to be tense and screaming all her life; that the misery would end.

Do you feel more unhappy than you did before you had the baby? We needed to move on from the shock of the birth. There were so many reasons to be optimistic, not least the stories rolling in about other children who had experienced a bad start. A friend of my brother's had suffered a bad placental abruption just a few weeks earlier, and the baby (boldly named Victor) was now showing remarkable signs of recovery. I took the mother's phone number but did not yet dare to use it. A friend of Jay's revealed that his stiff leg was the result of a nasty birth. Back in the 1960s, scrawny and blue with oxygen deprivation, he had nearly died, and now here he was, a strapping six-foot fellow. The hospital sent along a woman from a charity supporting parents whose babies had been in SCBU. She arrived, all spruced up and professional, to share her tale of anxiety and pain, and its happy ending: her asphyxiated daughter had just got a place at a very reputable university.

Imogen had been home for nearly a month. We thought we had been doing what the doctor advised, treating her like a normal baby, but now we could see that her abnormal birth had led to our behaving abnormally at home. We had been too intense, too earnest in trying to make up for the birth. Somehow we needed to relax about things, get out of the house, establish a family life for ourselves. All of us, including Immie, would be bound to benefit.

Before the baby's arrival I had imagined all sorts of activities for us. I thought I would be like other people at Ellie's toddler group, introducing my new addition as she snoozed in her car seat. I had fantasised that I would walk in there (exhausted but proud) and perform all the gestures for 'The Wheels on the Bus Go Round and Round' until my new sprog squawked and I would have to feed her. There on the floor, just like the other mums. But I still hadn't got round to it.

I still hadn't managed to bring my daughters together at all. It wasn't just the long, long feeds and the hours with my arms full, trying to keep Immie from screaming. Something had changed between Elinor and me. It was as if I had been on a retreat from her world and had still not found my way back into it. I felt a distance between us, a wariness from her. At bedtime, she started requesting Jay's company rather than mine. 'I like Daddy, I don't like you,' she announced, and I smarted. I had known this sort of thing might happen, that my dedication to the new baby would throw Ellie and Jay together. But I hadn't anticipated how bad it would make me feel. I reproached myself that my eldest daughter could no longer trust me.

The Cotswold Wildlife Park had been a regular treat for Elinor. So I got my act together to go again, to prove that everything was just as it used to be. On the chosen day, I gave myself plenty of time to feed Immie before we set off, plenty of time to gather the two-kids' paraphernalia. Papoose and nappies, baby wipes and baby hat, suncream and pushchair. Clean nipple shields (where was their box?) and Ellie's wellies just in case. Sunhat for the older sister. Oh, and money. Oh, and the front-door keys.

On the way, Immie slept – we were doing well. I sang the rhyme Elinor called 'Donald', with gaps for her to choose the animals.

'. . .And on that farm he had a . . .'

'Penguin!'

'. . . ee-i-ee-i-oh. With a waddle-waddle here, and a waddle-waddle there . . .'

When the car engine stopped, Imogen woke up, so I strapped her in the papoose and danced my shutting-up jig off towards our favourite spectacle: the penguins' feeding time. A huge holiday crowd had gathered along a low wall, behind which dozens of Arctic toddlers dived in and out of their pool. The keeper was trying to interest his audience in fascinating facts and figures, whilst being totally upstaged by one of his charges, who flapped at his trousers, hoping to get sprats without speeches. More significantly from my point of view, the infant down my front was doing her best to drown out the whole show.

A mother nearby gave me an insipid smile. I thrust Ellie into the pushchair and steered her away. Now I had two screaming children and could feel disapproving glances following me across the garden towards the glasshouse. Surely no one would be in there at the height of summer? As I pushed aside the plastic doorflaps, there was a blast of humidity and the sound of rushing water. And suddenly the screaming stopped. In the hot, wet embrace of the air, Immie felt better. She strained against the back of the papoose, as if she was trying to look up behind her. I unhooked the binding and held her head as she blinked into the light. She was more focused, stiller and calmer than I had ever seen her, enjoying the lushness of this man-made jungle, its extremes of dark and light. Above us was a thick canopy of vines and beyond, in the brighter atrium, a soaring banana palm, its leaves dripping with condensation. I parked Ellie's pushchair beside a bench and sat down. The three of us were concentrating together, listening to the water music around us. Under the high staccato notes of a small waterfall I could make out a baseline of deeper tones coming from some invisible source.

And I thought, this is happiness, isn't it? I've got such a lot to be happy about. I just need to hold on to this feeling. The colic is a passing phase, I know it is. Soon she will be calm like this all the time. Soon.

Rock-a-bye baby

Thursday, 25 July

'Pretty little thing, isn't she!'

Jay and I were back at the hospital for our internal inquiry meeting, and my obstetrician was back to his charming self. He was flushed, perhaps straight out of surgery, having just performed a few morning miracles. A laminated conference table laden with tea and biscuits filled the room, a row of matching chairs were pushed back against the windows. Immie was yelling as I sidestepped my way to an empty seat and sat down fast, groping about inside my jacket. Underneath the table I fumbled with nipple and shield, lobbing my child's head towards me. At last she was latched on and I could meet the consultant's gaze. 'Well, I suppose she deserves her say at this meeting,' I said.

There was quite a crowd assembled. All these people, so interested in why I thought their colleagues back in June had been so uninterested. Their papers were out, ready to reply to my list of questions about the birth. Why, when she first called me at home, had the midwife from my local midwifery unit not kept me on the phone? Why did we have to call the JR ourselves – shouldn't she have done it? And when we got through, why had they asked seemingly irrelevant questions when they should have enquired about my symptoms? I felt it would have been easy enough to diagnose my abruption and then refer me to a hospital that could cope with my baby.

Mrs Langridge, Comments and Complaints Manager, announced that she would be taking the minutes and passed round copies of my list. As she did so, a twenty-year-old memory came into my head: this same woman, my games teacher, standing behind me in the Saturday morning drizzle, holding on to my shoulder. 'You're OK,' she was saying. 'Keep bending forward. That's it.' I had been head down on the hockey pitch, tackling, when the hard white ball flipped straight up into my mouth. I remembered watching bright scarlet drops splashing down onto my hockey stick. It turned out that my teeth were intact; it was the gum above that had taken the impact, swelling overnight so it felt as though the ball itself had lodged there. When eventually it went down, a ridge of bony scar tissue remained.

Taking my notes from Mrs Langridge, I pushed my tongue up over my top teeth to feel the scar, wondering whether she remembered looking after me during that accident, whether she would look after me now.

One of the managers was explaining why the phone conversation at the start of my labour had been so brief. She was quoting from her notes: 'Midwife Murray did not want to delay Miss Hollander's transfer to the JR.'

I interjected, 'Why? Because she suspected I was in trouble?'

'Well, yes, she was slightly suspicious.'

'Then why didn't she say so?'

'She didn't want to cause you any undue anxiety . . .'

'But just hanging up on me made it all seem much worse. I felt abandoned.'

That feeling was still with me. Every time I went to the supermarket in town, I imagined bumping into Midwife Murray, on her break from the unit. Would I take the opportunity to confront her? Would I let the other shoppers know our story and warn them it could happen to them? Or would I scuttle away, too traumatised at the memory to say a word?

'I felt the same with the JR midwife,' I continued.

'Health care assistant.'

'What?'

'It was a health care assistant who answered your call to the JR.'

'So where was the midwife?'

Apparently, there had been two midwives sitting at the delivery suite desk, but they had left things to the HCA. They had assumed mine was a normal labour. Yes, the HCA should have handed over to someone qualified to diagnose my condition. With hindsight, she had been wrong to send me to the midwifery centre. The managers also agreed that Midwife Murray had been wrong to hang up on me, and wrong to leave me to phone the hospital myself. Neither woman had followed recommended protocol.

I was frustrated. I wanted the bureaucrats to take the blame for what their staff had done. But they weren't going to do that – and why should they? They weren't responsible for Immie's birth. The only person at this meeting with any responsibility was my consultant, but over recent weeks I had changed my mind about him. I couldn't really criticise him for recommending the midwifery unit. Not all obstetric consultants were open-minded about such centres, but this one had a reputation for being so; he gave lectures all over the world on the benefits of minimal pain relief and non-intervention. He had statistics to prove that a delivery in such places is no more risky than one in hospital.

It helped that he was good-looking, confident, charismatic even. He made me feel good about myself; he believed in my ability to give birth without clinicians like him around. After my night in hospital with the bleed at eighteen weeks, he agreed there was no need for me to be there – my baby was thriving. Walking with me down the corridor, he asked whether I had been head girl of my school. I was charmed. How extraordinary that my doctor should have unearthed this fact from my non-baby-making life! He knew, he said, because he himself had been at the school – a teaching assistant during his student days. We compared dates. I laughed. We were only a few years apart in age, had spent teenage times together. I trusted him.

In fact, I trusted him more than I trusted the midwives. Having had an exhilarating experience of birth the first time round, without a single doctor entering my delivery suite, I very much wanted to use the midwifery unit. But my mother was cautious; her first baby had died at a remote country hospital and my unit reminded her of it. So I got them to show me the resuscitation kit and the drugs for haemorrhage, just in case. During one of my check-ups, the midwife drew the curtain back from the window to reveal a bare patch in the car park where emergency helicopters could land: 'Don't you worry, you're safe here,' she'd said. But I knew from my friend Nerys that ambulances took for ever to get there; why expect anything different from the helicopters? The fact was, I could never be safe; there was always the possibility of disaster. I just didn't think it would happen to me.

We only managed to get halfway down my list before the meeting was over. They had given up their lunch breaks for us; they had to get back to work. Mrs Langridge said we could reconvene another time, but I wasn't sure – I was beginning to feel that the whole exercise was a waste of time. All we had done was rake over an experience I would rather forget. In conclusion, they agreed when I said the so-called 'care' had been a series of cock-ups.

I said all I wanted now was reassurance that what Immie and I had suffered would not happen in future – that their midwives were attentive to the possibility of abruption, that they would never hang up on anyone again. The managers promised that aspects of protocol would be adjusted, issues of referral and decision-making reassessed. The consultant even said that he would think more carefully about the risks involved in recommending the unit to other mothers. 'Well, I'm just a punter,' was my parting shot, and they laughed. It was true: I was merely a temporary visitor in their gigantic machine.

But when Jay and I got home and went over things, I had to admit my conclusion had been wishful thinking. We were very unlikely to be temporary visitors to the hospital because, as

Virginia Nicholas had warned us, it was going to take years to discover what damage, if any, the birth had done. 'This period before the outcome is known', one of the managers called it at the meeting.

In SCBU we had discovered that our daughter's likelihood of being brain-damaged was fifty-fifty; since then we had managed to put these odds to the back of our minds. But the meeting had thrust them forward again. We had to face the fact that there was as much chance of Immie being brain-damaged as not. One or even two years down the line, we could find ourselves with the bad outcome rather than the good one. With a brain-damaged child to care for, we would have to carry out our threat of suing the NHS. And suing meant blaming the obstetrics department. Everyone at the meeting, even my old games teacher, must have been thinking about this future, where a battle line would be drawn between their lawyers and ours. Damn, I should have been tougher. I shouldn't have fallen for all that 'protocol' stuff. I should have accused them of negligence – that's what they were expecting. The more we thought about the meeting, the more we began to feel that it had been held not to give us peace of mind, but as a starting point for a legal battle.

At one point someone had said, 'You suffered a major abruption,' and I thought back to the Banbury midwives carrying my placenta away. Had the bleed really been 'major'? No one had said so at the time. I took out the copy of the birth notes they had given us and ran down the list of facts about my delivery. Against 'Placenta' was printed 'Complete'; against 'Blood Loss', '200 mls'. And against 'Placental Abnormalities', in capital letters, it read 'GRITTY INFARCTED RETROPLACLOT'. I checked 'infarcted' in the dictionary and found 'a localised area of dead tissue resulting from an obstruction of the blood supply to that part'. The dead tissue bothered me; how long had it been there? Ever since the eighteen week bleed? And then the fresh blood loss, a modest cupful: it hadn't even made me anaemic, but what about her? What 'major' damage might it have done to my baby?

Jay and I were frightened by the idea of brain damage, so much so that we didn't talk about it. We could have leapt to the computer and searched out all sorts of information, but we didn't. We knew the spectrum of possibility was enormous, so we chose to stay ignorant. But ignorance was far from bliss – our fear still hung in the air.

Jay was annoyed about my defending the obstetrics consultant. He went on about my miscarriages and my early bleed, convinced these had been signs of impending haemorrhage that should have been picked up. Even the death of my mother's first baby came into the argument: shouldn't that have been factored into the risk assessment? I said that if my doctor had been wrong, then so had I in choosing him. I thought blaming the consultant amounted to blaming me – that Jay was trying to make me feel guilty. Well, I was just not going to go there. It wasn't the consultant, I insisted, it was the midwifery unit that should take the flak, along with the money-pinching bureaucrats who made people work twenty-four hours without a break.

And so we argued into the small hours, when Elinor was asleep and Immie whinging. As none of our culprits was there, we had only one target for our accusations: one another.

There weren't many other people in our lives at this time. The hospital crisis had kept friends away, and, now that we were home, they were probably waiting tactfully for invitations. But I thought things needed to settle down first – once Immie's colic had subsided and we felt calmer, once the summer holidays were over.

When people dropped by uninvited, I found it hard – 24/7 nursing had dried up any small talk I might once have had. Nerys arrived on a warm August afternoon with her strapping boy, born in the ambulance on the way to Banbury just two weeks before Immie. During our pregnancies she and I had gone to yoga classes and made music together, planning all sorts of baby activities to come. Now I led her outside onto the lawn to enjoy the weather. Sitting in the shade of the lime trees, breastfeeding, I tried to hide the nipple shield in order to seem as natural as my guests. But my effort seemed only to emphasise our difference. I was relieved that the combine harvester working just over the fence drowned out our attempts at conversation. Another day my yoga teacher visited, apologetically, bearing a saffron-coloured Babygro. She held out my sleeping baby at arm's length, with me hovering alongside, ready to whisk her away if she woke up. I didn't repeat my consultant's reassurance that her yoga exercises had nothing to do with the abruption. Intent on not feeling guilty about them myself, I didn't mind if she did.

But there was one friend I did not have to worry about: Nadine. She was different; she was part of the family. She had been ever since she appeared, out of the blue, on a summer evening two years ago (one of the first in our country idyll). Flinging her mountain bike down onto the lawn, Nadine didn't bother to knock at the front door. Handsome and strong in Lycra cycling shorts, she strode up the steps of the terrace: 'Hi, I'm Nadine. Are you the Londoners?' Several gin and tonics later, with baby Ellie happily dandled on her knee, she was already our granny next door. Nadine was full of stories of her Spanish childhood, her five grown-up kids, her Polish husband and his sudden death. She had lived in the village for more than a decade, inheriting her cottage a year ago from the old lady whom she had nursed there. She was a rich source of village gossip; she made me laugh.

If she felt bad about having turned up late at Imogen's birth, Nadine did not show it. She was not the type to look back. Now what we needed was her practicality, her uncompromising vigour, her generosity. Into the cottage she burst, to whisk my wailer away. 'Oh, my sweet pea,' she crooned, in her manly smoker's voice, 'what's going on with you today? What a little horror you are!' When other people took Immie they handled her like a fragile invalid, but not Nadine. She grasped her up against her clavicle, covering her whole face and head with the baby blanket, and swung her about. Up and down the kitchen floor she went, beating the baby's back in time to her dance.

Nadine did agency work as an old people's carer, but, on her afternoons off, there she was at the front door, offering to take

Immie out. My high-maintenance babe had been home well over a month, she said, and I needed a break. It was all very well, this stiff-upper-lip resolve, but mothers must take time for themselves. Time to recharge the batteries. She gave me a cold mask for my eyes and told me to go to bed for a couple of hours. Then away she strode, intent on getting some exercise as she propelled the roaring pram ahead of her.

Nadine said I was a typical second-timer. Like everyone, I had simply forgotten the bad parts of parenting; it was the only logical way we let ourselves in for the slog the second time around. When I rang her on the day I shouted 'I hate you' at Immie, she chuckled throatily down the phone and pronounced me totally normal. 'Show me a mother who hasn't done such things!' she declared. 'You'll get over it!' And I did, for a while. Until one lunchtime, I had just sat down to eat when Jay came inside with his bawling charge, saying he thought she was hungry. 'Take her away!' I snapped, and saw the shock on his face, and Elinor staring up at me. When she was tiny I had happily spent whole meals with her guzzling away at me under the table, but now I felt differently. I was determined to have this modest version of recharging my batteries. I got on with my meal, trying to savour every mouthful, even though Jay stood over me, waiting to hand back the baby the moment my knife and fork were down.

Not even two months into my second child's life, the pressures of caring for her were starting to get on top of me. The relentless broken nights made me grumpy and impatient, the constant screaming meant I was permanently on edge. And to make matters worse, I could feel the effects of the birth starting to seep into my consciousness. The physical pain had disappeared quickly enough, but, after a few weeks lying dormant, the emotions were ready for revival.

One morning in early August, a letter came for Jay telling him he had not succeeded in a job application. It was the sort of thing we would ordinarily have taken in our stride, with our uncertain freelance work, but this time the rejection really got to me. I couldn't accept my man's inability to control his world. Sitting at the breakfast table, with Ellie on the bench in front of me, I ranted: didn't they realise he needed to support a young family? He was by far their best candidate . . . Jay's shrug of resignation exacerbated my ire. I said he was giving in too easily; he should go back and tell them what he thought. But was he going to do that? No. He never stood up for himself!

In fact, Jay was quite capable of standing up for himself against me. He must have realised that this anger at him was simply an expression of my fears and frustrations about Immie. Why didn't he say so? We'd had rows enough before to know they could be resolved, that I would listen to him. But this time he was silent. He sat there, all hunched and hangdog, his beard sinking into his collar.

I let rip – how hopeless he was, always the victim, never able to grow up . . . He should be the family's rock, especially after what had happened to Immie. Ellie started to cry, but that wasn't going to stop me. My fury was in free fall, the frustrated house-wife, cut off from fun and friends by her impossible baby, I needed this outlet. When Jay tried to escape out of the room, I stormed after him until, finally, he took off on his bicycle. He didn't say where. I didn't care.

That night, he started sleeping on the bed downstairs. Less opportunity for inadvertently waking Imogen, we reasoned; less opportunity for us to fight. I remember arriving back after one useless dawn drive, dumping the whinging Immie in her baby seat in the hallway and escaping upstairs. I knew he would drag himself from sleep, heave the baby onto his shoulder and start pacing. From now on, he could do it on his own.

Mary the health visitor came every week, to keep an eye on Imogen's growth, she said. Suspecting that she was still on the lookout for post-natal depression, I worked hard before each visit to make sure the house was tidy and that I was wearing pretty summer clothes without too many milk stains on them. Jay was often around when she visited, showing Mary what a good team we still were.

I confided in Mary that I might be experiencing the emotional after-effects of the birth. She nodded, as if she knew it already — it was probably the commonest phenomenon in the book. Her suggestion was for me to write things down — a diary of Imogen's behaviour. That way, I might discover subtle improvements in her sleep pattern, the times she settled easily after a feed. If I could find the beginnings of a routine, I might start to feel more in control. The approach immediately appealed. I remembered the way life had settled down so reassuringly once teeny Ellie had begun to feed and sleep at regular times.

On Saturday, 3 August, I bought a little notebook with a pastoral scene on the cover and began the 'crying and feeding diary'. Using a twenty-four-hour clock, I noted down the times my baby slept, the times she fed and her moods in between. It begins:

02.30   Wake. Feed (right breast). Struggle to latch on. Sudden halt after 40 mins (tummy gripes).
03.30   Crying and crying. Rocking helps.
04.00   Sitting up and bouncing helps. Burps. Little sleep in my arms.
05.00   More crying after car journey. Feed (right breast again). Suddenly ASLEEP!
06.30   Wind. Nappy change (green poo). Griping.
07.30   Quiet on breast. Sleeps.

And so on, day after day. Often the date is left out, as days and nights merge into one another, but I kept the diary for a whole month. I think I assumed that the longer I went on, the more likely we would be to uncover a pattern.

Mary had been correct: keeping an account like this did give me a sense of control. Through it, I was able to observe my baby a bit more objectively, separating out her misery from mine. On 7 August, I write 'Panics over feeding', but above it, in bolder letters, Jay has inserted 'Mum was tense'. We argued over that. He thought he was supporting the poor, blameless babe; I wanted him to acknowledge that her moods weren't all my fault.

The diary became a regular outlet for our disagreements. For example, at midday on Saturday, 10 August, Jay writes 'Lots of calm looking and listening', and I then contradict him with 'Griping, tummy ache, refuses to feed, will not settle'.

It was around this time, a couple of weeks after the internal inquiry meeting, that I began being openly negative like this. I started saying things like 'We don't know how brain-damaged she is.' Jay didn't approve, reproaching me for my pessimism, as if somehow the words themselves might court bad luck. But I felt the opposite: that if I acknowledged how bad things were, read-ied myself for the bleakest possible outcome, then I could only be surprised and delighted when they turned out better. Come to think of it, I had learnt that trick at school. We ambitious girls had always moaned that we were going to fail our exams, only to be genuinely thrilled when we got top marks.

Then, on 12 August, out of the blue, there is a positive entry from me: 'More communicative feeding – eye contact – recep-tive'. I don't remember that. I know I was desperate to have it, staring down at her head for hours whilst she fed, willing her to look up. All I thought I got was a faraway gaze, but here is writ-ten evidence to the contrary. On reflection, I can only think I wrote it to make peace with Jay, or else for some future reader (Immie perhaps) who might want to discover what August 2002 had been like for our family.

I found it a real strain being upbeat. Much more of a strain than being negative, or even than the instant, thoughtless anger of rowing with Jay. Looking on the bright side seemed to take a huge effort of will.

One afternoon, outside the butcher's, I bumped into a kindly fellow who attended our village church.

'How's your baby?' he enquired.

'Oh, she seems to be well on the way . . . The doctors are really pleased with her progress,' I responded.

'What a relief. So our prayers are working!'

And I felt sick with dread. It was the thought of everyone praying for us, our being responsible for so many people's hopes. What if I let them down?

One night in the dark, with no moon and no candle, rocking Immie's angry little body back and forth, I feel myself swing just a little bit further. This is what it would feel like if I were to smash her head against the wall. It would be so simple: her soft skull would crush like a boiled egg, if I just swung that bit harder.

I must not tell anyone about my fantasy. It is too horrible, the ease with which I can truly imagine destroying my child.

Nadine had brought round a small blue dummy; I was not a fan. Having comforted baby Ellie with constant breastfeeding, I thought I had proved such aids unnecessary. But Nadine was not putting up with my prejudices – anything to stop the screaming, she said, and thrust it in the open mouth. It stayed in place for precisely thirty seconds before Immie spat it out in disgust. I teased Nadine that my child had better taste than she did.

One morning at the chemist's I spotted the colic remedies. They too were against my principles. During this home healing period, I had been proud to think of my baby cleansed of all drugs, made strong by my breast-milk alone. However, faced with a couple of panaceas sitting innocently on the shelf in front of me, I thought, 'what the Hell', and bought them, quickly. When I got home I phoned the experts at the feeding clinic to ask which cure might be most effective and whether they were a good idea for my drug-free babe. The woman who had taught me the colic-calming lift sounded quite amused. She said I could try whichever one I fancied; clinical tests had been done all over the world and the same results found.

What were they? I ventured.

'You probably don't want to hear this, but no trial has yet shown colic remedies to work,' she said. 'I'm afraid the best that can be said for them is that they work as a placebo for anxious parents. But now I have gone and told you, that's not going to be any use, is it?'

I was relieved not to resort to the drugs after all; I wanted to hang on in there, feel confident that, as her mum, I could still kiss my baby better. But the idea of some sort of cure for the crying, beyond what I could offer her, was now seeded. I had read about cranio-sacral therapy. The idea is that, during a speedy birth, the soft plates of the baby's skull are squeezed together so violently that the cranium becomes permanently compressed. A cranio-sacral therapist could use gentle, almost imperceptible hand gestures to release the pressure. Jay thought we should ask Virginia Nicholas's advice, but I preferred to steer clear of the hospital if at all possible; I was happy to pay an independent specialist to look at my daughter.

Tuesday, 14 August

I found the therapist's house at the end of a bumpy track, leading out onto open fields and the river valley below. I parked the car in front of the garage and walked round the side to the front door, past flourishing rose beds fringed with a soft, silver-leafed plant called woolly lamb's ears. As a child, I remembered sitting on the edge of my grandpa's rose border, stroking the fur on those leaves, imagining they really were little lambs. My mother's parents lived in a honey-coloured Cotswold house like this, upriver from here, with a similarly soothing view across the green, green valley. We used to visit every other weekend, without fail. Grandpa, like as not, would be out in the garden pruning his shrubs, with Granny in her kitchen, all a-fluster over Sunday lunch.

Clare came to the door, welcoming in a crisp shirt and a belted A-line skirt. She was probably the same age as Granny in my recollections, but a woman around sixty looks younger the closer one gets to it oneself. She was reassuringly unflustered. Gently, she took the baby seat from me and led me into her consulting room, setting it down on the massage table next to a pile of fresh towels. Clean, but not clinical, the room had sand-coloured walls and slatted blinds at the window.

We must have talked and she must have written things down; the main sensation I recall was of loving openness. Clare was slowly, gently feeling her way into my baby's troubles. When Immie awoke she gestured to the nursing chair in the corner of the room and came to sit beside me as I got out the nipple shields. My baby's body was locked in the arc of my arms as she fed, but her head was exposed and Clare began investigating the air around it with the palms of her hands. I remember leaning back in the chair and closing my eyes in order not to inhibit her. As she worked, I let hot tears roll down my cheeks and onto the baby. Then I felt her hand floating up towards my eyes, and without a sound she wiped the tears away.

The crying and feeding diary shows that from that day, when Immie was eight weeks old, we went to see Clare three times a week. One time Jay used the session to have a massage and came back saying that he had had a good wail. I tried it myself, but didn't come anywhere near wailing. I remember lying on my back and letting Clare shake my legs, pulling them up and round to release the tension in my pelvis. 'Golly, you did push hard,' she said. But I didn't want to think about that – it was the tension in my baby's body I needed her to treat. Only then, I felt, could I start to deal with my own.

Clare concentrated on Immie's head and neck but also her spine, bending and caressing her with thoughtful fingers. She talked as she worked, purring her words of reassurance. Sometimes Imogen's response was to yell louder than ever, but Clare would not give up until she had manipulated her into a position for sleep. Peaceful sleep was all we were after. I can recall one such conclusion with Immie naked and seated, her torso bent forward between her legs, head resting on the table, snoring. This perfectly balanced position had been achieved through a new silencing trick: Clare inserted her middle finger between Immie's lips and curled it up against the roof of her mouth, stimulating her to suck. With mouth clamped around fingertip, Immie's whole concentration was taken up with sucking. And, eventually, her face fell forwards into Clare's palm and sleep.

I remember another day in the nursing chair, with Immie at my bosom, watching Clare's hands hover over her skull. Every so often she would close a hand and withdraw it from the area round the head, as if she was carrying something away and throwing it out into the air. I asked what she was doing. 'I can feel black stuff,' she replied, 'and I'm getting rid of it.' I thought this must be the pain of the birth – the terrible headache it had given my baby; I trusted that, by removing it, Clare was freeing her of that past.

But then there was the dahlia. Clare's boyfriend gave Elinor a huge canary-yellow dahlia from his garden – such a generous gift. We cut off the stem and floated it face upwards in a dish of water, its frills overflowing onto the kitchen table. Within a day or two the outer petals began to blacken, and I had to push away the image of Immie's brain doing the same.

Each week, I watched from the bedroom window as the health visitor lifted her scales out of the back of her white Peugeot, crossing my fingers that we would pass this week's weight inspection. But, around the middle of August, the reading started going down. She was concerned: if Immie's weight didn't increase, we might have to consider supplementing the breastfeeding. She said the nipple shields inhibited the flow of milk and most likely they made the tummy gripes worse, so I should try to wean her off them.

The moment Mary had left, I set to work to get Immie feeding from my bare breast, but as usual she screeched and thrashed. It felt as though that one morning when we had done without a shield must have been some confused memory, harking back two years to the bliss of breastfeeding Ellie.

Reconciled to using the nipple shields, I was determined to get my baby's weight up before Mary's next visit. If I failed, all that work weaning her off bottles would have been in vain. I couldn't prove how much I was feeding her as I might have done with the calibrated bottles, but I could put in the hours. Now Immie's every waking moment was spent in my nursing chair, getting her latched on and feeding. If she threatened to nod off, I strove to wake her, tickling her bare toes, jiggling her about with a playfulness that belied my desperation. The morning Mary was due, I woke up especially early to put in a good three hours before my infant hit the scales. But when the dial came to rest, it was in the same place as last time.

Mary gave me the phone number of a breast-pump company and I ordered the most powerful machine available. Ermintrude II arrived by courier service next day and I rigged her up with two funnels so I could siphon off my milk as fast as possible, two tits at a time. But I could not resurrect the satisfaction I had felt in performing this task in hospital, and my breasts were not inspired to produce anything like the amount they had at the beginning. To my expressed milk I added the most expensive, most breast-milk-like formula I could find. That way I knew she was getting maximum calories along with my antibodies. But I loathed the plastic bottles she preferred to me. I loathed the smell of the formula milk and the rancid odour it gave my baby. Where was my 'sugar and spice' little girl? Ellie had always smelt as sweet as the rhyme proclaimed. Where was the nutmeg fragrance I had been waiting for since Imogen's incubator days?

Nadine cut through such self-indulgence. We needed to get the baby up and running – she needed food and that was that. Seating herself on an armchair in the middle of the room, she laid Immie across her knees, took the bottle of milk and wedged it in place. Then she swung her legs from side to side and chattered away in Spanish babytalk. Without the movement halting for even a beat, the feed proceeded. And, as I watched them, I chastised myself: this woman was a sturdy oak where I was a pathetic sapling, sagging under the weight of my tiny child.

I was exhausted. Life with Immie was less fun than I could ever have imagined it. *Do you feel more unhappy than you did before you had the baby?* The post-natal depression form had asked that question more than a month ago, and I had cried. Now there was only one possible answer: *Definitely. Yes, definitely. All of the time.* But I wasn't going to admit it to the health visitor; I could do without the antidepressants they had waiting for me. For now, there were more pressing matters to deal with. Most importantly, Immie's smile, or rather lack of it.

I knew the facts: of all the 'milestones' that twenty-first-century babies are given, the smile is the first. Elinor had been bang on time at around six weeks; most babies are. But Virginia

Nicholas was still waiting to tick it off on Imogen's list. Week six, then seven, eight, nine, ten . . . All went by without a sign.

Ellie said we needed to be funnier. Jay said he saw her smile whilst he was feeding her; I said it must have been wind. The lost smile became a family joke. In the back of the car Elinor would call out, 'She's smiling!' and when one of us turned to have a look, she would laugh: 'You just missed it!' When I was doing the up-down lifting, I would try to find exactly the right distance for her eyes to focus on my grinning face. Her big irises were no longer my blue colour; they were now charcoal grey. But they did not smile back; they stared unblinking towards the bold geometric patterns on the wall hanging behind me.

Mary said not to be perturbed; most likely her eyes had not yet fully recovered from the insult and if she couldn't see our smiles, then she couldn't learn to smile back. She demonstrated a particular way of stroking Immie's cheek, lifting the corner of her mouth with the tip of a forefinger to try to stimulate a smile, even when she was asleep. She said she had seen lots of babies take months to recover from a bad birth. And the scales showed that Imogen was starting to put on weight, which was something to celebrate.

I fished my baby out of the weighing tray – yes, perhaps she felt rounder and plumper. Now that I looked closely, I could see that the folds of skin on her arms were starting to fill out. Strange, I must be so familiar with her that I hadn't noticed her changing. Having relinquished the bond of breastfeeding, I was still holding her day and night, as if her body were simply an extension of my own. Perhaps that was the reason I was unable to get a clear perspective on her development. Because she was too close. If I could only prise myself away from her a bit, I might feel less anxious. At the very least I would get some more sleep.

Nadine said she'd have Immie over for a night. It was one positive result of stopping breastfeeding, she reminded me. She was used to working nights with her elderly clients; her cottage was just down the lane; I could call her at any time. The offer of a full night's sleep was too good to turn down. We sorted out the exact timings; we prepared the feeds, clothing and everything else. In the evening Jay took the pram over to her cottage, but, when he returned, I was in bed clutching Immie. I rang Nadine and apologised: I was bottling out; I couldn't be away from my baby for a whole night. She understood.

Mary brought along the nurse from Virginia Nicholas's clinic. Sally did not wear a uniform, but still retained a clean and tidy professionalism: straight blonde hair scraped back, file poised. She reassured us that all parents who'd had babies in special care said it was a roller coaster afterwards. We were doing really well; it was important to concentrate on the present and not worry about the future. 'Just hold on in there,' she said. 'Live a day at a time . . . Don't compare her to other babies . . . Don't think about the milestones. . . Take the baby on her own terms.' She took Immie from Jay and propped her up in a sitting position on her knee. Then she held a forefinger up a few inches from her face. 'She's fixing,' she declared, and started moving her finger slowly round in a horizontal arc. Jay agreed: yes, she was definitely following the movement. And I sat apart from them, as if they were the proud parents and I was some uncomprehending onlooker, telling myself I had to conquer these baby blues.

I had to conquer them because the month of August was ending, and with it Jay's period at home. During his days in London, I was going to have to cope on my own. The morning that he was due back at work, he discovered a puncture on the back wheel of his bike and set about the laborious process of mending it. Having psyched myself up for his leaving, I found myself irritated by the delay. I just wanted him to go, so I could get on with my new, solitary existence. Instead, one commuter train after another was passing through the station without him. At last, I watched from the kitchen window as he cycled up the lane and heard the tyre burst. Head down, he dragged his useless vehicle back towards the house and I went out to meet him. 'You're a loser!' I shouted. 'Let's face it, you're a fucking loser!'

Before he could reply, I was striding off to the vegetable patch to inspect the cabbages for caterpillars. When I found one, nestling in the silvery underside of a leaf, I flung it onto the stone path and stamped hard, satisfied with the bright-green ooze its body left behind.

How I envied Jay's being able to escape, doing something other than parenting. Meanwhile, day after day, here was I stuck at home in my nursing chair, a bottle pressed against my baby's hard palate. That was my only role in life now. And I could not see any way to change it.

Imogen was constantly ravenous, but seldom able to take more than a few millilitres of milk before the griping took over and I was forced to remove the bottle and calm her. I invested in an array of different teats, trying to find the one that worked best for her. Nadine said she had the greediness of a fat person but the stomach of a thin one.

Sally turned up regularly, on her rounds from one roller-coaster family to the next. From my chair I would hear her car grind down the lane, knowing I had a few moments to compose myself whilst she sorted out her paperwork. When she came in she would go straight to the bathroom to wash her hands – the old SCBU ritual. One day when my mother was visiting, she brought along her fixing-and-following tests: pieces of A4 white paper with simple black geometrical figures in the centre. She propped Immie in her lap and held up the bull's-eye, but Immie just wailed on and on. I eventually rescued her and folded my middle finger into her mouth.

'You're a saint,' said Sally.

'She's my baby,' I replied.

I wasn't sure about this saint business. Saint Julia. When I was a child my mother told me there was no Saint Julia in the Bible, and I felt rather relieved – in all the pictures I had ever seen, the saints were being tortured. When I was in hospital with Immie, waiting for her to wake up, a friend had said, 'This sort of thing always happens to the nicest people,' and I had laughed. Having a suffering baby had instantly made me one of 'the nicest people'. Now that she wouldn't stop screaming, I qualified for sainthood.

I couldn't see any alternative: this was how it was to mother Immie; I just had to accept the halo.

'I don't think she makes eye contact with me,' I said, wondering whether Sally would dismiss the idea as Virginia Nicholas had done. But she didn't; she just made a note in her file. I saw Mum's lips tighten. She was frightened that it was a symptom of brain damage; I knew it. My father was so terrified he wouldn't even enter the house whilst Sally was there. He stayed outside, scraping house martins' droppings from the windowsills, convinced of the importance of his task.

I didn't want the burden of my parents' anxiety; I had never wanted it. All those teenage years, refining my ability to climb the stairs without a creak so they would go to sleep believing I had got home at midnight rather than 4 a.m. – long ago I had learnt how to hide the worrying bits of my life. It was in my own interests: if they didn't know about such things, then they would stay calm and strong. That was what I needed from them.

And now that I was a parent myself, I valued the security they had given me more than ever; I intended to do the same for my children. Except that, with Imogen's arrival, things had got complicated. I couldn't conceal this baby from them as I had concealed other things. I kept on catching myself craving reassurance from my mother, wanting her to tell me everything was going to be OK. But she couldn't. In my arms was an undeniable reason to worry.

One morning, when the sun was up and blazing, Ellie came running into the kitchen: 'There's a baby animal on the fence; a baby animal.' I followed her out of the back door and round the side of the compost heap. In the long grass against the barbed wire fence, I could make out the prickly brown and grey back of a hedgehog. Only a two-and-a-half-year-old would be low enough to spot it. I parted the grass and saw that the little body had become impaled in a stretch of chicken wire along the bottom of the fence. It wasn't moving. I went to get a pair of gardening gloves and a trowel to perform a burial for the poor creature (and to satisfy my daughter, fascinated as she was with mortality and its rituals). But, when I returned, Ellie was shouting, 'It's alive, Mummy. The baby's alive!' And I could see the hedgehog's claws slowly pawing the hot summer air. I gently unhooked it from its rack and placed it in the shade, where it lay flat, too exhausted to curl up.

'Shall we give it some food?' One of my earliest memories, told to Elinor, was of leaving food out for the hedgehog in the strawberry patch. We took some bacon from the fridge and set it down with a saucer of water next to the splayed-out body. When we returned in the afternoon, meal and guest had disappeared. I told Ellie that meant the baby was better and had gone off to find its family. We each knew the other was thinking of Immie.

Nadine said I was coping well, but Jay thought we should buy in some help. I was adamant we couldn't afford it; Jay said it was not for ever. I said I didn't want to pay some stranger to look after my children when I had given up work to be with them. I said there was a principle at stake: we had made a choice to have children, and it had been hard enough with the miscarriages. Now that they were here, the least we could do was care for them.

'I want to be with my children, that's the deal, whatever they're like,' I said, feeling my halo glow.

'But we need to look after ourselves.'

'Looking after my baby *is* looking after myself. It may not be for you!'

Technically speaking, Imogen was my baby, but not Jay's. Because we were not married, I was the only one with parental responsibility. For him to get equal status, we had to sign official documents, but we had not yet found the time to do so. Now I could use such niceties against him.

'Maybe you don't want to be her father!'

'That's absurd. I adore my children. And I happen to think you're a good mother.'

'Well, you don't know how to show it.'

'You're impossible!'

'You should be supporting me, not palming off your baby onto professionals.' It was the professionals with their bottles and their milestones who had thrown us off course from the start. It was they who undermined me and confused me.

'Jules, it's not a crime! You're—'

'I'm fucking knackered!'

'And you think I'm not?'

He stormed out of the room. Ellie came running in: 'Mummy, stop shouting at Daddy!'

'You tell him to stop shouting at me!'

And she disappeared off to relay the message.

Calm down. You have to try to keep calm, hold on in there, spirit of the Blitz and all that. Don't think about Jay; just concentrate on the children; prove to him that you can cope. You can.

Alone in the big bed one night, I was holding Immie up against my shoulder, patting her back after a big feed, when she suddenly stopped crying. I turned to lower her into my lap and saw that behind me on the white sheet lay a huge puddle of milk, sticky with mucus. It took a moment to realise that she had thrown up her whole feed, without a sound – white on white, so thick and shiny that it did not sink into the cotton. The same thing happened twice more that night. I stripped the sheets and slept on the bare mattress.

It was another couple of weeks before the vomiting began again, but from then on it just became part of our life. We took to feeding her in the kitchen, where the lino could take the regular dousings. We became quite astute at recognising the signs of a vomit on the way – her face would redden, her cheeks puff out and her eyes swell. I would lift her away from me, turning her out into the open room as the blast of whiteness shot onto the floor. Jay would often make a run for the sink, in time for it to land there. I asked Mary whether it was projectile vomiting. No, she said, it had to hit the wall opposite to qualify for that title, and, anyway, it was normally boys who did projectiles.

★

Whilst Saint Julia was performing such duties, her toddler was expected to be equally selfless. Unfortunately, if I had accepted my halo, Ellie was intent on rejecting hers. Her most effective weapon was to wee on the floor. What a rumpus that created. I had been so chuffed to have successfully potty-trained her in time for the little one's arrival. But now she regressed to standing in the middle of the living room, feet wide, and firing a generous dose of urine into the carpet. 'Oh dear,' she sang, admiring the dark stain as it spread through the wool pile. I shouted at her – she wasn't responsible for paying our landlords to replace the bloody furnishings! Startled by my fury, her giggles turned to tears and then to a full-blown tantrum, in counterpoint to Immie's wailing. There was no use trying to comfort her, her kicks rejected my embrace. So I collared her and pushed her out into the garden like a naughty puppy. Lucky we had no neighbours to report us to Social Services.

Or that's how I saw it. From Elinor's point of view, with weeks of screaming baby turning into months, she was simply trying to reclaim some of her previous life. She was right: why should she sacrifice all her fun?

Bathtime, for example. That half-hour at the end of the day always used to be fun. Ellie would line up the rubber ducks and fish and a couple of plastic dolls, and then make cups of tea for them with bathwater poured from her yellow plastic teapot. I would be a VIP visitor to their party, accepting my cup with suitable protestations – 'Oh, thank you *so* much. Mmm. How delicious!'

But with Immie around, that game was out of the window. Knowing (since our hothouse visit) that she was calmed by the sound of water, I would extend the running of the taps for as long as possible. Ellie just had to wait. Once the water was still, my arms were full of baby, so there was no chance of accepting a cup of anything. Instead, I was constantly nagging the older sister to splash her water about, pour it from a great height – do anything to keep her sibling from creating a racket. Having complied with these demands, she would make me pay later, wailing, 'I want my daddy, I want my daddy.'

The school holidays were ending and the nursery no longer had extra room for Ellie. They needed to go back to her usual day and a half a week. I had thought that by now I would be coping well with two children at home, but I had to admit I wasn't. Already nerve-racked by the baby, I found myself constantly tense with my toddler, always anticipating anarchy. Perhaps the nanny idea was not so bad after all, I reasoned, just as a tempo-rary measure to bide us over until Immie was calmer. We would have to dig into our savings to pay for it.

Rocking Horse Nannies sent round an applicant on a sizzling September morning when I was indoors with the curtains drawn against the sun. I had been feeding Immie on and off for a couple of hours and was relieved to have company. Lorna told me she lived locally, a single mum but part of a large, supportive family. She took Immie in her arms and got her sucking from the bottle. When she asked about her birth, I thought she might as well know that Immie could be brain-damaged. 'Oh, but she's feeding – that's a good sign,' she responded. She knew what she was talking about.

Her niece, baby Joely, had been born four months previously at twenty-seven weeks and was seriously brain-damaged. Lorna's sister had had high blood pressure, so the GP sent her into the JR. And whilst she was on the toilet, she started to bleed. When she came round she was told the baby had been born by emer-gency Caesarean and she herself was lucky to be alive. Baby Joely nearly died several times. When they eventually left SCBU three months later, Lorna's sister was told the child would always have to be tube fed and would never walk or talk.

'They probably didn't dare tell her earlier, just in case she refused to take her home,' said Lorna. 'But my sister's not that sort of person. Ah well,' she sighed. 'I suppose with a family as big as ours, one of us is bound to have bad luck.'

I was shocked by the story. I liked Lorna, but it bothered me that, if she worked for me, she would be bringing news of her sister's baby. I felt that, somehow, baby Joely's fate and Immie's would become connected in this way. I turned her down.

A week or so later, waiting at the chemist's to buy a new soya milk formula (Mary had suggested it as the easiest one to digest), I spotted a young woman jigging her sprog up and down in a papoose. 'Listen,' I said to Elinor, 'other people's babies cry too.' The mother was asking for the same formula, so I butted in to ask her advice. Looking into the papoose to greet her child, I realised who it must be. 'Is this baby Joely?' It was obvious: feeding tube strapped to her cheek; her eyes very dark and staring. I explained how I had met Lorna and enquired about the birth. We swapped accounts of our JR dramas. I asked whether she would risk having any more children and whether they had considered taking the hospital trust to court. She said they had only just started thinking about these things. I remember referring to Joely and Immie as 'these abruption babies', but never once did I think that Immie would be as brain-damaged as this child. I agreed with Lorna: her strong suck was a healthy sign.

It turned out that Joely's mum and I used the same health visitor, so when Mary next came round I asked about the baby. 'I shouldn't really talk about other patients,' she said. 'But I'll tell you one thing – she's totally different from Imogen. Your baby's got life in her eyes.'

Nadine said we didn't need a nanny. What we needed was for someone to take the baby off my hands for a few hours so I could spend time with Ellie. 'Pay me my carer's rate and I'll look after Immie for you,' she offered. The hourly payment was twice our teenage babysitters', but I knew they were too nervous to look after Immie and they were right: she needed expert care. We were fortunate to have it in Nadine. But I felt her becoming more distant as we set out terms and conditions and formally agreed her hours. I regretted her changing from our granny next door into our carer.

For a couple of half-days a week, Nadine provided me with some Immie-free time. Time for Ellie. Time for Jay and me to see a couple counsellor. The counselling must have been Jay's idea; I would never have come up with it. I am sure I argued that it would only exaggerate the significance of our stupid rows, that we simply needed more social life, more fun together. But he reckoned we had reached enough of a deadlock to need a mediator, someone to listen to both sides of the argument; I owed it to him to try. On our first session the counsellor asked what we still had in common. We agreed: the children. She suggested 'family cuddles'. I remember getting back to the house and meeting Elinor on the front doorstep whilst Nadine stayed in the kitchen with the baby. Jay whisked her up and clutched her diagonally against his chest, her legs dangling down, longer and lankier than I recalled. I stepped forward and hugged the two of them, my arms around the crook of his back, my head against my little girl's. Our bodies moulded together, a perfectly steady triangle, so natural and so soft. 'It's an Ellie sandwich!' said Ellie.

The cradle will fall

IMOGEN WAS TWELVE weeks old – the time when the baby books say your baby will grow out of colic (overnight, some of them claim). We had set this as the date for a naming ceremony, in the hope that our daughter would do as the books promised. Though she hadn't, we couldn't cancel the arrival of thirty or so family members, plus godmother Fiona over from Australia with her three-year-old daughter. Anyhow, I wanted to conquer my misanthropy and show my parents that we were coping with our scary second-born.

After breakfast, Jay went over to the sink to wash up. As he did so, he began to whistle the jaunty theme tune from *Teletubbies*.

'Can't you shut up!' I snapped.

'What?'

'You have no idea, do you?'

'What?'

'Your whistling is incredibly irritating.'

'Oh, fuck off. I'll whistle in my own house if I want to.'

Out of the kitchen I stormed. It wasn't just the naming ceremony that put me on edge. Despite Nadine's help, and the counselling, I knew I was more argumentative than ever. Perhaps it was our imminent appointment with Virginia Nicholas. We were due at her monthly clinic the following day, and I knew Immie's delayed smile, her vomiting and general misery would all be under scrutiny.

I picked the last of my sweet peas – at the end of the season, more blue than pink – and arranged them on the living-room table. I printed out copies of a humanist ceremony that we had used for Elinor and tidied up for the guests. That grey lunchtime, our families squeezed indoors to hear parents and godparents take their vows:

Do you undertake to maintain a lifelong interest in Imogen, to give her help and support when required?

I do.

I remember ostentatiously kissing Immie's cheek as I levered her up and down in front of everyone. The formality of our ceremony protected me from any real contact with them. Jay had found something to read from Sylvia Plath:

> *Vague as fog and looked for like mail.*
> *Farther off than Australia.*
> *Bent-backed Atlas, our travelled prawn.*

I couldn't concentrate on his recitation; I thought everyone must be watching the baby and me, rather than listening to the poem. Now that I look back over the same page, I realise that the words describe Plath's unborn child, hidden in the womb. For Jay, Immie – the image – was still as mysterious as that.

Fiona stepped forward to speak. An old friend from teenage years, she had corresponded with me throughout my pregnancy, and received a long, shocking e-mail after the birth. When she mentioned to the gathered company that she hoped the worst was over for our new family, I felt my upper jaw tense with the prospect of tears. But mine was the next offering in our ritual; I couldn't lose it now. I held my solar plexus firm and stepped forward to sing my Mozart lullaby. I had chosen a boisterous one, not lulling at all. I imagined it sung by someone like Nadine –

practical and humorous, without a sniff of sentimentality. As Jay played the introduction on the piano, Elinor came over and took my hand; her presence strengthened me. I lost track of where Immie was (perhaps someone had taken her out of the room so she would not disrupt her own music) and focused out of the open window towards the copse on the other side of the stream. I could hear my voice resonating down the field: '*Schlafe, mein Prinzchen, schlaf ein.*'

The caterer from Ellie's nursery had come along with her daughter to provide lunch. They appeared now with trays of canapés and sandwiches, potato wedges and pizzas – delicacies to please all ages. Her fee seemed extremely modest for such a feast. I wondered whether it was because she felt sorry for us.

Whilst we ate and drank, Jay's mother clutched the baby tight and kept on announcing loudly, 'She's going to be fine, she's going to be *fine*.' My father folded his arms and sucked in the air between clenched teeth. Nadine sat and scowled at our lily-livered clan.

When the guests had left, I sat outside on the terrace, finishing off a bottle of bubbly and watching the house martins' bright white bellies flitting in from the fields. There seemed to be a constant flow of them, diving from different directions to serve the little blue-black heads that bobbed in and out of the door-way. It was more than two months since I had sat upstairs feeding Immie, listening to the birds doing the same. That brood must be out and about by now, as strong and independent as their parents, perhaps helping feed the next lot. And my chick? In all these weeks, nothing had altered: I was still struggling to get bottles of milk down her gaping throat; her limbs were as uncoordinated as ever.

Ellie clambered into my lap and I held her close. She was calmer, more contented than she'd been for a long time.

'Immie's our pet, Mummy,' she whispered.

Fiona and her daughter stayed the night, but clearing up the party and seeing to the children left little opportunity to chat. Once the girls were in bed, she joined me in the darkened kitchen, helping to calm my colicky babe. Her daughter had suffered from chronic colic; she knew what it was like. Fortified by shots of whisky, we took it in turns to hoick Immie up and down, demonstrating to one another the fitness benefits to be had. I remember laughing as my friend lowered the screaming bundle right down to the ground, and then swung her high up above her head with a weightlifter's groan.

Monday morning was sunny and mild, and we hurried breakfast to get the girls out into the garden. I had given it scant attention over the past months and my glorious July show was gone. The laughing viola flowers had been replaced by brittle pods. Snails had consumed the marigolds, leaving the stumps of stalks and a silvery trail behind them. The nicotiana plants had shriveled to nothing. But my neglect had given wild invaders the opportunity to flourish. Along the fence, forests of rosebay willowherb had grown up, their silky white seedheads disintegrating to the touch and sending out a cloud of fluff across the lawn. White bryony spiralled its tendrils through the netting, and our daughters delighted to discover its squidgy orange berries, bursting with poison. Eventually we persuaded them away from that danger and onto the climbing frame.

Fiona wanted photos of Immie to take back to Australia, so Jay held her high for the camera. Ever since her time in hospital, he had talked about doing 'flying babies' with her – one of baby Elinor's favourite games. But she had been so grumpy and he so anxious, he had not yet dared. Given this opportunity to perform, Jay at last lost his inhibitions. Placing a hand between her legs, another hooked under her arms, he flew her little body through the air like a jet fighter. 'Nee-ow,' the plane dive-bombed Ellie and her friend, who squealed in delight. I have one of Fiona's photos framed on the shelf above my desk: Immie's soft chubby cheeks against Jay's hairy arm; the cupid's bow of her mouth arching downwards to an elfin chin; the dark, serious eyes. She looks like any normal three-month-old baby.

That afternoon we were due at the clinic with Virginia

Nicholas. Jay and I dropped off Fiona and the girls at my parents' house and arrived early at the hospital. Sitting in the car, waiting until the last possible moment to go inside, I said, 'It's just routine, Sally will be there and she's told us everything already.' Jay laughed at my optimism.

'Always expect the unexpected!' he said.

The doctor was quick to voice her sympathy about our troubles. 'What you need is respite,' she declared.

I remember sitting down suddenly, Immie clutched against me. What did she mean, 'respite'? Respite was something people needed because terrible things were happening, because they couldn't cope. I looked over towards Sally, standing all neat and tidy behind the bed. Was that what she really thought? When she was with Mum and me at the cottage and she'd said I was a saint, had it been because, in truth, she knew how badly I was failing? She and the health visitor saw in us a case of serious post-natal depression . . . failure to thrive . . . respite case.

I don't recall what I said. Maybe nothing. My defiant glare must have been enough. The doctor sat down at her desk.

'I know you're doing your best. But Imogen is quite a tricky customer!'

Smile, please; I try.

'Sally, what kind of respite can we offer them?'

Sally looked down at the floor. 'I don't think there is any,' she admitted.

'Well, we'll try and look into it for you. Now, is there anything you would like to ask?'

I wanted to talk about the colic – was there really no treatment for Immie's sensitive digestive system?

'If I knew a treatment for colic, I would be a millionaire by now!' We managed to chuckle. 'Look,' she counselled us, 'if you were in a helicopter, flying over the Dreaming Spires in the middle of the night, you'd see all the bedroom lights going on . . . Parents just like you marching up and down. It goes with the territory, I'm afraid.'

Imogen had been sitting propped up in my lap, awake and

showing no signs of colic whatsoever. She seemed to like the strip lighting.

'Can I have a cuddle?' Doctor Nicholas took her from me. 'Now, let's take your hat size, young lady.' The doctor proceeded to wrap a measuring tape around her head. 'Thirty-eight centimetres,' she announced.

'Is that normal?'

No response. She was busy filling in the chart, with my baby snuck in close to her breast.

When she put down her pen, she altered Immie's position so she was facing her. Then she stroked the corner of her mouth upwards with her forefinger in the way Mary had taught us.

'Are you going to give us a smile, madam?' I felt a tightening in my gut.

Jay started to say, 'I think she has a happy face . . .' but the doctor cut in.

'It's very late. The smile is the first really important milestone . . .'

Jay was standing up to leave, gathering the changing bag and car seat. I took my baby back.

'Off already?' Her question brought us to heel. Jay sat down. I gave Immie my finger to suck.

'Does it mean she's . . .?' I said.

'Permanently brain-damaged?' The phrase landed pointedly, as if in a language I did not understand. Immie's tongue was pulling at my flesh. 'I have to be honest with you, Julia. Almost certainly.'

'But last time . . .'

'We have to look at the present. I'm afraid the signs are not good.' I knew her words were in plain English, but still they seemed to need translating, and my mind was struggling to do it.

'The colic – is that a sign . . .?' Jay asked.

'Possibly.'

'Will it ever go away?'

'We just have to wait and see.' She allowed the silence to sit. I suppose she thought she was letting the news sink in. But I couldn't concentrate on anything except the sound of Immie's slurp resonating around the room. Jay still seemed to be on top of things; his baritone cut through—

'Will she know us?' Pause.

'Nothing is written in stone. We have to take things a day at a time. Her motor and muscle reflexes are good.'

'What about your saying she would go to university?'

'I don't want to take that hope away from you, Jay.'

It was all too confusing; I needed to get out of there. Pile into the car, chase across town to the station where Jay had to catch his train to London. I drove as fast as I could through the rush-hour traffic, hooting at dreamy cyclists and slamming my hands on the steering wheel when a red light held us up. Jay found his Steely Dan CD and turned it up loud; neither of us wanted to talk. My thoughts were focused on the doctor: how her bad news seemed to come out of the blue when just five minutes ago she had been insisting we would know nothing for years.

As Jay left me in the car, his parting shot was, 'See, I told you: expect the unexpected!'

Driving on to my parents' house, I reproached myself for having deceived them with the ceremony the day before, with my composure and my hopefulness. As if I had lured them into loving Immie as a normal granddaughter when she was no such thing.

I stood on my mother's doorstep, holding my baby out like a broken doll. 'It's no good, Mum,' I said, 'Virginia Nicholas says she won't be normal.' Fiona hustled the girls away upstairs and my mother took Imogen in her arms. I felt suddenly exhausted. All I wanted to do was curl up on the sofa. It was just like the time I concussed myself falling off a pony. I remembered how the tiredness had hit me an hour or so afterwards, yet Mum wouldn't let me go to sleep, just in case I didn't wake up again.

Fiona came back downstairs and we followed my mother into the conservatory, where she sat looking at me with her lovely grandchild in her lap. I could see the strain in her eyes, the way the lids drooped downwards exaggerating her sadness. She wanted some explanation, but I had nothing to say, so she turned back to the sleeping cherub, bathed in September sunshine.

'She doesn't *look* disabled, does she?' my mother pleaded. Fiona had a Down's syndrome brother, though we all knew Immie didn't look like him.

At last I said, 'She looks like me. Except I'm OK and she's not.'

On the long straight descent into our village, the ash avenue's bright summer green was fading. Bunches of yellow keys at the ends of the branches were turning brown, dragging the filigree of leaves downwards into ugly clumps. Those leaves had done their work for the season, and soon they would fall away to expose elegant silver limbs. But now I realised this was not so, that the trees would never be free: every trunk was clothed in a dense skirt of ivy and its little pompom flowers hung from every bow, ready to burst open and pollinate. Surely someone should cut that ivy back, to give the ash a chance. If they didn't, come the winter storms or a heavy fall of snow, the trees might not be able to stand the strain.

When I got home, I packed up the breast-pump. I couldn't go on giving Immie my milk – I wanted to cut that tie with her. Like the ash trees, I needed not to be needed any more. My breasts didn't complain, they'd had enough. In the bath that night I inspected the dark line that had appeared during pregnancy, linking my tummy-button to my pubic hair – the *linea nigra*. It had faded over the past three months and now was almost indiscernible. Gone was this piece of evidence that I had had a baby, that I had been anything more than me – singular me.

Next day Jay was in despair. For the past few weeks he had been so optimistic about Imogen; now he said he couldn't see anything positive in her future. I realised this change put me in a new position. There wasn't space for my negativity any more; I needed to be strong. I said we didn't know anything; the doctor didn't know anything; we should be brave, for Ellie as well as for Immie. We must take Sally's advice and live a day at a time, not let anxiety overwhelm us.

I felt I was holding the family together; I couldn't afford to engage with Jay's distress. A friend of Elinor's came round with her mother and I took them outside into the garden, leaving Jay alone in the house. Whilst the girls played, we mothers chatted. The mother assured me that her daughter had been a terror as a tiny tot, either screaming or like Immie now – flat out. She said she was trying to get pregnant again, but had just had a second miscarriage; my success in bringing this baby to term made her more hopeful. She took Imogen from me and clutched her against her bosom. Lots of people think that if you hold someone else's newborn, it will bring you childbearing luck; I couldn't let on that this charm was broken. Inside the house, the double-glazing kept the truth at bay: Jay was howling, his big, strong body floundering on the living-room carpet.

Later, Nadine and I took Immie for a walk down to the Mill House and parked the pram next to the thundering waterwheel. Nadine said my daughter was going to be different from other children, that it would be hard work. But thousands of people did it. Oh God, what if she's incontinent? I said – the rest of her life in nappies. Were there really people who had to use nappies all their lives – and me the eco-warrior who couldn't even bear Pampers for my babies! With all her years of caring for the old and infirm, Nadine must have thought I sounded a real wimp. She said, look on the bright side: if Immie was brain-damaged, then there was much less likelihood of the usual parenting nightmares – unsuitable boyfriends, nights out who knows where, dangerous cars . . . 'You've got a CP baby!' she announced.

Cerebral palsy. Of course: my closest experience of cerebral palsy had been a boy in my year at university. He had a lolloping gait, and his speech was slurred, his features crooked. But he was still charming and funny, and he got all the top marks. I rang a friend whose son had been diagnosed with cerebral palsy after a premature birth. 'The proportion of CP people with a high IQ is the same as the proportion for normal people,' she said. 'In other words, Imogen has as much likelihood of being intelligent as anyone else. In fact, more so because you're her mum!'

When friends phoned, I had to give them the news. Having practised saying 'brain-damaged' in the past, without having to face what it really meant, now I could not bear its force. 'CP' seemed too vague. I wanted to be as clear as possible, once and for all.

'They think she's going to be disabled,' I declared.

'How do they know . . .? Can they prove it . . .? You don't trust doctors, do you?' they responded.

They were fearful for me, and guilty, and sad; I did not feel any of those things. I was almost excited at the challenge that lay ahead.

'How could we have sunk so fast?' Jay kept on saying. But we hadn't, I responded, irritated by his defeatism. OK, so we had sunk below the halfway line; we were in the fifty per cent of out-comes that we had hoped to avoid. We just had no idea where. We simply didn't know. Immie was so much better off than baby Joely – everyone told us that. She wouldn't be that bad. So what were we going to have to cope with? Wheelchairs, maybe. Well, that wasn't so bad; this cottage was made for wheelchairs with its big ground floor. Just a couple of years ago Jay had composed music for a disabled dance company; we knew wheelchairs need not ruin your life. I pictured my daughter as one of those joyful dancers, spinning in their chairs. And then there was Fiona's Down's syndrome brother. I knew the story of his mother being told to give up on her disabled baby, to put him into care and forget him. But she had refused, and the result of her bravery was her busy forty-year-old, who had a job and drove a car, was an increasing help to his ageing parents and kept everyone laughing.

Someone had left a large brown envelope on the windowsill with a red brochure in it, 'just in case'. The title was 'When Your Child Has Special Needs' and above it was a photo of a family: balding dad; mum with a new haircut. Their three sons were also pictured, the middle one propped up against his father, with his eyes half closed and mouth drooling. The youngest brother was kissing him and the mother was smiling. Jay scoffed at the picture: 'As if having a brain-damaged child is such a wonderful thing!'

I liked the charity's name, 'Contact a Family', and rang the local branch. I gave a brief rendition of Imogen's birth and Virginia Nicholas's concerns about her not smiling.

'What's her diagnosis?' the woman enquired.

'We're not sure yet. I think it might be CP.'

Didn't I have anything more specific? Well, no. I waited an age whilst the volunteer went down her list of possible problems and the charities that might help – but without a diagnosis she was not sure what she could do. Had I tried SCOPE? What was that? It used to be called 'The Spastics Society'. Of course, I would try them.

That evening Jay went on their website. He quickly found the 'forum' and began to trawl through discussions between parents of CP children. I remember there was a long correspondence about babies who would not stop crying. When he got to the mother whose baby had screamed non-stop for four years, I decided I could do without the internet for now.

We cancelled the couple counseling; attempting to analyse our relationship just did not seem right in the face of Immie's news. But I saw no problem in my taking up work again.

I had a grant to write a book about the street theatre of India, which had been lined up before Immie's birth. During the 1990s I had visited the subcontinent regularly, directing shows and workshops with urban theatre companies. Having developed an interest in the street entertainments, I spent lots of time travelling to remote villages in search of it. I loved the vibrancy, the roughness of the performances, and the book was an opportunity to describe them.

I had planned to fit in some writing once Immie was nine months old or so. Instead I began when she was just over twelve weeks, three days after our being told she was brain-damaged. I told Jay I had learnt my lesson: I needed this outlet, it was healthier for me not to be holed up with the children all the time, a nagging housewife. Though I could work at my desk in the corner of the living room, I accepted the offer of a studio space from friends in the next village. I think that, like my father cleaning the windowsills, I was busy escaping from the brain-damage worry. But there were other reasons too. Where caring for

Imogen over the past months had been so erratic, so chaotic, the writing allowed me complete control. If I worked at it, I knew there would be some sort of result, whereas after so many weeks with my baby there seemed to be nothing.

The weather was warm – a really vibrant Indian summer, and it felt good freewheeling my bike down the hill to my writer's hideaway. I was touching a little of the old, baby-free me. Jay became calmer and more positive again. I remember getting home one golden evening and there he was, Immie between his knees with a bottle in her mouth, Nadine-style.

'I told Nadine she could go home. It's fine,' he said. 'I feel fine about looking after her.' He was back to his upbeat self. Thank God. Now we could get some balance back in our life. Nadine was going to her place in Wales for a week, but if Jay was prepared to look after the baby, then I could focus on my book, at least for part of the time. Everything would settle down.

It was ten days after the clinic visit, the day before Nadine went away, that the impact of Virginia Nicholas's news hit me. I had taken Immie for cranio-sacral therapy with Clare and she had fallen asleep quite early in the session. Clare used the spare time to tell me about a charity for brain-damaged children that had been set up by a woman in her village. The woman's son had fallen head first down the stairs when he was a teenager and had been permanently paralysed. I had a vivid picture of such an accident – it was something I feared might happen to Ellie on our cottage stairs, with the terracotta tiles at the bottom. I started thinking about that woman's strength at being able to make something positive out of her tragedy. Then Clare said, 'You know, there is help if you feel you can't cope.' I was surprised.

'What do you mean, "help"?'

'Well, I could look into it for you . . .'

In the car, accelerating hard across a glorious late-summer cornfield, I turned up Aretha Franklin to block out Immie's wails. We had played the CD a lot whilst I was pregnant, singing along as if our little family were the Soul Queen's backing vocals. Ellie's favourite was always 'Baby, baby, baby, I love you!' Leaning into our fist-mics, Jay and I trying to catch the harmonies, we were all thinking of the baby in my tummy. And now that she was here, the anthem had become my rallying cry, filling me with its defiance, its reckless joy. The throb of the bass line must be echoing across the fields.

What exactly did Clare mean, 'if you feel you can't cope'? Everyone needed me to be strong, that's what a mother does. Like the SCOPE mother, I would be there for four years of screaming and puking and sleepless nights. I could love my unlovable baby, my fearful man, my wayward toddler. '*All you got to do is snap your fingers, and I'll coming running – I don't care.*' As I drove into the sunshine, I felt a wave of weakness coming at me. Some 'can't cope' feeling was pushing against the wall of my anthem. '*Boy, you're goin' to get it.*' Aretha's voice couldn't compete with the screams, which were higher and louder, splitting the air. Permanently brain-damaged. My child was permanently brain-damaged. It broke over me suddenly, in one crashing sob. I was giving in, allowing my brittle strength to dissolve away. Freely, I bawled at last.

By the time I got home, the panic about my inability to cope had advanced to panic about Elinor. If Immie was too much for me, then what did that mean for her sister? What had I foisted on her? What if I had given her an impossibly retarded sibling; no loving companion, instead a burden and a shame? Leaving Immie in the car, I went and wept down the phone to friends who tried to reassure me.

When Nadine arrived to take care of Immie, I got out of the house. I remember striding along the lane; I didn't know where I was going, just that I needed to get away. I could hear the tractor up in the big fields and stopped to catch the smell of barley on the breeze. They must be bringing in the straw; like Ellie's stacks of wooden bricks, the bales would soon be cleared away, the stubble bare.

Next thing I remember, I was sitting in the back corner of the church, crying. I must have been there a while before the door scraped open and I pulled back my sobs. Along the central aisle came a woman carrying armfuls of sycamore and beech, their leaves beginning to turn. It was Anne from the neighbouring farm, who bred the lambs in the field by our house. She was decorating the nave for the harvest festival, oblivious to my presence behind her in the gloom. With such gentleness she arranged the branches at the foot of each pew, strapping them with twine to the polished oak. As she completed her task, there was a sudden sweep of light from the west window, and for a moment the leaves glowed red and gold against the pink walls of the church. But she did not stop to relish the sight; already she was sweeping the flagstones clear.

Anne had cared for the church for years without recompense, devotion embodying its own satisfaction. Was this what God expected of me? My child might never smile, might never satisfy me with anything more than the peace of sleep, but still I must care for her as this woman cared for the sacred building. I thought back to the first day in hospital when I had imagined Immie to be God's child, not mine. She had been sent to teach me true devotion, was that it? Never giving back anything, to me or to anyone. *To give and not to count the cost.* That was what Sally the nurse had seen when she called me a saint. Could I go on doing it for the rest of my life?

Slipping out of the church, I headed into the sunshine and over the graveyard wall. Concentrating on the regular rhythm of my steps, I walked down to the mill, but did not stop to take in the thrill of rushing water; I could walk onwards like this for ever. At the gate into the spinney, the ground was strewn with crab apples – I should gather some. Already I had passed by fat purple sloes, and deeper into the wood would be blackberries and scarlet hips. But no. I would have to make time for them another day; now I wanted to get to the mushroom field.

I took in the circular expanse of meadow, framed on one side by ragged willows and on the other by a hedge of ash and hawthorn. Through the trees I could see pale arable, sweeping away onto high ground. Straight ahead lay the line of the railway, and above it the forest, black against the horizon. I skirted anticlockwise around the pasture, keeping my eyes to the ground in search of fungi. The grey mare watched me warily as she grazed, nose to the ground, ripping and chomping. This time last year the mushrooms had been easy to find, but now every flash of white was a false alarm. Each time I got closer, it turned into a clump of thistledown, or a stray feather. I was on top of one seeming-clutch before I could make out the bare hollows of eye sockets inside the perfect white orbs of an empty badger skull.

The rooks that had picked it clean were now roosting in an old oak at the centre of the field, their rough chatter echoing around. As I approached, they scattered on the wind, wheeling out across the cornfield. Only one remained, lower-voiced, croaking above my head. Though I had not known it until now, this was my destination – this tree standing over me. How old was it? One hundred years, perhaps. So many flocks it had harboured, so many storms withstood. There was a rust-coloured gash down the centre of the trunk, as if perhaps it had been struck by lightning. But its sides were still strong, able to withstand another hundred years or so.

Between the tree's ridges of bark grew prickly, pale blue lichens. As I leant out to touch them, I spotted the mare approaching, eyes shiny behind her ragged forelock, white blaze expectant. I thought of stretching my hand to stroke her muzzle, whispering into her ear. Instead I held fast to the tree, motionless and silent. The horse gave up on me and lumbered away towards the stream; from this angle I could see her swollen belly – she must be pregnant.

Alone again, I leant back against my oak and looked up towards the forest, submitting myself to the landscape. 'Please don't test me like this,' I heard myself pray. 'I can't do it. I can't take such a burden. Please, God. I beg you, God. I beg you.'

Tuesday, 1 October

Immie needed to go for her three-month jabs. The GP had a good look at her and said, 'You'll be a very pretty little girl once you stop yelling.' She was calm, got me to talk about my anxieties. She had lots of children of her own, I knew. She said we had to trust the paediatricians, and I nodded. As I came out of the surgery, I saw Mary.

'How's it going?'

'A bit wobbly . . .' And I started to cry.

She apologised that her room was occupied, so we must sit on the bench in the corridor. I told her about our out-of-the-blue diagnosis, how Jay and I were taking it in turns to go to pieces. She must have known most of it – surely the GP had been notified by the hospital. But I saw the shock on her face.

'You poor things.'

Her sympathy opened up a new deluge of tears.

'We don't know how brain-damaged she's going to be. But I can't stand the wait.' I said, 'Oh God, it's not fair. It is not bloody fair.'

'But she's been doing so well. You just don't know . . .'

'I feel I'm looking after an animal,' I blubbed again, almost delirious with my outpouring. I had never cried so freely and so publicly in my life.

Afterwards Mary told me this was the decisive moment, when she realised we needed help. I suppose the animal idea came from Ellie's calling Immie 'our pet, Mummy'. I didn't think it so very shocking, but Mary did. She asked whether I would like a visit from Social Services. It meant nothing to me. I had never had any dealings with them, nor had anyone I could think of. Mary asked whether I would like to talk to the GP again and I said that might be a good idea.

Back in the doctor's surgery I felt safe, passive even. She asked me whether I had considered taking antidepressants, just to tide me over and get me through the worst of the worry. I started on about trying to avoid drugs unless totally necessary, then I looked at her (pen poised) and said, 'If you think they're the right thing.' She filled in a prescription and handed it to me. I said, hadn't I recently seen a programme on television that associated this particular antidepressant with suicide? I wondered whether it might send me even deeper into despair than I was already. She had heard similar claims but said there was no firm evidence, at least not for adults. Lots of her patients benefited from this medication. I told her I thought we needed help from Social Services – it seemed the right way to acknowledge this new inability of mine to cope. She said, 'It's very hard to get anything out of Social Services.'

I rose to the challenge. 'How do I do it?'

'They have to believe that the baby is in danger.'

Thinking of my head-smashing fantasy, I looked her straight in the eye and said, 'She is!'

Next day, Mary rang to say someone from Social Services would be with us first thing in the morning. Whatever she had told them, their response had been incredibly swift. I was meant to be going to join a book group in Oxford that evening, but I wasn't sure I could face it. Jay said he would manage – I needed to get out. He was right: more than three months since Immie's homecoming, I had not once been out on a social date like this. So I sprayed perfume over one of my mothballed dresses and rooted out a lipstick. Then I drove into town like any childless chick on a girls' night out.

This was the first time I had attended the group, with women I hardly knew; I think my mother must have put me in touch with them. No one knew about my recent troubles. They were discussing *The Blind*, a gruelling fantasy about a plague of blindness where those who fall victim are locked away and start to destroy one another. I had managed to read almost half of it, often by wedging Immie's bottle upright against my chin so one hand was free for the book. Now I pitched in enthusiastically; I must have been enjoying the fact that my own world of disability and incarceration was a full half-hour's drive away. The conversation soon turned to amiable chat, welcoming me as the new participant. People asked about my life in the country and about my children. There was united admiration for the fact that I had left my three-month-old in order to come to their book group.

'Gosh, when my baby was that tiny, I just couldn't escape,' one said. Everyone laughed in recognition, especially me.

At nine o'clock next morning, there was Alison from Social Services sitting in our kitchen. I remember her fluffy blonde hair and blue eyes (pure English rose), her glamorous clutch-handbag standing on the table next to her. She wasn't here as a social worker, she explained, but as an assessor from the children and families team, come to see what sort of help we needed. She asked about what had been going on, and, as I tried to describe my worries, she said, 'You haven't really bonded with the baby, have you?' That got the tears going: I was giving in to my shame. Alison sat there, respectfully silent, eyes lowered. I could see she was wearing blue eyeshadow. And a part of me floated away to watch myself the distressed mother performing her role.

I thought: if only I had done this when I was in labour. If only I could have cried 'I can't cope!' down the phone to the midwife, maybe then she wouldn't have hung up on me. Maybe we would have got to the midwifery unit earlier, soon enough to catch the ambulance before it went off to its cardiac arrest. But instead, there on the living-room carpet I had borne the pain, allowing myself to become paranoid rather than aggressive. Well, I had learnt my lesson; from now on no more stiff upper lip. In front of Alison, a complete stranger, a social worker, I sobbed and sobbed.

She apologised for having to fill in her 'Disability Service Priority Matrix'. They were meant to be replacing it with something simpler, she said. Nevertheless, the form would give the disability panel vital information to work out what sort of help our family needed. I still have a copy, two sides of A4. Down the left-hand side of the page is a list of family characteristics: physical health, mental health, quality of life, etc. Against these are vertical columns, labelled 'X', 'Y' and 'Z', containing different statements about those things, with little boxes next to them to be ticked or left blank. Each column scores a certain number of points. In column Y (a tick scores three points) we have ticks for 'Child has chronic ill health or medical condition which is likely to deteriorate' and 'Conflict between family members'. Column X (five points, the highest score) is full of ticks: 'Family totally unable to participate in basic social functions when the child is present' and 'Carer currently unable to view child at all positively'. How did Alison get these statements from me? Did she simply read them out and get me to confirm? All I wanted was some help. It didn't need the score-system, the columns, the sophisticated 'matrix'. They just had to respond to one thing: I CAN'T COPE.

'Sixty-seven. You have scored high!' said Alison. 'I think we need to get you some help.'

'What kind?'

'What do you want?'

'I don't know. I don't know what's available.'

In the matrix there was a statement ticked that read: 'Immediate action needed to avoid family breakdown'. I asked what exactly that meant.

'It's a way of getting the panel moving,' explained Alison. 'I think you are a severe case, and that means we need to find you help as quickly as possible.'

'How soon might that be?' Pause.

'Well, where are we?' she said, looking at her watch. 'October the third. I'm afraid the panel has already had this month's meeting, so we can't expect a response from them until November. Then a suitable foster family needs to be found . . . I'm going to recommend they offer respite care every other weekend.'

She seemed to think that was a lot – perhaps it was the most anybody got.

I knew I couldn't afford to worry about what kind of respite in what sort of place. But I was concerned about the wait.

'Are you saying this respite might not happen until the Christmas holidays?' Pause.

'I'm afraid so. I'm sorry.'

'But we need help sooner than that.'

'I'll do everything I can.'

She picked up her handbag and I accompanied her through

the darkened sitting room where Immie lay in the pram. We looked down at her, sleeping peacefully.

'Such a sweet little thing, isn't she?' said Alison.

As I closed the door I felt the ache in my gut. It had been there ever since the meeting with Virginia Nicholas. Now I realised that the pain came not from my digestive system but from my womb; the same place that poor Immie's brain had been damaged, it was the seat of my anxiety about her. And it was aching worse than ever.

What was I meant to do now? Having admitted to my terror, exposed my despair, I had nothing to show for it. I felt cheated: the system had stretched out a hand to help me and then withdrawn it. That was worse than never having offered it in the first place. How did I live from day to day with this rising panic of not being able to deal with her, our damaged child? What if I smashed her head in before they came back?

That evening I answered the phone on the terrace, watching the house martins above me forage for insects. There was quite a family now – almost a dozen birds swooping about, practising their aerodynamic skills on whatever midges and flies remained in the air. Alison was on the line. She said she had sorted things out; she had got round the red tape; Immie could go to a foster carer in Banbury this weekend. I thanked her over and over again, but couldn't take in any of the details. I was so grateful that, after all, she had understood; she was looking after us.

It was Thursday. All I could think of was our liberation less than forty-eight hours ahead. We had done it – we had achieved this respite that Virginia Nicholas said we needed and that the nurse had thought so impossible to get. Once Ellie was in bed, I trawled the internet to book a luxury hotel on Saturday night for Jay and me (my mother would have Elinor). I found an old manor house describing itself as 'a perfect retreat from the twenty-first century', with twelve acres of 'peace and tranquillity'. I imagined us pampering ourselves with its every luxury: the swimming pool, the spa, the three-star restaurant. Hell, we might even rediscover romance.

On the Saturday morning we all drove over to Banbury, the first time we had driven along that road since the birth. Alison had given us detailed instructions how to get to the foster family's house. If we'd had more time, she said, there would have been a formal introduction with a social worker present. But this carer was very experienced; we need have no worries.

Tracey was younger than I had imagined, short-haired and slim in tracksuit and trainers. Her husband had taken their three children out, she said. On the sitting-room floor was a little boy playing with building blocks – this weekend's other foster child. We sat for a while going through my list of things-to-do: Immie's crazy feeding habits; her wild routine; her need to be held, and how. I tried to be dignified; I smiled and was grateful and handed my baby over, kissing her on the forehead. Tracey followed us to the door. She would let us know how they got on, she promised – she never lied to parents. We could phone her whenever we wanted, but she would only contact us in an absolute emergency.

'Have a nice time!'

I knew this respite was a good idea: Tracey was a carer, a rather better carer than me. It was not so strange, handing Immie over to a babysitter for the night, just as I had planned with Nadine a month ago. I needed a break. Poor little Im. Would she miss my songs and my smell? Would she notice the difference between my love and her foster carer's? I suspected not. Or was my depression confusing me?

In the car driving away from Banbury, I wept with shame: I was a mother who could not care for her child, a hopeless, frayed, weeping child myself. The confident head girl, capable, intelligent – I had sunk this far. I had handed over my baby to a stranger because she had the compassion that I lacked. She knew how to love my baby. It was much worse than letting the nurses care for her in SCBU; then she was ill and needed help to get better. This time I was handing her over willingly, not because of her need, but because of my own. And only now that I had committed the act did I realise its significance. For Social Services to have provided emergency help like this meant much more than babysitting. Openly, publicly, they had allowed me to confess: I have not bonded with my child; I cannot be trusted with her. 'A severe case,' Alison said. It meant that, out of all the families in the UK, we were at the bottom of the scale – the most broken, the most dangerous.

And where might we go from here? I kept on imagining what Jay said I must not: a future where I was obliged to give up my baby for good. A future apart from her. How would I bear it?

Like soldiers on leave, Jay and I were determined to squeeze as much fun as possible out of our freedom. We took Ellie to a swimming pool in Oxford and splashed around in the shallows with her. I lowered my face into the water, growling along the surface like a crocodile circling its prey, whilst she bobbed up and down in her rubber ring.

'Eat me, Mummy. Eat me!'

When I grabbed hold of her, she squealed with delight. Jay's games were even more boisterous – lifting his laughing nymph aloft, he threw her into the air, catching her only just in time as she hit the water. 'More,' Ellie cried, and up she soared again.

We packed in the retail therapy: books and make-up and clothes. Elinor's lunch menu offered her favourite sausage and chips, with ice cream to follow, but the excess of pleasure seemed suddenly to overwhelm her, and she would not eat. I had booked her into the most expensive hairdresser in town for her very first haircut, but when we got there she wouldn't let them touch her. Instead, she sat in my lap whilst I was restyled. The tresses left over from pregnancy, when my hair had grown long and thick, were hacked to a short back and sides.

Leaving our little girl forlornly holding my mother's hand, we drove northwards out of the city. On the pavement I spotted a teenage boy in a wheelchair. The woman looking after him was surely too old to be his mother. She had stopped to move his head; it looked as though it had lolled out of its padded rest. I saw that his tongue was hanging out.

'Do you think Immie will be like that?' I said.

'No, not that bad,' Jay responded.

The hotel lobby was brimming with Japanese tourists on their way to Stratford-upon-Avon; Jay and I slunk up to our room. Even before I had entered, I was tapping Tracey's number into my mobile 'just to check everything's OK'. By the time I came off the phone, I regretted it. Tracey was totally reassuring, but the call had reminded me of my confusion and shame. I sat with Jay on the sill of our mullioned window, smoking pot and throwing the roaches down into the cobbled courtyard below, like rebellious teenagers. Though I had started taking the doctor's antidepressants – red and yellow capsules glugged down with my tea each morning – they were unlikely to take effect for a week or more. Jay had got hold of some cannabis in London, and its numbing power was instant.

Stoned enough, we descended to the basement for our luxury spa treatments. The place was deserted but for a group of young women playing water polo at one end of the pool. Jay decided to have a sauna, whilst I plumped for my second swim of the day. After a couple of half-hearted lengths, I struck up conversation with the girls. They were there for a hen party, out for a laugh, they said. And so was I, I said. They glanced towards the door of the sauna and giggled.

Jay and I didn't get it together to walk out in the twelve acres of peace and tranquillity. We booked an early slot in the salmon-pink restaurant, where we found ourselves alone, tended by a superabundance of waitresses. In front of me they placed one huge platter after another, with some morsel stranded at the centre whose menu description I failed to recall. A few months ago, we would have exchanged mouthfuls, guessing at the ingredients, playful in our judgement of the food. But now we could not summon up interest. Having agreed that we wouldn't talk about the children, we failed to pursue any subject of conversation for long.

Before my first glass of wine was finished, a headache came over me – a perfect excuse to retreat back upstairs to bed. We knew we must be easy on one another, how frail each of us was, we refugees from parentdom. I remember that night as a coming together, of quiet forgiveness, and of sleep. I suppose, in a way, it was romantic.

Next day we drove to a National Trust garden nearby, famed for its hornbeam hedges and grand vistas. We crept away from crowds and grandeur to the comfort of the orchard and huddled together in the dappled light under the trees. Sitting there, silent, we noticed a thudding noise, irregular and muffled. It took a while for us to realise that it was the sound of ripe apples falling on the grass. And as we did so, both our minds turned to Immie.

When we got back to Tracey's place, she didn't lie to us. 'Poor little thing,' she kept on saying, 'she must be in such pain. She's just not right, is she?' Oh God, what did I know? Immie lay whinging in a car seat that they had got down from the attic. Tracey's husband was there, rocking it back and forth with his foot. He didn't say anything. 'My husband can't stand all the crying,' she admitted. Tracey insisted we take the seat: 'We don't need it any more, and it seems to help her.' I lifted up the seat and carried it out to the car.

As we headed home, the back of the car full again with our daughters, it began to rain. As I hurried to the front door, I unbelted Immie and clutched her to me. But her body would not mould itself to mine; she seemed to be pulling away. I realised that, after a day and a half apart, I had lost the habit of being with her, and my muscle memory had regressed to the way I used to be with baby Elinor, soft and pliant. Throughout the months of nursing Immie, my body had been tense like hers. Now it had loosened, while hers had not.

I stood under the porch for a moment, letting the baby stay rigid, apart from me, as if I were carrying someone else's strange child. I looked up at the landing window where I had fed her at night during those first hopeful weeks at home. There was something strange about it – vacant, haunted. Then I realised: the house martins had left.

A-tishoo! A-tishoo!
We all fall down

Monday, 7 October

NADINE WAS BACK. Maybe she was shocked to hear about the emergency respite; maybe she thought it would not have happened had she been there; she didn't say. The fact was that she wasn't going to be our granny next door any more; she was returning to Wales for good. The news was not completely out of the blue. She had been getting estate agents to value the cottage for so long that I had begun to think it was just a way of reassuring herself of her assets. But now someone had put in a serious offer and she had made up her mind to go. Nadine admitted she hadn't enjoyed taking money from us; she wanted to go back to being friends, and anyway we couldn't rely on her even in the short term. She needed to spend more time in Wales now, preparing for the move.

The prospect of Nadine's departure seemed to fit with the general change that had come about over our respite weekend. By resorting to help from Social Services, I had stepped away from all that Nadine offered: her optimism, her strength. In truth, my whole attitude had shifted away from hers.

It was Virginia Nicholas's phrase, 'I don't want to take that hope away from you', that stuck in my head. Hope. It had kept Jay and me going, investing so much in Imogen. But what had it really done to us? Every time Ellie called out, 'She's smiling', our hearts lifted, only to sink even further (behind the laughter) with the crashing disappointment. I was convinced that Jay's determination to stay positive had made the brain-damage news harder for him. I wanted to be free of hope's seduction. I needed to find another way – an openness, an acceptance of what Imogen might be. Not hope.

The hunt for a new Immie-sitter began without discussion. I calculated that, if we paid the usual babysitting rate, we could afford twenty hours a week – twice the number Nadine had done. A friend of a friend recommended a local girl who had just qualified as a nanny, and I invited her round. Holly was strong, with attractive, open features. The daughter of a childminder, she had a natural calmness that would be good for Immie. I hoped she was patient enough to take her charge through the laborious feeds and endless calming tactics. I didn't say anything about Virginia Nicholas's prognosis. I reasoned that, as nothing was certain, I should not burden Holly; in truth, I was frightened she might not take the job if she knew.

The nursery reported that Ellie seemed more withdrawn than before. There were times when she would sit alone, pensive, unable to join in with their play. I took her to a friend's third birthday party and she sat in my lap, watching the other children dance. Of course she couldn't join in; she inhabited another world from them – one where sisters fell down and broke their crown, where Mummy was not such a reliable little nut tree after all.

It rained every day. When Holly came to the cottage I took the opportunity to be with Elinor. The straw bales had been brought into the long barn and we went there to play. I thought she would like to jump around as I had at her age, leaping off higher and higher bales into a mattress of loose stalks below, but she seemed to have lost her taste for falling through the air. Instead, she wanted to play 'houses', allocating parts of the stack as rooms for different members of the family. I had to be the mummy in bed, and high up under the corrugated-iron roof she found me a hollow to lie in whilst she prepared breakfast below. I pulled out an empty ear of corn and crackled it between my fingers to release the sweet savour of summer. Slowly, carefully, Elinor climbed up the staircase of bales, bringing me a plate-sized mound of straw.

Holly started taking Immie off to her mum's place, sometimes for eight hours at a time. The absence was a relief, the silence a healing balm. I lit the woodburning stove and brought tender pelargoniums in to their wintering place on the windowsill above my desk. I tried to use the time to do research for my theatre book, forcing my mind to escape into events far away. But the fire's warmth made me sluggish, and each page I opened blurred before my eyes.

I remember feeling constantly tired during this period, which I put down to accumulated sleep deprivation and the shortening October days. It might have been the antidepressants. Often I would go to bed at the same time as Ellie, but would be disturbed a couple of hours later by the sound of Holly's car returning. I did not care to wake fully; the sleeping baby would drift to my bedside and into the crook of my arm, her haven, where her dreams might mingle with mine. I dreamt my mother and I were standing over her and she was saying, 'You can cure her. She looks just like you did when you were a baby. You're the one who can make her better.'

Perhaps my dreams were part of my medication haze. Each morning I looked forward to that rhubarb-and-custard capsule; I reckoned my GP was right – it was helping. My feelings couldn't overwhelm me any more. It was as if all my emotions, the loving ones as well as the fearful, no longer belonged to me. I knew they existed, but they inhabited a separate world, as if locked away behind glass.

I kept thinking about the incubator, Immie's and mine. I am alone in a glass case. People move around outside, in slow motion. They communicate – they laugh and cry; they are full of hope and of fear. But I am cut off from it all.

★

The experts turned up regularly at the cottage. I was getting used to having them around; in fact I preferred their professional jollity to the fear and the guilt I sensed in friends and family. Sally's and Mary's weekly visits were always on a particular pretext – to give Imogen her immunisation jabs, to take a urine specimen, to reassure me of her weight gain. They suggested her seeing a speech therapist 'to help her development'. A friend whose father had been paralysed with Parkinson's for decades rang to say 'Don't trust speech therapists'. But I wanted to give Immie every chance; I couldn't let other people's prejudices inhibit me.

The speech therapist brought along a selection of dummies, all of them huge. They would help stimulate Immie's mouth muscles: at this stage, for feeding rather than speaking, she explained. I welcomed them, thinking they might spare my oversucked digits and the awkwardness of being forever attached to my baby's mouth. After half an hour of dummies flying around the room, I wedged my usual finger in place and said maybe she wasn't ready for them after all. We organised for the therapist to come back in a month or so.

A physiotherapist from the hospital rang to make an appointment. I wasn't keen. I thought Immie was getting excellent therapy with Clare, and after two months with her I didn't want to change. However, Clare disagreed, saying it was 'important to get into the system'. I was very sad to leave her; I had grown to believe that Clare's intuitions about Immie were better than any of ours. But I knew we couldn't afford her fees indefinitely. Somehow, sometime, I was going to have to transfer my allegiance.

Judith, the physio, got down to work, shaking the sparkly rattle and calling Immie's name to attract her attention. Jay and I stood over her, impatient for our daughter to relax as she had done with Clare. She screamed and clenched her fists, but Judith was unfazed, picking her up and holding her over her forearm to investigate her musculature. 'I can't feel any spasticity,' she said, and Jay and I felt a huge sense of relief. Afterwards, she stayed to watch me feed the baby. 'Look,' she said, 'she is gripping the bottle!' By the time she left, our spirits were higher than they had been in weeks.

After that, Judith came every Wednesday. Often she would hang around after her session for a cup of tea. She wanted to know what Virginia Nicholas had told us; I said, not a lot. Everyone was advising us to 'wait and see'. Her eyes went ceilingwards. I asked whether she could tell what Immie was going to be like in the future. She said, no. On another occasion I confided in her about my trying not to hope any longer. I told her it was hard to invest everything in a child like Immie. She nodded; she seemed to understand. I said I knew that baby Joely was her patient and asked why she was doing physiotherapy with a child who would never walk or talk. 'Because the doctors might be wrong!' she said.

I couldn't shut my ears to this sort of thing. When it came down to it, there didn't seem to be any way of mothering Immie without hope. She was the child in whom I had invested even before my pregnancy with her. The very condition of parenting was an investment in the future. During the many hours I still spent alone with her, especially late at night and into the early morning, I found myself behaving in exactly the same way as I had always done. After the back-patting and the jigging around, if she was calm I would stroke the corner of her cheek and chatter away in my sing-song voice. 'Come on, little Im, we know you can do it. Come on, my grumpy chick.'

The antidepressants must have numbed me to the disappointment.

I asked Sally about our October appointment with Virginia Nicholas: would the doctor have important issues to discuss? No, she said, all we would talk about at this stage was the feeding. We even had good news to report: over the past couple of days Imogen had stopped throwing up. We decided there was no point in both Jay and me attending the clinic; I would go along on my own. He left for London that morning in a cheerful mood, saying he felt really optimistic about Immie.

In the waiting room I sat under the 'Give Your Baby a Head Start' poster and wondered whether anyone with a brain-damaged child had ever complained about it. The woman who ran the support charity for parents of SCBU babies was drifting around and I signalled to her; she made her way over. I explained that the doctor had told us Imogen was likely to be permanently brain-damaged; she was very attentive, very serious. I reminded her that she had sent a mother to see me whose baby had recovered from a terrible birth; now I wanted to get in touch with families who had a damaged child. She looked taken aback, said she wasn't sure whether her charity could do such a thing, that they must take advice from the paediatrician

Virginia Nicholas was calm. Did her usual tests and filled in her files. I noticed that the head measurement − thirty-eight centimetres − was the same as a month ago.

She smiled, said she'd had a letter from the physio and thought we should help Imogen along with some baby-friendly drugs: a couple for her tummy ache, and one to help her relax. I did not object. My inhibitions about drug-taking were now consigned to some previous life.

The doctor moved rapidly on. How was Imogen sleeping these days? Well, things were better, but we were up with her most evenings until midnight. In that case, here was another prescription − chloral hydrate; it would make her 'much easier to manage'. The name rang a bell. Had my head been clearer, I might have remembered the painter Rossetti and his addiction to the drug's hallucinogenic properties. I might have questioned whether it really was so 'baby-friendly'. But I doubt I would have turned it down. The prospect of 'managing' my nerve-frazzling infant was just too attractive.

Dr Nicholas asked whether I had any questions and I asked whether there was anyone I could get in touch with who had a child like Immie. She said she would 'have a think'. There had been one family whose response had been 'very sensible'.

I thought, what about the rest? How 'unsensible' had they been?

The doctor leant back in her chair. I looked across the room to Sally, who was trying to dissolve into the floor, just as she had last time. She had promised there would be no heavy scene. But I could see it coming.

'I'm afraid Imogen is not developing as well as we would like.' The blood was pumping loudly in my ears. 'Her head is too small for her age. That means that she has something called microcephaly. I am detecting some spasticity in her arms . . .' I supposed I knew it already. 'We have to be prepared for major problems.'

'What do you mean?'

'I mean that, as Imogen gets older, she is likely to develop major problems . . . because of her brain damage.'

'Like what?'

'We can't be sure.'

'Will she walk and talk?'

'I really can't say.'

'Incontinence?'

'I'm afraid it's still going to be a while . . .'

'It's possible she won't be able to do anything, isn't it?'

'She can tell the difference between light and dark!'

We weren't getting anywhere. 'Major problems' sounded bad, really bad. It definitely meant that Imogen was getting worse, not better. Yet the doctor wasn't giving me any facts. Whilst she carried on being vague, I was the one who had to walk out of here and look after her patient, without any certainty except this horrible uncertainty. I picked up my daughter and strode to the door. I think my parting shot was 'Thanks' (with just a tinge of sarcasm).

I carried Immie across the car park to the main hospital building, dawdling behind a bed trolley that sailed along the corridor, a big bag of drugs swinging from its mast. I thought of all the pain harboured in this place – where did it all go? The painkillers and the antidepressants covered it up, but it had to come out somewhere. In some hidden ocean of agony.

I handed the bundle of prescriptions through the pharmacy

window and set down the baby seat on the chair next to me. Two girls sitting across the way came over to baby-gaze. 'What a lot of hair she's got!' they agreed. An elderly lady further along the row grinned. I knew what she was thinking: what a lucky young woman with her beautiful new baby. So I grinned back. Yes, here we are, Mummy and Baby, bringing Hope into the world.

When at last the drugs were delivered and their administration explained, I headed outside fast. I lifted my face up to the sky and let my tears join the drizzle. In the car I pulled myself together to phone my parents; they would be eager to hear what had happened. I wasn't going to offload onto them, what was the point? So I tried to make light of things. I said the paediatrician was still being her evasive self . . . 'She keeps on saying "problems" but she won't say what . . .' I didn't want to phone Jay. I thought it better to tell him the news in person rather than leave him stranded on his own with it. I imagined us later that evening, cuddling Immie together after I had reported her doctor's prediction.

At home I rang Nadine and told her what had happened. 'I'm coming round,' she responded, and within a couple of minutes there she was, taking the baby off me as she stepped inside the door.

'Poor little Im, my poor sweetheart,' she murmured, clutching her up against her cheek.

When I returned from putting Elinor to bed, Nadine was standing with Immie against one of the hi-fi speakers. 'Look,' she declared, 'she likes Paco de Lucia.' It was true: swaddled in a shawl, ear to the amplifier, her charge was listening to flamenco. The clapping of cupped hands shifted to a sharper metallic clatter as long nails scurried across the strings, and still Immie was calm. Nadine caressed her head and murmured soft words of Spanish love along to the music. I got the stove burning and we shared a fat spliff, waiting for midnight and Jay. He thought she was getting better; now I had to tell him she was not.

Nadine was still holding Immie against the speaker when Jay

got back. Suddenly there he was in the doorway; I stayed sitting on the sofa. I delivered the news calmly, economically, aware that the cannabis might be making things seem more absurd than they really were. Jay looked at Nadine, as if somehow she was to blame, turned around in the doorway and disappeared into the darkness.

Totally ignoring his daughter, he had scuttled away to phone his mum. That got my goat. When at last he returned, Nadine went home, leaving me to my outrage. We should be in this together, supporting each other; we were her parents! Jay couldn't see it. He was suddenly far, far away.

Microcephaly

The term microcephaly simply means 'small head'. It usually reflects an underlying reduction in the size of the brain. The effects of microcephaly may vary considerably. It may cause delay in the child's development which can vary from very mild to profound. Severely affected children frequently have cerebral palsy, epilepsy, visual impairment or feeding difficulties.

I downloaded the information from a medical website. I had to. However horrible, knowledge was better than uncertainty.

From what I could see, my daughter was only four months old but already suffering everything on the 'severely affected' list. The epilepsy had been treated in SCBU, but presumably it could return at any time. Would I be able to recognise it second time around? As for the other major problems, they were already obvious enough. She couldn't see my face; in future she might even lose interest in bold, abstract patterns like the wall hanging. As for feeding difficulties, I found it hard to imagine anything much worse than our current hassles: three or four hours to give Immie a bottle, with her regularly vomiting up a whole feed.

First on the list was CP. No longer a vague acronym, it meant something very tangible to me now: paralysis. I could see it in her fingers, always curled inwards, nails digging into palms. I had been wrong to think they clung to me for safety; it was simply because they were in spasm. The stiffness in her arms and legs was now undeniable. Though her limbs and digits pulled inwards, her back thrust outwards, mangling her poor body. When I rang Mary to tell her what the paediatrician had said, I added that I thought Immie was 'already a spastic quadraplegic'. The health visitor gasped, but she didn't contradict me. I went on the internet to find out what spasticity in all four limbs might entail – major hip operations in early childhood, most likely. But I still couldn't be sure; not until a specialist looked at my daughter and confirmed it.

I put my palm against Immie's curly locks and eased her forward to release the tension in her spine. Her head was burning hot. Now that I knew about the microcephaly, I did not want to interpret her screaming as common colic, nor as 'irritability' (as the professionals term it). I wanted to acknowledge that it was anguish. Anguish at what she had been through and what was to come. She had been expressing it ever since she came out of the coma; it was just that no one wanted to admit it. When she arched her back and stiffened her legs, she was suffering – her head was throbbing, letting her whole nervous system know that it had been shocked. Zapped. Now I was sure that the 'black stuff' Clare felt coming off Immie's head was useless dead matter, floating away like smoke from an incinerator. How much of it was there?

Virginia Nicholas phoned to see how we were doing. I told her that we felt very low about Imogen's future. She said, 'I think you need anxiety management.'

I said, 'I'm taking antidepressants.'

'Do you think they are working?'

'How can I tell without stopping?'

'Oh no, I wouldn't do that if I were you.'

The anxiety came from the uncertainty, of course. If only Dr Nicholas could give me a definitive diagnosis, corroborate what I'd read on the internet. If only she would give me baby Joely's rhyming phrase, 'She'll never walk or talk', then I could start preparing. I could do the research, meet other parents, phone Contact a Family and get in touch with the right charities.

Despite my lack of diagnosis, I rang the SCOPE helpline. The girl on the end wouldn't commit to what major problems might mean. I remember asking the question that most preoccupied me: 'How am I going to communicate with her?' And the girl reeled off the ways: sound, touch, music, dance . . .

'But that would be in the very worst case,' she said, as if mine wasn't. Eventually she admitted that prescribing drugs and predicting major problems so early in CP cases was unusual.

Unusual. I had never expected this in baby-making. Everyone had said that having a baby made you part of the crowd. Whatever your background, whatever your talents, becoming a mother was absolutely ordinary. I remembered, at the height of my first labour torture, consoling myself with the thought that this outrageous pain was what women had always put up with. It was completely, utterly normal.

But Immie's birth had proved itself not so. She was at the bottom end of the fifty per cent of those babies in SCBU. If only this unusual experience had been a fortunate one. Couldn't my daughter have been chosen to sit at the other extreme of childhood: a child genius, why not?

Now the mornings were misty, the nights threatened frosts. I strode out across the fields with Immie strapped tight to my tummy and Ellie at my side, eager to show off her new Thomas the Tank Engine boots. Down at the stream the sheep had been churning back and forth across the stone slab of the bridge, and the mud was smooth as Cotswold honey. Ellie's boots were soon stuck fast, and she had managed to step out of them into the morass. I plucked her up under my arm, ripped off her socks and let her paddle herself clean in the freezing brook. She had always loved cold water.

Up the slippery slope, Ellie squelching ahead, calling, 'Anne, have you seen my new wellies?' Anne came to the door of the farmhouse and beamed in admiration. Then she turned to me and asked how things were. 'Fine!' I answered, perhaps too brusquely. I knew by the way she held my eye that she had heard our news.

And I thought, you could do it, Anne. You would invest in your daughter, whatever she was like, however frightened you were about her future. You would trust the doctors and wait for their opinion, not get yourself worked up with worry and Web-trawling.

We gathered windfalls from Anne's orchard – bulbous Bramleys and downy quinces. It was good to be outdoors and busy. Ellie helped me load the fruit into plastic bags and we set off for home. But my not-yet three-year-old was whining, demanding to be carried down the slippery path through the hazel wood. I held the heavy bags in one hand and used the other to dangle her upright. Under our feet was a scattering of red hawthorn berries; over our heads, the leaves created a golden canopy against the flat white canvas of the sky.

I could feel the pain in my gut, exacerbated by my awkward clamber. A month ago I had identified it as anxiety, but now we'd had the major problems prediction, I'd changed my mind. Now it felt like a faint, perpetual echo of the abruption. I imagined that my womb (the part of my body that made me a mother) was reminding me of what it had done, harming its own fruit.

Out of the copse at last, I adjusted the bags so I had equal weight in each hand, leaving Ellie to drag her way up the hedgerow. As well as the womb ache, between my shoulder blades I was feeling the strain of the papoose. And Immie had started yelling.

'Come on,' I called back to Elinor. 'Just as far as the big tree.'
'Which one?'
'That one, it's about ten steps.'
'Then will you carry me, Mummy?'
'Yes, I'll carry you.'
I crouched down in the mud and she clambered aboard. At least my body was balanced: a bag in each hand, one child at the

front and the other at the back. The baby's hectic shrieks spurred me homewards, where I would be able to loosen her from me, get a distance from the noise. Head down, I stumbled through newly ploughed furrows of clay, my whole body aching. I could do it. After the abruption, no pain was unbearable. I was Mother Courage, indomitable, trudging from one battlefield to the next.

It wasn't my body, of course, it was my mind that really hurt. It wouldn't stop beating me up. It said I was the one who should have been damaged by the haemorrhage, not my healthy baby. She had been a perfectly normal child until the moment my placenta broke down. If only that moment had been mine rather than hers – I would willingly have perished from loss of blood in order to preserve the next generation intact.

Every day I told myself I just had to get through it, this one waking span. For the first time in my life I was needing all my concentration just for that, just to reach the end of the day. I reckoned the antidepressants got me up in the morning, and from that moment I tried to hold on to my routines: preparing meals, getting Ellie to nursery and back, getting her to bed. Most of the time with screaming Immie in tow.

When I was out in town, I kept on seeing ordinary babies with lovely, round, full heads. I wanted to go up to their pushchairs and stroke them and gloat over the big brains that were growing inside their skulls, and warn their mothers to take care.

Meanwhile, I knew people were looking at me and saying, 'It's a tragedy.' I didn't like that. Tragedies happen in newspapers and on television, they make a person into a public hero. I rejected the role. I felt the word 'tragedy' was an attempt to exalt our anguish, giving it a dignity it did not deserve. I wanted everyone to realise that this microcephaly business was real – it entailed banal realities like vomit on the kitchen floor. I also rejected their pity. Being pitied made me feel weaker and less able to cope. It made me feel sorry for myself, and that was no way to get through the day.

Determined not to give in to their image of the tragic mum,

I made sure I wore make-up and flattering clothes. Weight had been dropping off me ever since the birth; proud of my skinniness, I bought some designer-ragged jeans to show it off. When people asked how I was, it took huge concentration not to crumble. I could feel the skin around my eyes pulled taught with the strain, like a bad facelift.

At home, when I had time to myself, writing was out of the question. I couldn't even concentrate long enough to watch a television programme. I stood at the sink and watched Jay outside on the lawn, pacing up and down as he talked into his mobile. He was always on the phone now – to his parents or to close friends in London. He stayed outside, so I could not hear what he was saying. Having given up cigarettes at Elinor's birth, he had started chain-smoking, chucking the stubs around the garden. He didn't bother to join us for meals; he was afraid to get involved with our domesticity. I had no idea how to get him back, how to find the love I had once felt for him.

A childhood friend rang to find out about Imogen. 'Well, at least you're a believer!' he concluded, as if that made it all more bearable. I was surprised by his assumption. God had hardly entered my head over the past months, and when He had, it had been at moments of panic, in prayers of desperation. True, as a child I had believed in a powerfully Loving God, but adulthood had taught me circumspection. And now, with what was happening to me, I couldn't think how He could possibly console me.

Once the phone was down, I bundled Immie into a luxurious winter Babygro, hands and feet buried in its folds, and carried her down the lane to the church. By the time we entered the old building's half-light, she was rigid and screaming. I strode straight ahead, along the aisle to the rail, and held her up to the altar.

'Look what you've done!' I shouted into the gloom. 'Why?'

I didn't expect any answer, but all the same I waited a moment. Immie's wails rang out against the empty walls.

'Why? What have we done to deserve this?'

Still she shrieked.

'How could you do this to a child? What's the point? What's the fucking point?'

Slamming the door behind me, I felt stronger for my railing.

Virginia Nicholas's drugs had to be administered using plastic syringes squeezed into the corner of Immie's mouth. She hated it; she roared, throwing her head back, legs rigid. And as she did so, a shower of thick pink syrup would came splashing back, all over me. It reminded me of forcing medicine into horses when I was a teenager, their jaws clenched shut against the horrible taste. I used to find it easy enough, motivated by the certainty that it was doing them good. Not any more. Protected by my own drug, I could do Mother Courage; I could face the microcephaly, I could rant and rail. But when it came to drugging my baby, I was just too soft.

I had to ask Jay for help. His strange new state of mind, cold and uncommunicative, willingly assumed the role of doctor. Hooking one baby arm behind his back to stop her thrashing, he held her body tight across his front. His sunken eyes glared out into the room, away from the child. I handed him the full syringe and he shoved it into her mouth, aiming at the back of her throat. Before she could gag, he grabbed her bottle and pushed the teat firmly against the roof of her mouth. Her lips closed around it and she began to suck, ingesting medicine along with milk. Once she was settled, Jay's hand was out, fingers clicking impatiently for the next dose.

This routine must be performed every morning and every evening. In the morning we made it as swift as possible, but in the long, dark evenings we dawdled. There didn't seem to be anything else to do. I would line up the medicines in front of the living-room fire, alongside a large bottle of whiskey. Once Jay and I had each consumed a measure or two, the baby got hers. Our operation completed, Jay folded her into her sitting position with one palm cupping her bottom, the other supporting her chest, and began his levering duties. He tried to make the movement as clinical as the drug administration, but I could see him slipping back into softer habits. As she rose up towards his mouth, he took a beat to kiss her, absent-mindedly, on the top of her head. Her drunken face lifted in response.

Once she was calm, he handed her over and I gave her my finger to suck whilst he rolled a spliff. If by 8.30 she was not asleep, she could have her sedative, with its faint chloroform aroma reminding me of the biology lab. A good shot was guaranteed to render her comatose within half an hour. Then we could sit, all three doped up to the eye balls, listening to the hiss and spurt of the fire.

The agony of waiting. I watched the beautiful, innocent child in my lap and couldn't believe she would be so disabled. Epileptic, blind, paralysed – surely not. And again that demon Hope slipped through: will her eyes one day communicate? Will she talk, even just a little? Will she smile? If only Immie would smile. If only she would show me some sign of being here in the world with us, her family.

Everyone advised us to get on with our lives. I really wanted to, but Immie's was the only life I could think about. So I got on with doing things about that. Most importantly, there was the business of suing the NHS for compensation. We were here now, sooner than expected, at the 'outcome' they had mentioned at the internal inquiry meeting. I rang Mrs Langridge and told her Virginia Nicholas's prediction. 'Oh, Julia, I am so sorry,' was her response – my kind teacher's response. But I knew the Comments and Complaints Manager couldn't possibly be on my side. I was curt: the situation meant that we would be pursuing a clinical negligence case against the obstetrics department. I imagined her rushing off to the lawyers' office to go over her official version of the minutes.

Of course, compensation was not what I was after. The cliché was true: no amount of money would ever compensate Immie for her suffering. No, it was simpler than that. She already needed expert care and, as her major problems developed, she would need more of it. That meant money: money that Jay and I did not have. So, if we could prove the hospital had been negligent at her birth, they would pay. There must be thousands of families with children like Imogen who can't blame anyone, but possibly we could. We should count our blessings. I already knew that protocol had been violated, cock-ups made; now I must turn it to my advantage.

Jay said I was naïve. He said NHS lawyers were experts at guarding their coffers; the vast majority of clinical negligence cases are in obstetrics and they're always fending off mothers like me. And anyway, how would it make me feel, making the hospital my enemy? From now on, every time I went there for help with my sick child, I would be thinking of how they had let her down. I said I thought he was right: in my moment of greatest vulnerability, in labour, I had discovered it was possible for the National Health Service not to care. That was exactly why I had to go to battle.

Nadine brought round envelopes containing the seeds of my favourite perennials – fragrant lupins and dark blue delphiniums. She had gathered them from her garden as a farewell present. Now she proposed a final outing up the fallow field to the damson tree. We had done it every autumn and Nadine felt we shouldn't let this one go by without a visit.

Ellie was refusing to leave the house; eventually I persuaded her to accept a piggyback, whilst Nadine strapped Immie to her, whinging. We trudged to where the damson tree rose only a little higher than the hawthorn hedge, its branches gnarled with age. Alongside the main tree, we found lots of younger offspring, intermingled with hips and brambles. Their leaves had atrophied, but the fruit was firm and dark on green stems. We carefully extracted them from the prickles, polishing off the greyish bloom to reveal shiny blue skin. I showed Ellie how to peel this back with her teeth, finding the film of red, like blood-filled veins, on top of sweet yellow flesh. Whilst I hugged Nadine and told her I'd miss her, Ellie stood amongst rusty docks and thistle heads as tall as she, spitting out stones.

Jay had gone to London for a friend's concert. I managed bedtime without too much trouble, lifting Immie up and down in the dark whilst I sang Elinor her string of nursery rhymes. I had just completed the horrible drug-squirting when Jay rang to say that he had walked out of the concert. He couldn't concentrate, was thinking all the time about Immie and how he couldn't give out any more love to her. I wasn't in the mood for commiseration. There he was, swanning up to London with his friends whilst I performed gruesome duties alone. What had he to whinge about? He wasn't the one who'd had the accident, the one who was suffering.

'You're free!' I said. 'Why are you complaining? You've got a life – get on with it! You don't have to give her any more love than you want to. *She's* the one with no choice. I'm the one who takes the responsibility. *All* of it!'

I hung up to seethe alone. I was furious with him for not loving his baby. It reminded me how much I did, how trapped I was in an impossible, unrequited love for her. Without a smile, or even a look, Immie had me in her thrall. It was like being in love with someone who you know loves someone else.

Later Jay phoned back. He sounded drunk and angry in a way I had never imagined possible. Jay was not a violent man.

'I'm coming home,' he said. 'I'm going to pick up my things and I don't want to hear a word from you. If I do, I'll beat the shit out of you.'

I started to laugh, but he had hung up. Then I cried. I cried because I really thought he would leave, or beat me up, or both. I must have believed I deserved it. I remember thinking there was only one thing worse that he might do, and that would be to throw himself under a train. In a panic, I rang him back, but only got the answer machine, so I ranted at that: 'You hate me, I know you hate me, but you can't abandon me . . .'

The tears were good. So often during these weeks of confusion I had kept wanting to cry but nothing came out. Something seemed to dam me up, perhaps the antidepressants, I couldn't tell. I would be walking along, perfectly fine, coping, and suddenly my throat was mangled, my upper jaw throbbing. The blast of misery came all of a sudden, from nowhere, surging through my skull and then becoming trapped there, like a whirlpool, a gigantic scream that couldn't get out. I reflected how my labour with Immie had lacked any waves of pain, how in retrospect that abnormality had been a sign of the haemorrhage going on inside me. Waves are part of the ebb and flow of life, they are part of every living being. When a huge wave of tears smashed through me like this, then at least it was flowing, at least the process was natural.

The next morning Jay returned home, and we got on with duties and routines, trying to mask the worst of our misery from Elinor. Neither of us had ever felt such grief; we were having a crash course in it. If it had been for a parent, or even a sibling, then only one of us would have been experiencing the full blast. The other would have been on the edge, in the shallows, maybe outside it completely. Our partnership had not yet been put to such a test, but I could imagine one of us holding firm whilst the other got buffeted to pieces. The trouble with grieving for our child was that we were both doing it at the same time. And we were discovering how selfish grief can be.

I rang an obstetrician with whom I was vaguely acquainted. I wanted to know whether he thought that the NHS calculated nationally that it was cheaper to give the odd brain-damaged child compensation than it was to provide adequate ambulances and midwives in rural areas. He said he did.

A friend of Jay's parents was an expert witness for clinical negligence cases and recommended a law firm. When I rang, the solicitor explained that CP cases were always problematic; even if our NHS Trust had been negligent in the way they treated me that night, it might not be possible to prove that Imogen's brain damage was actually caused by the negligence. He warned that a case like this was 'a huge mountain to climb'.

The solicitor said I must start by writing down my account of everything that had happened on the night of her birth, getting hold of phone bills so we could be sure of the timings, keeping receipts for the money we were spending on nursing care and treatments . It was worthwhile launching an investigation now, as cases often lasted many years. Finally, he said, the amount of compensation we might get would depend on the estimated 'outcome' of Imogen's condition, which would not be known until she was five or six years old. This 'outcome' meant life expectancy.

Immie might well die during my lifetime. The idea was not such a shock. It made sense that major problems might cause her death. In fact, the certainty of death would be preferable to this mixture of uncertainty and grief. Jay said he wanted her to die now, to end her suffering; he said he wished she would die of a cot death. I said maybe she would. But no, he said, she was strong – that was how she'd managed to survive her terrible birth. If we wanted her to die now, she would need help.

'What do you mean, help?' I said, thinking of my wanting to smash her head against the wall.

'I've checked on the internet. There's no difference between cot death and suffocation . . . We have a window of opportunity,' he said. 'The longer we wait the less likely it would be for her to die like that. At four months it's not so strange for her to just stop breathing . . .'

'You'd put a pillow over her head . . .?'

'And leave her. No one would know.'

'We would.'

'What's the alternative?' He was absolutely serious.

'A parent can't kill a baby, Jay. You wouldn't be able to live with yourself. We can't kill our own child.'

'Who else is going to?'

I knew it was his despair speaking. I remembered how he had so recently adored Immie, how he had dedicated himself to her. Only a few weeks ago he had been more loving, more optimistic than me, but, since the 'major problems' news, these qualities had distorted into their opposites. It was not his true self that desired her death, but a desperate, grieving one. Although I understood what was going on, I didn't do anything about it. As a loving mother, surely I should have defended my baby, yet I felt strangely indifferent. Then I thought of the tales of people made suicidal by my antidepressants – planning their own deaths with this sort of detachment; I wondered whether there had ever been an infanticide. I lay in bed that night with Immie asleep in the crook of my arm, gazing at her inert body and imagining her dead.

The technicalities of the legal process were welcome refuge from such morbidity; I eagerly immersed myself in them. The way to apply for compensation was for the offended party (Immie) to sue the people who had caused her suffering (the NHS Trust) – little, brain-damaged Immie against the Goliath of the NHS. Because she was a minor, she could get a grant from the Legal Services Commission. Brilliant: one public body funding an attack on another public body. Thousands of pounds of taxpayers' money down the legal drain before anything might come to the needy child.

And such an emotional toll the case would take: this nerve-racking uncertainty until she was five or six years old; six years reliving the birth; six years conjecturing about her death. If we won the case, Imogen would have the best nursing care money could buy. But, while all that time went by, I would have to care for her myself. Could I do it in the hope of getting the money? It would mean six years of suspended life, my work ambitions set aside, the greater part of my mothering taken up with her problems. By then I would be forty-three, past any realistic likelihood of having more children.

When I imagined that future I was frightened, but the alternative was even worse. If we didn't win the case, or if we decided to withdraw from the process now, then I would be her carer until she died. It was Clare who had said to me, 'You're a carer now,' soon after the first brain-damage news arrived, and it had taken a while for me to work out what she meant. I decided the difference between a parent and a carer must be the difference between nursing a child who would get better and one who would not. A parent sits by their child's bedside, administering drugs, singing songs, cuddling them, because one day that child will get up and play. In contrast, the carer (me) has no such hope. This lack of hope was what I had been struggling with since

Virginia Nicholas's first brain-damage announcement. How did people bear it when it continued for decades?

Cold winds had shrivelled most of this year's blackberry crop, but the thicket outside the back door was in a sheltered spot. A few berries at the very end of each clump were still edible; there were even some pretty pink ones, unlikely ever to ripen, but useful enough for cooking. I took the high stems whilst Ellie worked down below, carefully pinching out the berries. I remembered first noticing that pincer movement when she was less than one – how fascinated I had been to witness a landmark in her development, how unconscious she had been of its significance.

We piled the fruit into a baking dish, using our stained fingers to mix them with the remains of Anne's windfalls. Flour and butter sprayed between Ellie's palms as she attempted to rub the crumble together; sugar crunched underfoot. I wanted to be patient, but the mess irritated me. Ignoring her protestations, I lifted her up to the sink and washed her mucky paws clean. Once she was in front of the *Maisy's Farm* video, I carefully reconstructed her creation. On hands and knees, I spent an age levering lumps from the lino and sweeping up. Unfolding a stiff new J-cloth, I wiped the surfaces clean. I wiped and I wiped.

Round the corner of the lane sped a familiar car, belonging to Mark the vicar. Though I had not attended church services since Immie's birth, he had recently started calling round. A passionate person, full of energy and idealism, he had come to the area the year before, taking charge of five local parishes. His inaugural sermon had been at the harvest festival, when he discussed the ethics of food production and the imperative to buy locally. I didn't know what the old ladies had thought, but I had appreciated it.

Mark had young children of his own, a past life working in inner-city Liverpool. He had been chaplain at a children's hospital where he came into close contact with sick babies and their families. As with Mary, our health visitor, I reckoned there wasn't much that could shock him, though I had kept quiet about railing at God in his church.

I made him a mug of tea and laid Immie in my lap to feed her. Mark and I watched her gulping away at the bottle. Thinking of his congregation praying for us, I described a recent shopping trip when I had thought perhaps she was getting better: there have been no screaming and she had gazed up at the pinspot lights for nearly an hour. To Immie, he said, 'I bet you'll always love looking at those lights, won't you?' Turning to me, he went on: 'When times were really hard at the hospital, I used to go to their sensory room and lie down on the mattresses. Sometimes they played soothing music. It was very dark, and you could look up at the ceiling with all these mirrors and starry lights. Magic.'

Christmas lights were already on sale in the hardware shop. I bought a set with a big dial that altered the speed and rhythm of their flashing in countless combinations and spent a morning weaving the wires through the playpen bars, hanging little bells from the bulbs. I set my light bower close to the hi-fi speakers, put on Paco de Lucia and laid Immie down inside. She arched her back and yelled, not seeming to notice any of it. Ellie took her sister's place, delighted with the stroboscope effect she could make by turning the dial round and round.

When Jay came home that evening, he said, 'What's the point?'

'At least I'm trying to do something for her.'

'Why not face the fact she can't see them?'

'Because that would be giving in.'

'It wouldn't, it would be facing the truth.'

'How do you know? No one has said she can't see.'

'Then why doesn't she respond?'

'You were the one who said she was smiling at you.'

'That was before I knew . . .'

'But you don't know. We don't know anything for certain yet.'

'I know she's suffering.'

'Which is why we need to do something for her.'

'It's harbouring false hopes, Jules.'

'It's being a parent.' Silence. Sally the nurse would have been proud of me; I could feel my halo glowing. And then, just to add insult to injury, I added: 'There's no way I'm going to give you parental responsibility if all you can think of is killing her!'

As arguments about Immie had escalated, I had begun to see my solitary parental responsibility as a symbol of our difference – me with my legal status, soldered to my broken babe, and Jay without it, indulging his freedom.

'Would you put the pillow over her tonight?' I sallied.

'If you let me,' he parried.

'Then you'd be a murderer.'

'Yes.'

'You're a fucking murderer, Jay!'

'If you say so.'

'You're mad.'

'I can't live with her.'

'Then I'd better take her away from you . . .'

'All right.'

'. . . if you can't be in the same house as your own baby . . .'

'Go on, then—'

'. . . without wanting to *Murder* her!'

'Take her!'

Grabbing the baby and the changing bag, I went out into the cold and darkness, still fizzing with indignation. I knew Nadine was back for the night. That was a bit of luck – there was nowhere else to go.

Her cottage was full of packing boxes, the rooms chilly without the insulation of books and curtains. She sat me in the alcove next to the open fire and we spent the rest of the evening spooning sugared water into the baby's mouth – she had vomited a lot that day and would not take the bottle. Around midnight we lowered a mattress into the middle of the bare floor, and Immie and I snuggled underneath the eiderdown. I felt as though I had run away from home to be with my lover.

Next morning, Nadine and I huddled next to her Rayburn and talked. She said I needed to be patient – Jay would eventually come round; he was a kind man. I felt a little ashamed of our drama. She said I needed to make the baby a less overwhelming part of my life, to compartmentalise. But I instantly rejected her advice: for the rest of my life, everything – the healthy members of my family, my work, my hobbies – would all have to be arranged around Immie. It was perfectly natural, I was like a she-wolf defending her sick cub, I said.

But later, alone, I thought again about the she-wolf. If I really were such a creature, then at some point I might well stop protecting my cub. Animals aren't compelled to nurse their young if they are not going to get better; in fact, a wolf's natural instinct might well be to get rid of a sick baby, destroy it. Animal mothers know that profound neediness threatens their own and their other progeny's survival. I remembered once seeing a magazine article about an orang-utan baby that had been rejected by its mother because it was brain-damaged. I was less interested in the tale of its adoption by a human mother than in how its biological mother had abandoned it. In evolutionary terms, I knew there wasn't much difference between my genes and an orang-utan's.

The impulse to reject my baby had been there ever since that morning in July when I threw her across the bed. Hating her had been a natural, animal compulsion. Wanting to smash her head against the wall had come from some primitive survival mechanism. There was no reason why such feelings should not arise again.

Immie was well sedated in her cot next to my side of the bed. Jay was sleeping on his side again. Gently, I moved closer to him and put my arm around his waist.

'Jay . . . Jay,' I whispered.

'Yes.' He was so calm that he must have been awake already.

'We can do it together, it would be so simple.'

'. . . Yes . . .'

'. . . We'll suffocate her. Now. With a pillow.'

He sighed and turned towards me in the dark. 'We'd go to prison.'

'I'd claim diminished responsibility.'

He grasped my arms. 'We can't take that risk. Think of Elinor.'

I rolled away again onto my back. Neither of us could possibly sleep now. We lay on our separate sides of the bed, listening to our baby breathe.

I hardly left the house. It was much better to hide from those undulating hills where Immie's brain cells had been destroyed. I thought bitterly of how I'd once imagined this region as a little Eden where nothing horrible could take place; its innocent loveliness was a major reason we had come here. When Mark the vicar visited, I said, 'Things like this don't happen in the Cotswolds, do they?'

He answered, 'Believe me, in my experience, they do.'

And then I remembered Hannah. Hannah who lived in the Cotswolds. She must have been the first child with cerebral palsy I ever met. A girl of about my age, she lived in the farmhouse next door to my grandparents. On our weekend visits it was often a treat to go and see her – this strange girl who could not speak but moaned and flapped her arms against the flagstones. Her body was long and thin, her face had a crooked smile and her eyes rolled up under her brow. When her mother turned on Radio 3, she listened hard and sometimes, if the music was in a minor key, she wept. Hannah knew the difference between major and minor. I thought of her as an angel who had fallen to earth.

Although Hannah's mum didn't leave the house much, people like us would drop by. I remembered the mother's smile, broad and welcoming. But her teeth were rotting; her hair was so thin that you could see the skin on the top of her head. Only now could I see how hard it must have been for her, holed up with her child.

I described to Mark my not wanting to go out, feeling lonely. He said it reminded him of the way people are when they have been bereaved. His word 'bereaved' struck me – of course, that was exactly what we were. Allowing myself to admit it was a huge relief. My experience of grief had been passive, but bereavement was active. I needed that. I needed to acknowledge the child I had lost: her intact brain, her perfection – a perfection she never had outside of me. Mark had granted me sanction to do it.

When I sat down at my computer to write my account of the

birth for the clinical negligence lawyer, I allowed it to become part of the bereavement. Thinking back over the route between the midwifery unit and Banbury, I imagined Immie's brain gradually perishing with the oxygen deprivation. I pictured it like Clare's dahlia – layers of yellow petals dying one by one from the outside in. What abilities had been contained in each petal? Fine motor skills first. As we sped past the Hook Norton turning, her pincer movements, perhaps . . . Now she would never pick a blackberry. At the Deddington turning, the nerves controlling her arms; as we rounded the corner at South Newington, her legs . . . No more walking, little girl. And then what? As we accelerated up into Banbury, her potential for language – first full sentences, then short phrases, then, as we reached the brow of the hill, even her ability to articulate names. Gone. How many of Immie's thoughts and feelings died even as I was borne on the wheelchair into the delivery suite?

It's a very confusing business, mourning for someone who is alive, there in front of you. You feel you shouldn't really be doing it, because, after all, she's not dead. Not yet. But every day some little thing would come up. Something to do with my hopes for the future and the way the major problems had dashed them. For example, each time Ellie said 'Mummy' – which was ten, maybe twenty times a day – the mourning self would tell me, 'Immie will never say that.' Virginia Nicholas would have said that I couldn't be certain, but I wanted to be. Mourning for such a thing was so much better than hoping.

I dream I am holding a bunch of brightly coloured balloons – they are like huge boobs, floating above me in a limpid sky. Slowly, carefully, I let go of one and watch it float away out of sight; it represents breastfeeding Imogen. The second one is let loose; it is my face, or rather mine and hers combined in a smile, that blissful love-smile between mother and baby. The third is the curve of my arms as I embrace her and comfort her . . . Each of these balloons represents a part of my body and the expectation it once held for Immie. Gradually I let them all go and stand staring up at the empty blue heavens.

All the king's horses,
And all the king's men,
Couldn't put Humpty together again

Thursday, 31 October

FOR HALLOWE'EN I had saved a couple of Hubbard squashes from the vegetable patch. Rather than hollow and carve them myself, I handed my project to the babysitter in the hope that she would enjoy it. I felt bad about Holly – I still hadn't revealed much to her about Immie's brain damage; it had been such a boon having someone in the house not weighed down with worry. But she was young; she loved children. Even though she tried to hide it, I knew she was bored with her joyless charge, hoicking her up and down hour after hour. It was amazing she'd stood the monotony all these weeks.

I watched as she and Elinor spooned piles of pith and seeds out of my pumpkins. Holly took my smallest kitchen knife and from each shell she cut perfectly symmetrical eye sockets and neat shark-toothed mouths. Even little circular troughs were carved at the bottom of the heads for nightlights. I was sad not to be sharing the occasion with Ellie, but pleased to give Holly some job satisfaction. At last, two glowing faces stood on guard by the front door. Once darkness set in, the trick-or-treaters appeared, a clutch of masked local kids, banging on the door and chanting their rhyme:

Trick or treat,
Smell my feet,
Give me something good to eat

Ellie squealed with delight and trepidation.

The spooks inspected their takings and dissolved back into the dark. Next morning we discovered one of the hollowed heads kicked across the lawn, and a mess of porridge daubed across the car windscreen. I couldn't see anything funny about it. In fact, I was outraged that our property should have been vandalised after we had doled out bloody treats. When I told Mark the vicar about the attack, I said it felt as though the Ku Klux Klan had been round. He assured me that everyone else in the parish would condemn it. That calmed me down a bit; I realised I was probably overreacting, that frustration and distrust were spilling out into every part of my life.

Mark had come to talk about baptising Immie, and swiftly this became the subject of our conversation. For a while now, I had felt it would be a good thing. I very much wanted her to have his blessing; I thought perhaps Elinor should be baptised too. Jay joined us and the talk turned to Immie's future. When we were alone these days, Jay and I did not dare to touch on such a theme, accustomed as we were to its erupting into a row. But, with Mark present, we were safe, knowing we wouldn't lose it completely. Now Jay confessed that he could not see himself continuing to care for Imogen. I felt my hackles rise. I wanted to say that I thought whatever happened to us was God's will, but I could not bring myself to use the word 'God'. Instead I said, 'I think it's my destiny to care for her.' Mark was silent for a moment, and then he said, 'Perhaps it's somebody else's destiny.'

It wasn't the response I was expecting. I'd thought he would take my side, criticising Jay's rejection of a vulnerable child. Wasn't my motherly self-sacrifice something Christianity approved of, invented even?

'Somebody else's destiny'. I recalled the humiliation of the respite weekend, when I'd left Immie with the Social Services carer. The worst thing had been imagining that the foster carer might be more loving and caring than me, that I was dispensable. If that's what Mark meant by 'somebody else's destiny', then I rejected the idea. I never wanted to feel such shame again.

Friday, 1 November

The shape of my life had changed for good. My friends were now the string of experts who came to see Immie; the others were on permanent hold. If dirty dishes were overflowing in the sink, if I was still in my dressing gown when people arrived, I no longer cared. Mary the health visitor brought along the disability living allowance application form. There were lots of boxes where I must state Imogen's feeding difficulties, her drugs, her constant care needs. Patiently, laboriously, Mary led me through the questions, helping me find the right words. She thought we would probably qualify for the top allowance, £56.25 a week. I instantly calculated that the money would cover eleven hours' babysitting from Holly, though what we would do when she moved on I had no idea.

Judith the physio came round with a colleague to let us know she was leaving and would be handing over her responsibilities. I was upset; I told her so. I said I didn't usually confide in strangers. What was I meant to do now: simply transfer my loyalty? I reminded myself not to be so naïve in future.

The physiotherapists laid Immie down on the bed and took it in turns to stretch her legs about, grasping her calves and revolving the joints. The muscle relaxant was definitely working, they agreed, though children often responded well at the beginning and then the beneficial effect wore off. The replacement physio asked whether her eyes always flickered like this. Flicker: that was the word Candice Walker had used in SCBU, on the day Immie started fitting. The Banbury incubator resurfaced in my mind, my baby's legs pumping away, my hand trying to calm them.

Immie was propped up on a pile of cushions, her head lolling down onto her chest. Suddenly it swung up and round over her right shoulder, and as it did so her eyelids fluttered as if something might be irritating them. I drew the curtain across the window to reduce the glare, and excused my daughter: 'Her eyes do all sorts of weird things.'

'Like this?'

'Well, she can go cross-eyed when she's trying to focus . . .'

The three of us watched as Imogen repeated her head roll. It definitely wasn't what she had done as a newborn.

'I can't be sure,' said Judith, 'but it's possible she is fitting. I think you should phone Virginia Nicholas.'

Oh God – how could I be so blind as to not perceive my own child's suffering?

Picking her up off the bed, I held her in front of my face. Her face circled downwards, anticlockwise as before, and I had to admit that her eyes were flickering.

The nurse who answered the phone said that Virginia Nicholas was busy in SCBU, but the return call came soon enough. When I described the movements, she said, 'I think you should take her in.'

'Where?'

'To A&E.'

'Why A&E?'

'That's the way to get admitted to the paediatric ward. Good luck.'

That 'Good luck' sounded final. We weren't going back to SCBU; this was full-blown paediatrics. I assumed we were being referred to A&E because they had to act fast with babies. The drive to the JR was long and straight – just as it should have been five months ago, on the night of Imogen's birth. Jay dropped me at the entrance and went off to find a parking space. A&E was being rebuilt, with half the hall masked off with dusty plastic. There were long queues up to each of the admission cubicles. Seeing that I was carrying a baby seat, someone hurried me to the front.

'Yes?' said the clerk, without looking up.

'I think my baby's fitting.'

No response.

'Look!' I lifted Immie's seat onto the shelf and turned it to face my adjudicator. She peered over her specs.

'Name?'

After five long minutes of form-filling, I was taken back along the queue and into a side room. The sign on the door read 'Relatives' Waiting Room'. Inside, it was crowded with people, eyes wide with worry. I made my way towards the far corner where I intended to crouch on the floor and give Immie her bottle. Next thing I knew, all the relatives were being ushered out – to worry in the corridor, I supposed – and Immie and I were alone.

A quarter of an hour later, a disarmingly junior doctor turned up, looking distracted. I wondered whether she was at the end of one of her twenty-four-hour shifts; I noticed that the roots of her auburned hair needed touching up. She said we would be able to go up to the ward in a little while, when Imogen's bed was ready. Probably thinking she should put me at my ease, the young woman tried to make conversation. 'Is she crawling yet?' Crawling! Most normal babies weren't crawling at five months, let alone epileptic ones. My icy 'No' shut down the chit-chat.

It was getting late. Someone needed to pick up Ellie from nursery. I wanted to go, but Jay reminded me that I was the only one with parental responsibility for Imogen – doubtless I would be required to sign more paperwork. I reckoned he was getting back at me for using my legal status against him in our rows; if I so valued my unique position, here was my chance to prove it. Meanwhile, he was off to look after our healthy child. Damn. I could feel my commitment in danger of turning into claustrophobia.

At last, the children's ward. There was a bed in the corner for us – full size, but with bars on the side to stop a baby falling out. Imogen immediately seemed to calm to the warmth and gentle bustle of the place, comforted by mechanical bleeps and fuzzy lighting – maybe they reminded her of SCBU. It wasn't long before the nurse brought over the neurology consultant. Middle aged, with a gentle lilt in his voice, he was sober, without smiles, but kindly. He asked me to undress Imogen and lie her on the bed so he could feel her leg muscles as the physios had done that morning. I was surprised that she didn't scream. Being on her back usually infuriated her, but here she lay, totally calm and relaxed, a bigger, stronger version of the way she'd been when I first set eyes on her.

After the examination, Mr Randle wrapped her in a blanket and handed her back to me. I sat in the armchair at the bedside while he questioned me, jotting down notes in his little book. He asked what was my profession, and Jay's, whether our parents were alive and what they did, how old our other daughter was. He seemed interested that music was important to us. I thought he must be getting quite a comprehensive picture of Immie's family – our sensibilities, how we would cope with bad news. I wasn't frightened; I remember being grateful that he saw her as part of our family.

The interview completed, Immie's nurse hovered behind the consultant, attentive to information about her charge. Simply, directly, he explained that she was likely to be very badly brain-damaged. He had read her notes, had pieced together her medical history. It was now a case of scanning her head and taking tests to establish exactly what was going on. His tone was respectful; I felt completely calm, able to take in everything he was telling me.

Mr Randle said that Imogen probably was fitting, constantly, with what are termed 'infantile spasms', and she should begin treatment immediately. In his experience, the majority of children with this condition went on to develop full-blown epilepsy by the time they were two. Nothing surprised me. It all seemed to tally with the microcephaly information I had downloaded. I asked whether she would be spending a lot of time in hospital. Yes, he said, children with her level of brain damage spend most of their lives going in and out of hospital. This news brought a sharp wrench to my gut; I was surprised how much it distressed me. Today being Friday, the doctor continued, he would not be able to scan her until the following week, but then they should be able to give us a full prognosis. All I could think of was the baptism – we had planned it for Sunday. I suddenly wanted to baptise her more than anything else. I said, please would he let her come home for the ceremony.

The doctor turned to the nurse: 'She must be allowed home. Just for the day.'

Then he turned back to me. I remember how communication was suspended for a moment, a second, perhaps. Something significant was about to be said. Then it came, straight and clear: 'It's likely Imogen will never walk or talk.'

At last, I thought. At last I have it – the certainty I envied Joely's parents. All these weeks of confusion, all my pessimism and my tears have been in preparation for this. The hindsight lifted me, buoyed me up onto a pool of calm. My mourning muscles were already so well exercised that now, instead of weeping, my body started to relax like Imogen's. The tension that had wound around my womb began to loosen.

It was already dark outside. Immie's nurse brought me sweet tea in a styrofoam cup. 'You mustn't be frightened,' she said, 'it's not as bad as you might imagine. My neighbour has a child who can't walk or talk. He's a lovely lad.'

'How old?' I said.

'Oh, eleven or twelve, I suppose. She gets lots of help . . .'

'What kind?'

'Well, I think he's at boarding school some of the time . . .'

She didn't know. Nobody working in this controlled environment knew what life was like for families like us. She hadn't seen the everyday turmoil inside our home.

I looked around the ward: it held maybe a dozen sick kids. In the armchairs sat adults with ashen faces, some of them holding the hand of their loved one, wishing they could kiss it better. Many of the children were wired up, some were whimpering. A girl of eight or nine was being unhooked from her drip and supported by her mother as the nurse put an overcoat around her flimsy body. The mother and nurse chattered away encouragingly.

The child grinned as she was lowered into a wheelchair – despite being so ill, she was being taken home.

At the bedside next to me a young woman caught my eye; she wanted to talk. Her little boy was three years old; he still had no diagnosis after a week in hospital, she said. She and her husband had been taking it in turns to sleep beside him. Though the television above was on, the boy lay on his side, gazing into the distance. I knew this mother wanted my story in return for hers, but I didn't want to tell it. Luckily, my silence was interrupted by her husband's arrival, laden with plastic bags. The couple spread out tubs of food across the bed and began supper; the boy showed no interest.

It was the everyday details that got to me: the overcoat, the supermarket provisions. They contrasted so sharply with the neutrality of the hospital, especially back in SCBU. There, the babies had been hidden in those plastic cabinets, their movements (and their suffering) hardly discernible – ethereal beings, *farther off than Australia*. But here you could see exactly what was going on, and hear it. These children had been out in the world already, they had known what it was to run and eat and play. They knew what they were missing. If SCBU had been Limbo, then there was no getting away from it: the children's ward was Hell.

The nurse came over to my corner.

'We have a parents' room. I have organised a bed for you – there's a locker for your things.'

I looked at Immie, dozing in her huge expanse of bed. I thought: my presence here is irrelevant. I can't hold her hand like the other parents – she wouldn't even notice if I tried. She's happy here; I'm not.

'I don't think I shall stay the night,' I said. The nurse looked surprised.

'Most parents do,' she urged.

'I have to get back to my other daughter. I can show you how to look after Imogen . . .'

'*Somebody else's destiny*', Mark had said. Nadine, Holly, the foster carer, the nurses . . . Ever since Candice in Banbury, my baby had been cared for by someone else. I had to accept that, even though I was her mother, I was not indispensable; I never had been.

As I walked past the parents with their picnic, I did not meet their eyes. I was hanging up my halo.

Anne was at home, sitting at the kitchen table. Many times she had walked past the cottage on the way from church to her farm-house, but she had never come in before. She said she wanted to do something to help and thought perhaps we would like her to decorate the church for the girls' christening. I was really touched by the offer, said I would pay for the flowers. No, she insisted. Then she hurried away.

I made the most of my freedom, stretching out bedtime with Ellie. She wanted me to share a bath; we filled it with bubbles and created a snowy mountain-scape on the water, our heads adorned with Father Christmas wigs and beards. Freshly bathed, her skin downy and hot, she sat on the bed and let me twist her hair into smooth wet ringlets.

'Tell me a story about when you were little,' she said.

'You start,' I said. 'You tell me what I'm doing.'

'You're in bed.'

'And what happens?'

'There's a tiger. A tiger's coming . . .'

'To eat me?' My mouth and eyes opened wide with horror.

'Yes! Quickly, hide!'

'Oh no, a tiger's coming. A tiger's coming . . .' And we buried ourselves beneath the duvet.

There in our cosy den, I clutched her and told her I loved her. And she said, 'Mummy, you're squeezing me too tight.'

Once she was asleep, Jay and I sat by the fire without a baby to nurse. He was not surprised at the news from Mr Randle. We agreed that Immie's life was going to be really, really hard – we had witnessed almost five months of it already. We talked about abortion. If this sort of brain damage had been caused by a con-genital defect, and had been detected in my womb, then the obstetrics department would have offered to terminate my pregnancy. Even late on, during all the months she was inside me, they would have been prepared to kill her. It would have been seen as an act of mercy.

At that time I would not have agreed; I had strong, virtuous feelings about protecting the life inside me. But now that Immie was here, I no longer possessed the luxury of virtue. My body had destroyed her prospect of a healthy life – it had proved itself viciously destructive, not nurturing at all. To avoid the anguish ahead, the act of abortion would indeed have been merciful.

And so we came, easily enough, to our conclusion: that it was no kindness to keep Immie alive, that she needed releasing from her painful existence. During the previous weeks, ever since my first fantasy about smashing her head against the wall, this had been our feeling; instinctively, we had known that her life was not worth living. Now that she was in hospital, now that they had given us proof, they must allow her to die.

Next morning Jay and I waited for the consultant at Immie's bedside. Seated on low armchairs, side by side, we felt closer than we had for a long time. He took my hand, and we sat there silently, more like a fond elderly couple than two people who had recently produced a baby together.

In the bed opposite, a little boy, bald and naked but for a nappy, was being helped to his feet. I had failed to spot him the day before. The nurse took his hand and led him barefoot up the ward. His whole body was darkest yellow, the colour of turmeric powder. His chubby face smiled back at me. I thought maybe he had liver cancer or some other killer. Where were his parents?

Round the corner came the flock of white coats – the consultant and his team. Jay got out his notebook containing a list of things to say, ready to note down the consultant's responses. Our meetings with Virginia Nicholas had taught us how hard it was to retain information when in a state of panic. But it was not Mr Randle, it was the Saturday team, headed by my parents' neighbour. Of course, I knew he worked here – he had come to see me when Immie was in SCBU. I could trust him to comprehend my horrible decision. I watched him turn away to speak to his colleagues; he must have been briefing them about us. Then he led them over to our corner.

'I'm sorry you have to be here,' he said.

I looked up, and said in a meek little voice, 'I don't want her to have any more medication.'

Pause. His gaze slants away from mine, as if he is avoiding eye contact. All my senses are heightened, trying to pick up what he is thinking. At the same time, everything is in suspended animation, far away and hazy.

Somehow, I'm not sure how, maybe immediately, he says, 'You would like her files marked "Not for Resuscitation"?'

'Yes.'

I remember his explaining this meant that, if Imogen got an infection, she would not be treated with antibiotics. But I had intended something much more. If only I had the zeal to tell him to leave her epilepsy alone, to allow it to grow and grow. At some point, I imagined, some huge seizure would take hold of her and stop her breathing. That was what the infantile spasms were for, to end the suffering.

If only I could say all this, but I didn't dare; I was small and weak like her.

I watched the doctor approach the desk and take Immie's file from the nurse. It was such a simple thing, a bit like observing a waiter making out a bill, but in slow motion. Everyone seemed to be watching the words as they were written. I thought they must already have me down as a bad mum – the one who had walked out on her child, the one who didn't care. And now the evidence was there in writing.

We went to the canteen and bought cups of black coffee to accompany our cigarettes, outside on the dreary rooftops. There in the rain was a man we recognised from the village – Graham, the local furniture-maker. His face was swollen from weeping. He told us he'd come to see his father who had started severe rectal bleeding the evening before but had had to wait all night for an ambulance. We said we'd had similar bad luck with our emergency five months ago. Graham thought he knew why this might have happened. 'Have a look outside A&E when you leave,' he said. 'There are ambulances queuing up on the slip road with patients inside them. It was debated in the House of Commons months ago. But what has the NHS done about it? Fuck all, as far as I can see!'

As we passed A&E on our way home, we spotted the line of ambulances.

My daughters were being baptised in the morning. I rang Mark and told him about Immie's never walking or talking. I thought, now he'll have to go over his sermon and take out all the hopeful bits. Ellie's brand-new dress was spread out ready on the bed, her stripey tights still unwrapped. For Immie, my mother had given me a long Edwardian christening gown; a family heirloom, it hung on the cupboard door in its dry-cleaning package. Granny had worn it for her baptism, then my mother and then me. Now it was my baby's turn.

As I eased the garment from its plastic, I recalled the connections between its first wearer and its last: how Imogen had been born in the same hospital where Granny had died ten years earlier; how we had given her the same second name – Cecile. And then I thought about their mothers.

A century earlier, in Ireland, Great-Granny dressed her bonny babe in this gown and took her to church to be blessed. A year or so later she abandoned her. Just upped and left, no one knew why. The Edwardian father didn't have much idea how to cope, and his daughter suffered. She was tripped from pillar to post until, aged eleven, she turned up alone on her mother's doorstep. By that time my great-grandmother had married a chartered accountant and was living in London. She could have taken her daughter back, but she didn't – she sent her packing. Everyone said she just didn't give a damn.

Rejection was the skeleton in our mother-cupboard. Down the generations, one after another, we mothers and daughters must surely find echoes of that hundred-year-old cruelty. When I left Immie in the paediatric ward, when I handed her over to a foster carer or nurse, my confusion was compounded by the legacy. I felt it was a terrible thing to do, that only someone who 'just didn't give a damn' could commit such an unnatural act.

Granny was highly strung, everyone said. And that was because of her mother, they said. After the second rejection, Granny spent the rest of her childhood in full-time boarding school and eventually got a job as a governess in Africa. Meeting my grandfather there and having three children must have brought her some sort of happiness, but the abandonment had left its mark. Mum (the third child) said she couldn't remember ever being hugged by her mother. She said Granny was very needy, often ill. At Mum's birth she got mastitis and sent the baby off to be nursed by an African nanny.

I remembered Granny's last couple of decades, retired in the Cotswolds – a beautiful woman, but with her emotional life hidden away. She didn't cuddle or play like other people's grandparents. She liked doing the *Guardian* crossword and reading first editions of heavy intellectual tomes, inserting pencil notes in the margins in her elegant handwriting. When I was eleven, I sat next to her at a school performance of the musical *Oliver*. The urchin sitting alone on the steps downstage was my brother. With choirboy innocence he sang the abandoned child's lament for his mother, 'Where is Love?' The audience applauded and I tugged at Granny's sleeve to share my pride. But she pulled it away; her features were all crumpled with crying. For a long time after that, I thought Granny's tears must have been my fault. Until Mum said they were her mother's.

Sunday, 3 November

Jay went off early to fetch Immie from hospital. I chose to wear my new skinny jeans with a black silk jacket more suitable for a funeral than a christening. When Immie turned up she was dressed in the same fleecy Babygro she had worn when last I'd gone to the church – that furious day I took her to rail at God. I decided not to bother with Granny's gown, to leave her as she was.

It was a sunny November day, unseasonably warm. Though my plants were now mere remnants of their summer selves, the lawn had made a final burst of growth. As I hurried the children down the lane, Jay hung back with his family. He had retreated again into his cold, aggressive mood; he didn't want to join in with my ceremony. There to meet me at the church were my parents, my cousins, friends from Ellie's nursery, and even some friends from London. Nadine had driven down from Wales. Clare, Immie's cranio-sacral therapist, turned up in a white Mercedes, very glamorous in a suit and sunglasses. Holly brought gifts and her cheery mother. I was amazed how many people had come, though I was too distracted to communicate with them. Nadine escorted the children and me down the aisle, greeting the rest of the congregation as we went. I thought probably they were still praying for us every Sunday. Once settled in the front pew, I looked back and saw that the rose-coloured, sunlit church was absolutely packed.

Gawky in my inappropriate garb, I stood to sing the first hymn, *'Dear Lord and Father of Mankind / Forgive our foolish ways . . . Take from our souls the strain and stress . . .'* I could feel the power of the voices behind me, singing in unison. Over the months since Immie's birth, I had lost touch with these people and their importance in my life. Now I could feel their love coming forward to cradle me and my sick daughter. The trouble was, the sensation overwhelmed me. As the string of notes rose higher, a sob lurched into my throat. I couldn't sing any more; it took all my concentration just to stop the sob. From that moment on, every time I thought I was in control and tried to join in, my voice would catch with tears.

As the congregation crowded around the old stone font for the baptism, I fixed a grimace to my face – the one I recalled my mother wearing in church when I was a child. The font was crowned with white freesias and Michaelmas daisies, dusty pink roses and the skeletal leaves of Silver Dust. Anne's figure shone out from the crowd, pleased to have given us such beauty. Mark lifted each of my daughters up in turn to bathe their foreheads as so many thousands had been bathed before. Ellie was shy, Immie calm – she must like the feel of the holy water, its tinkle as it fell back into the bowl. In the same clothes she had worn when I accused God of such cruelty, she now received His blessing. And I remembered the idea I'd had on her very first day, looking at her on the resuscitation table: that she was God's child, not mine at all.

At Communion, we filed up to the altar through the choir stalls, past the oldest tomb in the church. For nearly four hundred years the stone knight had lain there, side by side with his wife. The tomb always fascinated Elinor: the couple's living children knelt above them, and along the rim lay three miniature figures, all packaged up in lacy bonnets. Those were their dead babies.

Monday morning: the hospital machine was running at full throttle. I did not question the process; it was easier just to obey. First, down to the basement where Immie was sedated and laid at the opening to a huge white scanner. The radiographers disappeared into their protective cubicle, leaving me in the toxic atmosphere as my child was borne away down the tunnel. It must have been this exact same process that was carried out all those months ago when she was in SCBU: they were X-raying slices of her brain, cross-wise, from the bottom up. Later, Jay and I drove her across town to another department where dozens of electric wires were glued to her head and the doctor went behind a television screen to watch for signs of seizure. 'What a good girl,' everyone kept on saying.

On the ground floor of the main hospital again, we waited to see the feeding specialists, surrounded by other CP children and their families. I was fascinated by these bigger versions of Immie and their parents. One lanky lad flopped over his father's shoulder, his arms reaching almost to the floor. A glamorous young mum pushed her boy of six or seven in a three-wheeled mountain buggy, surely meant for a much younger child. She seemed to be great friends with the nurses, and I heard shouts of welcome as she entered the consultation room. The father lowered his son into his lap and gently, patiently, he fed him a banana. I felt very moved by such tenderness. I remembered Hannah, the angel of my childhood, on her kitchen floor.

When we eventually got to see the Professor of Nutrition, he was seated at a desk with a group of students beside him, slumped in their chairs, arms folded. The professor asked me to describe Immie's feeding eccentricities, and I obliged, a bit bothered that they were not fascinating enough for this high-powered audience. When I was done, the professor presented his acolytes with a string of phenomena that my daughter might be suffering. I felt the panic rising: that I did not understand, could not take it in. If only I had brought the notebook with me. There seemed to be various long-term options they might try, but for now a young woman was delegated the job of creating a feeding programme to reduce the vomiting. She accompanied me back to Immie's corner in the paediatric ward. 'Soon enough you're going to be the real expert in your daughter's feeding, medication and all,' she assured me. 'Mums always know more than the doctors.'

I sat with Immie asleep in my lap until Mr Randle came round. He said he had heard about my request for her files to be labelled. I thought this was probably my last chance to push home my conviction about Immie's being allowed to die. The christening had confirmed my feelings. I said, 'I want nature to take its course.' He was thoughtful; perhaps he understood.

Then he said, 'You can't be sure what might happen. Without medication, the infantile spasms might prevent her from feeding, but such a process would be extremely slow and quite possibly painful for her. No one in this hospital could stand by and let that happen.' He cast a look behind him where the nurses were gathered around the desk. 'Her nurses would object to treatment being withheld. It is their job to look after children like Imogen.'

I looked down and saw what the nurses saw: a cherubic little girl who needed looking after. But they must also know her future. They saw severely brain-damaged children all the time, their anguish. Did they never think that the process of death was part of their duty of care? Surely being a good carer might sometimes entail letting someone go.

In 1963, they let my brother go. The hours of labour had been so traumatic, his look so manifestly dead, that they didn't try to resuscitate him; they simply took his body away. They judged that the baby (Martin, they named him) would be likely to have a very difficult and painful life, and it would be better to spare him such a thing. My parents always insisted it was better that Martin had died, that he had not gone on to lead a life of suffering. The way they consoled themselves after their first-born's death had been to imagine it was for the best. It is the same consolation one uses with miscarriages – the babies were damaged in some way, one says; it's better that they died.

But, all these decades later, the JR paediatricians would try to resuscitate a newborn like Martin for twenty minutes before giving up on him. The doctors say it's worth taking the risk of resuscitating every infant, because the majority, once treated, will turn out fine. They insist there are loads of happy outcomes for the most horrific and incompetently handled births.

I think there are other reasons why Martin was not resuscitated, but his niece was. Thirty-nine years ago it was the baby boom, and people like my parents were producing more babies than the UK knew what to do with. Nowadays, economists say we're seriously short of them – so we're not going to throw the next generation away unless we absolutely have to. In the twenty-first century, a doctor allowing a newborn to die has the power of the courts to contend with and the courts are most likely to judge any life worth living, whatever its quality. Finally there are the NHS managers: in a competitive market, infant mortality is bad for a maternity unit's profile; live births are what they are aiming for, whatever the future.

These ideas are too cynical, perhaps, born of my anger. Yes, I look at my parents and envy them their son's death. Its simplicity; its finality; its consolation.

★

Tuesday, 5 November

When I arrived with Jay in the morning, Mr Randle was waiting on the ward – he had the CT scans to show us. As we made
our way to his office, I saw him beckoning to the nurses at the
desk. They were shrugging their shoulders, getting him to decide
which one should accompany us. 'Whoever knows Mum best,' I
heard him say, and Imogen's nurse stepped forward. I felt sorry
for her; looking after distressed parents was most likely not her
vocation. Once the door was closed behind us, Jay and I sat in
the row of chairs opposite the desk; the nurse tactfully left one
seat between herself and me.

There, pinned to the wall, was the series of X-ray images, a sto-
ryboard of Immie's head. From left to right across the page was
one monochrome photo after another, showing cross-sections of
her brain. All the shapes were perfect ellipses. On the photos
across the middle of the page it was easy to discern the two big
bulges of her eyeballs breaking the perfectly smooth, pale cir-
cumference of the skull.

Mr Randle took us on the journey the scanner had made: first
the spinal cord, then the greyish bulge that was the lower brain –
the control centre for basic impulses, the part that told her heart
to beat and her lungs to breathe. We could see that, as the machine
moved upwards through her head, gradually the grey shape was
shrinking inside its regular oval frame, replaced by blackness.

By the time his finger reached the row where the eyes jutted
out, the shape was entirely black, with a lacy edge that looked to
me like the frills around a black doily. It continued like this to
the end of the page, where we reached the crown of her head.
The neurologist explained that the blackness was the space where
Imogen's cerebral cortex should be, the lacy edge its torn
remains.

Black – the end of the spectrum. No uncertainty, no confusion. The colour was deep, seductive, complete. The beauty of the
image drew me in. I felt I was at the calm epicentre of the vortex
where I had been spinning all these months. The confusing

numbness I had felt at her birth transformed at last into stillness, innocence and love. We had reached some point of purity, Imogen and I – a place no one else would ever enter.

Jay took up the discussion,

'Could the brain have developed like that from conception?'

He was trying to put the blame on himself, on some faulty sperm.

'I don't think so. This type of damage is typical of a birth trauma.'

Well, Jay was off the hook then.

'Could she be like Christopher Nolan?' Jay remembered the CP writer's autobiography: the expression of his internal life, despite the limitations of his external one. A triumph against the odds; a mother's dedication.

'Locked in?' said the consultant. 'No, that's not possible. The damage is global; Imogen's cognitive powers have been destroyed. Strictly speaking, she has no intelligence.'

'How long will she live?'

'If she survives the next eighteen months, then probably into adulthood – twenty years, or more.'

'Will she ever know us?'

'Parents of children like Imogen tell me they do recognise them.'

'What about caring for her? What do parents say about that?'

'They tell me it is hard. There is never enough help.'

I had a question now.

'Can you tell from these pictures what she might have been like, without the brain damage?'

'What is your other child like?'

'Sparky. Playful . . .'

'Well, that's how Imogen would have been.'

He went on to talk about the infantile spasms – random electrical pulses shooting through her skull – and explained the complexities of treating epilepsy: trial and error, the side-effects of the drugs, but reassuring us that within a few days Immie would be ready to come home. I felt suddenly angry.

'Am I just expected to take my baby home and feed her?' A gentle pause.

'Yes.'

'I don't think of that as parenting.'

'Many parents do.'

Mr Randle said he would keep Imogen in hospital for a full week more. I understood that he was giving me space to come to terms with things. All I recall after that is the intense concentration it took me to cross the ward, one foot in front of the other, find the release button on the security door and make my way out to the car. Jay drove in silence to my parents' house where Ellie was waiting. As we turned into their street, I saw my mother coming to meet me. I got out even as the car was still in motion and walked towards her embrace. Mum says I kept on repeating one phrase: 'I'm sorry, I'm so sorry.'

Determined to continue life as normally as possible, in the days following the scan I kept to routines: cooking, cleaning the house, trying to occupy Ellie. Though my womb-ache seemed to have gone for good, I now had a permanent headache – that's Immie's empty head, I thought. Nor would the CT image go away. Holly was organising a big fireworks display, and, as part of our determination to keep life normal, Jay and I took Elinor to see it. There was a festive atmosphere, laughter in the damp and chilly air. I remember eating hot dogs and wandering through the crowd with my excited toddler on my shoulders. When the fireworks began, I craned my neck back and she kept her balance by clutching her hands around my neck. Faces close, we watched bright circles of fire burst against the pitch-black November sky. And in each explosion, I saw the beautiful lacey remains of Immie's grey matter, haloing the black hole of her lost consciousness.

At night, the scan loomed even more vividly. The dark walls of my bedroom resembled the blackness inside Immie's skull, and as I tried to fall asleep, they would slowly start to contract, closing in like the aperture on a camera. Just before it closed completely, the blackness would start to slide away again, but too far, forming a huge hollow space in which I lay stranded. When I reported these terrors to my mother, she said, 'They shouldn't have shown you the scan. It was too much.' But then how would I have known?

On top of these visions came the thoughts, haunting me over the days and nights following Mr Randle's diagnosis.

'Strictly speaking, she has no intelligence.' I had to accept that the part of Immie that processes ideas and feelings had been destroyed. I tried to imagine what it meant to have lost all these fundamental characteristics of being human – *Homo sapiens*. What is a human being who cannot think? Without its thinking part, all her brain could do was control her most primitive compulsions: keep her tummy filled, get her to sleep and to breathe. Perhaps she sensed warmth and light, softness and hardness, things that affected her physical state. If she felt sadness or loneliness or fear, they arose only in relation to her need to survive. She had no comprehension of who or what she was, or what she was experiencing.

Brain transplants; I thought a lot about them. These days you can transplant a kidney or a heart from one person to another without too much trouble, but never a brain. You can spend years on the plastic surgeon's operating table, having every bit of your external appearance altered. But your brain is a constant; it belongs to you alone, you can't change it. It's what makes you you. Without it, in a way, you cease to exist.

I decided that Mr Randle's answer about parents saying their children recognised them had been diplomatic, but non-committal. As a doctor he must know perfectly well that Immie's lack of cerebral cortex meant she could not have a relationship with us. Lacking self-knowledge, she could not possibly know others, not in any meaningful way. But he had listened to parents, and he knew that their deepest need was to be known, or at least recognised by their children. They couldn't go on caring for them, having lost all their hope and expectation, without that connection. That projection.

Refusing to buy into other parents' projections, I searched for another way to accept my daughter. I decided that Immie's destroyed brain meant that she had indeed lost her uniqueness as a person; but I still believed in her soul. I pictured it as a floating spirit that had landed in a useless child's body, with no means of expression. This soul was something apart from me, the bit of her I had always regarded as God's. And the place it had found to live was a mangled body, the flesh and blood that I had created.

The Latin word *mater* from which we derive our word 'mother' is also related to the word 'matter'. Matter is the stuff from which we are made. 'My own flesh and blood', we say of our children. It was this flesh and blood that had grown inside me for all those months before anyone else encountered it. And then, once it appeared, I had nursed it so close that I still felt it was part of me. Even now, her body contained cells from mine, and I held cells from hers. Her pale, brand-new body was like a branch, grafted to the deepest core of me.

I sat in the paediatric ward with my sedated babe in my lap, and yet again I imagined her dying. This time my fantasy was not about the release of death, but about resurrection. I looked at the turmeric-coloured boy in the bed opposite and I thought: all he needs is a liver. Maybe he's dying just because they can't find him another child's liver that is compatible. If we gave him Immie's, he would lead a happy, active life. Just that one little liver, easily transplanted, and his parents would have a chance of bringing him up – a perfectly normal, healthy boy.

But in the same moment that I thought it, I knew I must not. No one was going to let me donate my daughter's body parts to another child. No one was going to let her die, least of all Imogen herself. I had to accept her existence, here and now, in this stark and simple form. Though I regarded hers as a death-in-life, she, thank God, could know no better.

So they all rolled over, and one fell out

HOLLY TOOK ELLIE off to her mum's place, leaving me in grown-up silence. I had forgotten how quiet the cottage could be without Immie's screaming. But I wasn't going to sit around. I had less than a week before her return, during which time I intended to get on top of things.

At least the CT scan was definitive; it was the diagnosis I had lacked when I first tried contacting the disability charities. It gave me the chance to discover what our future entailed.

I started by phoning the SCOPE helpline again, to see what they had to say about caring for someone as badly brain-damaged as my daughter. The man at the end of the line was attentive; I remember feeling immensely grateful for his unjudgemental, informed responses. He advised that I see a social worker as soon as possible; they would put together a care plan for us. There were 100,000 children across the UK receiving the highest level of disability living allowance, but no one knew the total number of children as profoundly disabled as Immie. It might well be more. Every region did independent assessments, providing different levels of help, he said. He agreed with Mr Randle that they never provided enough. I had to be prepared to fight every inch of the way. He gave me his first name, Gerald, and said I should keeping phoning the helpline with whatever problems and worries came up – I could always ask for him.

I wanted Jay to engage with this next stage of Imogen's life, hear from the helpline himself. He returned from his call, saying they had told him they weren't a counselling service.

I had not thought of SCOPE as an emotional outlet; I supposed I had been calling them simply for information. Yet counselling was just what Gerald was offering me. Each time I rang, there he was – intent on hearing whatever I needed to say. Mainly our chats focused around the scary future, but sometimes I would voice present preoccupations.

I remember one time confessing, 'I feel so jealous of all those people whose babies don't have brain damage.'

And he said, 'You're going to have to get used to that. When people her age are taking their GCSEs, or having children of their own, your baby's not . . .' He trailed off. I felt a lurch of panic: what about those experiences? Whom would I talk to then?

The only counselling I'd ever had were the couple of sessions with Jay in the summer. I had never considered it solo before; now maybe I should. Perhaps the helpline was not enough; I should go somewhere safe to weep and talk about my baby. Luckily for me, Mary the health visitor had already cottoned on. She turned up with a leaflet from an Oxford charity for parents and babies suffering the effects of post-natal depression. Tactfully, she agreed that mine was not exactly this situation, but that it was a very interesting project, an important piece of national research. She made it seem as though my going there would be as much a favour to them as it was to me. I rang and made an appointment.

However, counselling was a long-term project for a vulnerable, mourning me. In the short term, I had to be stronger than ever. With my deadline of next Tuesday fast approaching, I needed to launch my fight for help. Armed with my antidepressants, like a Perspex riot shield, I was ready for battle.

★

Along with the counselling literature, Mary had brought round a fat, green, wipe-clean file with the title 'Children with Special Needs – Information for Parents'. Even before I opened it I was in a bate: how I loathed that word 'special' – its soggy sibilants, its sentimentality. I hated the fact that Immie was now labelled 'special'. The dictionary definition is 'distinguished, excelling all others of its kind'. People really are prepared to claim that children like her possess these qualities. 'Ah,' coo the Bleeding Hearts, 'look at them, they're really *special*.' They can afford to; they don't have to change their unconscious offspring's nappies for twenty years. They don't have to fight every inch of the way. What else would they label her? 'Disabled'? No, Immie was entirely 'unable'; 'learning difficulties' – you can say that again, it's tricky learning anything when you haven't got a brain. To me, the language seemed chock-a-block with euphemisms: pathetic plasters to cover gaping great wounds.

I opened the file with its sturdy clips ready for updates, and flicked through the pages. It was set out as clearly and consistently as it could be, with an opening glossary of terms and a list of acronyms to help me on my way. I skimmed through the section about 'Getting into the System'. There was a diagram dedicated to the complex assessment of *special* educational needs, a string of *special* schools to choose between, comprehensive descriptions of paediatric services and social services, speech therapies and occupational therapies.

Perhaps if Immie had been at home, I would have leapt straight in there; with her shrieks racking my nerves, I'd have picked up my action pack and charged ahead into the system. But her absence gave me space to think. And, I thought, this isn't for me; it's for people who know their children, who know what they are looking for. All I'm up to is quibbling with their jargon.

Thursday, 7 November

The anniversary of my older brother's birth and death. The social worker arrived; she explained that she was not the family's social worker, but Imogen's. I sat in my feeding chair, arms pathetically empty, whilst Jay paced about on the other side of the room, describing our fears and differences. The social worker said nothing, and I thought: this is where the fight begins. So in I launched, complaining that Alison the assessor had visited many weeks ago, but after the emergency respite we had heard absolutely nothing. She had said we would be getting the same thing every other weekend. Where was it?

Immie's social worker tried to reassure: she and Alison would be filing a full report and from there they would work out exactly what help we were eligible for. Unfortunately, these things did take time. As well as respite weekends, we would probably get one session a week from the Home Care Service. Her jargon bounced about: a personalised care plan, the right to appeal, signposting . . .

I cut her off to say I knew Oxfordshire was a rich county and unpopular jobs were often left unfilled; even the local supermarket had problems recruiting staff. I wondered about the care industry; I imagined it was unpopular and unlucrative. I didn't tell the social worker that I had discovered that weekend foster carers like Tracey got paid around £1 an hour. There was no point in having a care plan if no one wanted to do the work, I said. She admitted this could be a problem . . . She promised she'd come back next week.

According to the official line, it was just a case of waiting. Except that I didn't want to wait. I distrusted the jargon and the information packs, all the explanations and reassurances. For months now, everyone had been saying, 'Live a day at a time,' but I felt that advice had simply been a way of hiding the truth from me. The professionals, with their single focus on Immie, needed me not to think about the future. That way, my overweening love for my baby would thoughtlessly transmute into full-time nursing care. Just waiting was how families found themselves ten, twenty years down the line, still slogging away with a newborn who had failed to grow up. At no cost to the public coffers. Well, I was not going to fall into their trap.

Turning to the green file again, I searched for independent

charities that might give me a truthful picture. The lists gave numbers for family centres and support groups, residential respite care and family-based respite care. When I got through to the local authority resource centre, the receptionist started to explain their complicated new set-up: they were run by the children's charity, Barnardo's, in collaboration with the council. Immie would not be eligible for respite until she was seven, and then just for the odd weekend, depending on her care assessment. I asked why, if they were run by a charity, they took referrals only through official channels. I said that, so far, I had found little to reassure me in Social Services.

She must have heard the note of desperation in my voice. Her own became softer, more confidential.

'It's so hard for families like yours,' she said. 'There are just too many people needing help. Did you know that only 6 per cent of families with disabled children get anything at all? And that might just be a couple of hours' hoovering. If you want residential respite, you're going to have to fight tooth and nail. Across Oxfordshire, there are six resource centres like ours, but three are about to be shut down. We're closed for refurbishment, but when we reopen there will be all the extra children to look after . . . That means everyone getting a smaller slice of the cake.'

'Why are they reducing respite?' I asked, to cue her inevitable punchline.

'Cost-cutting, it's always cost-cutting, isn't it?'

She gave me the number of a local parents' group campaigning for the respite needs of families like mine, and I wrote it down in the back of Immie's disused crying and feeding diary.

Then I rang Gerald on the SCOPE helpline and reported what I'd been told. Did he know about care provision in better areas than Oxfordshire? I said we didn't have the money to buy in professional help, but we did have the freedom to move house anywhere within a reasonable commute of London. I was quite fired up with my strategic approach. His response was tentative: well, yes, Cambridgeshire was meant to provide care packages that were a little more generous . . . but had I considered the impact such a move might make on my other child? I confessed that I had not. He went on to point out that the care system was always changing; having moved, I might find my new area altering its budget or, more likely, its eligibility criteria (the level of disability at which a child qualifies for state help). That's what had happened in my region. Gerald thought I'd be better off staying put and trying to establish a good relationship with the social worker so she would get us the best help. Here in Oxfordshire, he said, we had friends and family. I would be depending on them just as much as the system.

Friends and family. Gerald's comment sliced straight through my fighting spirit. I couldn't think of a single friend who would help me with Imogen now that Nadine had gone. Many offered to help with Elinor, but she wasn't the one I wanted taking off my hands. Although Holly had done her job amazingly patiently, now that the diagnosis was certain, we couldn't go on pretending it was regular babysitting. She needed to take her talents elsewhere. I could picture my future, unable to afford a special needs carer, permanently holed up alone with miserable Immie whilst my sunny older child was farmed out to all the friends who wanted to help.

And my family? I imagined that if I had an extended one like baby Joely's, then my sick child would have aunts and grannies around to look after her. But my family wasn't set up that way. No one lived just round the corner; they were all busy with jobs, separate homes, individual lives. I couldn't depend on them.

Then there was the emotional fallout. I was acutely aware how much Immie's condition had stricken people close to me. Ever since Virginia Nicholas's first brain damage news, I had witnessed their sadness and their fear. I imagined theirs was a double burden of grief – not just for her, but for me too. More than anything I wanted it to cease.

A friend who had not been in touch for a few months rang to say he was passing by and would like to drop in. 'How's Immie?' he asked. Laughter clattered like machine-gun fire from my mouth. I had noticed that laugh evolving over the past few weeks.

'She has no cerebral cortex.'

'Oh!' And he was gone. The short sharp shock was best. Best to shut out other people's emotions, blockade myself in. That way, at least I stayed strong.

My carapace was seldom broken; those who got through had to be especially resilient, like me. Some tried the practical approach. One friend sent a leaflet picturing a crookedly smiling child; it advertised a local physiotherapy centre that provided parents with 'intensive daily programmes' for their palsied offspring. Another left several messages on the answer machine, describing a miraculous training regime: a long rota of exercises to help brain-damaged children towards their milestones. I added them to the contact list that was fast developing in the back of the diary. But I couldn't see myself using them; maybe my friends couldn't either – they were simply trying to show support.

A neighbour I hardly knew posted some contact details through the door; they belonged to a Londoner with a brain-damaged daughter who had won her clinical negligence case after seven years. I added these to my list, but didn't have the guts to pick up the phone.

Jay kept out of all of this. His attitude was straightforward: Immie was at the extreme end of the disability spectrum; she needed professional help. He insisted that he was not retreating from his responsibilities; he was simply accepting his own limitations as her father – which were that he could not bear to nurse a child without consciousness. Now that we had seen the scan of Immie's skull, we had to accept that she could not comprehend who we were, that she had no idea who was caring for her at all. Obviously, nurses coped much better than a family in such a situation, Jay said. I should leave things to them.

'But no one spends their whole life in hospital!' I said. 'Mr Randle says she's well enough to come home.'

'How are we going to cope, Jules?'

I had no idea. With Imogen's return would come not only her wail, but also the drugs, the sour milk bottles, the therapists, the tension of her body infusing mine. We would be back to our constant state of stress, physically and mentally.

If Mr Randle had said she was definitely not going to survive the next eighteen months, I might have done it. I might have shut myself off from everything and dedicated myself to my dying baby. But I reckoned she was going to hang on in there, get through this early stage and claim her twenty years or more. Twenty years of family life as it had been before she went into hospital. No, worse, because now I had seen from the scan that there was no relationship to be had with her.

If only our case against the NHS looked positive. If I thought there would be money at some point in the future, then perhaps I could find a way to get through six years of legal battle. We would borrow money and buy in whatever help we needed. But the clinical negligence case had not even begun; the hospital Trust had not yet released our records.

'Where are you going?' asked Ellie.

'To the hospital.'

'Why?'

'Because I need to visit Immie.'

'Why?'

'Because she's sick.'

'Why?'

'Because her head isn't working properly.'

'Why?'

'Because of the accident.'

'Why?'

'Because she had a terrible accident when she was born.'

'Yes, but why did she have the terrible accident?'

'Accident' had been the right word to choose: it was random fate that had affected Immie in this way. But how to explain that to a small child who needed reassuring answers to all her Whys? If she did not have a good enough reason for her sister's brain damage, she would be sure to find one. And quite likely she, like me, would find a way to blame herself. How many surreal scenarios might she create in her mind to convince herself she had caused the accident?

'It's no one's fault,' I kept on saying. 'It's just something that happened. Sometimes horrible things happen and this time it was to Immie.'

Each morning I drove along the well-worn route to the hospital, seeing how efficiently I could accomplish my mission: into the ward; over to Imogen's corner; locate her nurse: 'Everything OK?'

'She's doing fine!'

'Sorry. I'll try and stay longer tomorrow!'

Then away again to my urgent business – the warm car.

The roads were slippery, the commuter traffic almost as impatient as me. After the extended summer, the frosts had sent leaves falling fast, and now they formed a lethal mush on the camber of the road. Sometimes I drove carefully through such hazards, responsible-mother style. But mostly I was careless. Alone in this roaring machine, I defied destiny to pick off my worthless little life. As I approached speed cameras, I delayed the brake later and later, its last-minute force testing the heavy car. This time surely it would veer out of control, spinning me against another lump of metal. What if I don't bother to slow down at the blind turning, just stay in top gear as I swing over to the other side? Who cares! It must be how teenage boys feel, foot down, burning rubber: not the ones who think themselves immortal, but the ones who don't care one way or the other. Nihilists.

Home again, I sat in the sitting room, bundled up in a shawl close to the fire. Home was my bunker, the babyless burrow where I could hide. Outside, daylight came and went but I, like the hedgehogs, was indifferent.

My mother rang to say, 'I have been thinking: Immie has lost her creativity; you owe it to her to pursue yours.' Creativity. What creativity? I had set out on this parenting journey with Mum's notion in mind: that bringing up children was the most creative thing one could do with one's life. Now she was looking at me and wishing I hadn't. If only I could plunge back in there, drown my sorrows in the busy, childless life I'd once had. The thought that such a thing might compensate for the loss of my daughter's creative life was compelling. But I just couldn't see a way; I wasn't ready.

Ready to go back to work. When Ellie was six weeks old, I happily sped off to work two mornings a week. At three months, I handed her over to a childminder every day for six weeks so I could direct a show. I was glad when it was over – I could see that she missed me and I her. This time around, I had planned to be much more sensitive to the process, watch my baby's increasing independence and accommodate my work to that. But now I knew that Immie would never be independent of me, not just because of her great inability, but also because of her lack of under-standing. If she was incapable of making a meaningful attachment to me, then she was also incapable of detaching in any way.

Despite its logic, the idea was very hard to accept. Alison from Social Services had been wrong to say I had not bonded with my baby; I had, deeply and lovingly. But it could not be the unre-quited love I had once imagined, because Immie did not possess understanding enough to reject me. Instead, my love existed in a vacuum. I could imagine never being ready to go back to work, because the half of the relationship that should move away, demonstrating her diminishing need, was just not there.

Jay was trawling the internet, rooting out the scare stories. He printed off a report from Australia, listing the impact a severely disabled child has on an average family. The term 'chronic stress' jumped out at me even before I went down the list: families were likely to suffer from very little social life or time off; a lack of hol-idays; reduced career opportunities; feelings of low self-esteem in siblings and parents . . . Jay pored over the material and com-posed a long list of reasons why Immie should not come home, ending with 'sanity threatened'.

I imagined that the life of Saint Julia, where I endured twenty years of nursing my poor daughter, would most likely entail all these sacrifices. To what end? Because I had a duty to her, the person I had (so bunglingly) brought into the world. Because there was no alternative; because I loved her. But I also loved Jay. At least, I had done once.

It struck me that, since Immie had been in hospital, Jay and I had stopped rowing. The only time we had come near to it had been the day she came home for the christening, as if her very presence catalysed dissension. I saw that since her birth I had been pouring love into my baby, emptying myself of anything I might have given to Jay. He had said he couldn't love Immie any more, but I knew that was not so. It was his impotence in the face of her suffering that blocked the love. And so he had turned away from both of us, too distressed to express any kind of tenderness. Love, in each of us, was locked away behind the armour required simply to cope with Imogen and her world.

I wanted to find it again. More than ever, I needed Jay's love and doubtless he needed mine. It was the foundation of our family.

Jay pointed to an American report asserting that people in our situation needed to uphold their rights and liberties as a family, as well as for their disabled children. The two might not always be compatible.

The greatest happiness for the greatest number. I remembered the phrase from my student days. It kept on jumping into my head. Life with Jay should be full of creativity and laughter, not the angry conflict that had begun even before Imogen's diagnosis. We should be planning a course of action for our family where we achieved the greatest overall happiness in the future. Jay's list pointed out that such a thing would be hard-won. How did families achieve happiness without holidays or career satisfaction or self-esteem? Maybe I felt guilty enough about Immie's brain damage to think I deserved twenty years of unhappiness. But Jay did not deserve it and neither did Elinor.

Mark had given me the phone number of a woman down the road with an eleven-year-old severely disabled daughter. Tussie

Myerson would have a lot to tell me about coping with Immie. I picked up the phone. The woman who answered sounded extrovert and energetic; in the background was the cacophony of a busy family. It was true, she began, that there was never enough help; looking after Immie was going to be bigger than anything I could imagine.

Our conversation quickly turned to the macabre: wanting our children to die, managing to persuade doctors of that, or not. Tussie had spent years in paediatric wards, hovering behind the nurse with the file marked 'Not for Resuscitation', waiting to see whether her daughter would come round from the latest epileptic crisis. It was a great relief to talk to someone familiar with the dark, confusing world I had so recently entered. I could feel my guilt starting to lift as I heard it expressed by someone else.

I confessed that I was fearful for Ellie and the stresses she would suffer because of Imogen. I described the way she had closed in on herself over the past months. Tussie admitted that the needs of her two able-bodied children often took second place to their sister's. However, they loved her dearly and generally found ways to get by. Recently her son had been teased at school for having a spastic sister and they had put a stop to it by inviting the teaser home for tea.

I told her Jay was determined not to have Immie back, that I thought he felt trapped by her.

'Already!' she cried. 'It normally takes a few years. But there you go – it's quite a strange journey, this one. Everyone does it their own way, though most of us reach breaking point in the end.'

After eleven years of fighting, she knew how to cut the bullshit. When the conversation turned to Social Services, she sighed. 'They've got it all wrong,' she said. 'It's just about saving money. Social workers have to function as gatekeepers, when they should be providers.'

For the past few months she had been taking part in a television programme for *Panorama*. The cameras had being covering the ways in which her family could no longer cope with their very sick daughter. According to a MENCAP survey, the results of which were to be launched in June, eight out of ten parents caring for a severely disabled child admit they are at breaking point. Tussie's programme followed her efforts to get her daughter into residential care, something Social Services were resisting in all sorts of long-winded, bureaucratic ways. Although they had tried to persuade her that foster care was better, she did not believe them; it was just much cheaper. True, the local residential school was expensive, but it was the right thing for the family.

I understood Tussie's objection to foster care. Even when they were paid as little as £1 an hour, it was possible for foster carers to do an excellent job; my experience with Tracey had proved that. All the same, the respite weekend had been an agonising humiliation for me. I was still smarting from the shame of handing my baby to someone who was better at mothering than myself. A foster carer was a replacement mother, the embodiment of Social Services' judgement that my child needed saving from me.

In the back of my mind was also a fear that, behind the closed doors of a long-term foster home, my daughter might be mistreated in some way and no one would know about it.

A residential home, though, was different. An institutional form of care, it entailed no single, alternative mother. It was anonymous, professional, controlled – somewhere that could contain my huge Immie burden without my being any less her mother. In such a public place, I imagined, it would be much harder for carers to abuse their position than it would be in a private home. I had not considered residential care before because no one had suggested it. I had assumed that children's homes were Dickensian places where disabled people were hidden away, unloved and forgotten. But Tussie was describing something very different.

In a home for children with profound physical and mental disabilities, there are therapists and nurses, as well as a raft of trained experts to see to their every need. I imagined uniforms and corridors, and all the technological paraphernalia of a hospital. I had seen Immie in SCBU and in the paediatric ward – she seemed to like those places. We could visit her whenever we wanted; she could come and stay, having her needs met by a team of professionals. It made a lot of sense. Why wait eleven years as Tussie had done? Why not send her there now?

The internet soon threw up loads of names, loads of numbers to ring. Within a day, glossy brochures were pouring through the letterbox. This was material with which to confront Imogen's social worker; she couldn't wriggle out of it by pretending such homes did not exist. I would tell her I couldn't hang about any longer for her non-existent help, that I had made up my mind.

Jay didn't believe it. He said, 'You won't ever be able to give her up.'

'Why not?' I retaliated. 'It would be as if a bit of me had been cut out. I would survive.'

Immie was my flesh and blood. I thought of her not as a baby growing in independence and ability, but as a permanent, integral part of my body. Ever since her birth I had imagined her being severed from me. If I had a rotten lung or a diseased kidney or something, a surgeon would remove it. And then, living carefully and respecting my body's weakness, I would still be able to lead a happy life. I would be different from other mothers; something fundamental would be missing. Some days, like any invalid, I would have to stay away from people, nursing myself. But from what Gerald, my SCOPE confidant, said, that would be the case anyway; Imogen's very existence was a wound to be tended.

On the Friday, the social worker phoned, and I told her we wanted Immie to be cared for permanently in a home. Very patiently, she explained: 'The local authority doesn't tend to put children like Imogen into residential homes.'

'Why not?'

'Because they don't think it's the best place for them.'

Gatekeeper, I thought.

She must have realised. 'You know, we are here to help,' she said. 'People see the horror stories on the television and they think all social workers are out to get them. But most of the time we're not. We *are* listening to you.'

Well then, she would have to take on board my decision about the future. I was going to be clear-cut and uncompromising, like the black hole in my daughter's head.

Two days before we were due to pick up Imogen from the hospital, I stopped going to see her. I remember waking up and thinking that I just couldn't face the charade any more. It was Sunday; I knew there would be different staff on the ward, just a couple of junior doctors who would get on with things without enquiring where I was. So I stayed cocooned in bed with the curtains drawn. My Immie headache was worse than ever, squeezing like a clamp around my temples. It was my version of her palsy, the heaviness of her world bearing down on me.

On Monday morning, despite a cocktail of painkillers on top of the daily dose of antidepressants, I was no better. I lay on the sofa with Ellie, watching her *Babe* video with the sound turned down. A car coming down the lane roused me. There on the doorstep stood a woman, tall and strong in the pale November sunlight. She said she was from the carers' centre – an independent charity providing support for carers.

Perhaps I had organised it in one of my bouts of research, perhaps my health visitor had contacted her for me: I had no idea. All those charities out there, all those dedicated volunteers – I needed them to lift this weight off me.

We sat together by the fire. I didn't bother to change out of my pyjamas, I just let her talk. Sheila described in detail the vast problems in the local care system, the way families struggled. She told me about the 'tripartite system' of care, how children like Immie were supported by three different public bodies: Health, Education and Social Services. All regarded themselves as underfinanced and readily palmed off responsibility onto one another, given half a chance.

She was surprised by my residential home idea, saying it was generally felt that foster care was better for babies. She told me that she herself had been a foster carer for a family whose son was badly brain-damaged. On the day he was delivered to her home, the mother decided she wanted to care for him after all. But Sheila had stayed in touch, regularly having him to stay for the weekend until his death at the age of nine. I saw how this woman's generosity must have helped the family. She had given them regular respite but had been more than that – a safety net, security. 'You were their extended family,' I said, and she smiled.

She told me she had adopted a CP girl (much less damaged than Immie). I asked whether she knew the mother and she said she had met her. I was thinking of my great-grandmother and of all the millions of other women who have abandoned a child. Back in September, Lorna had said that her sister, baby Joely's mum, was not the sort to leave her daughter in hospital. But there must be many who were; maybe I was one of them – it was in my genes.

'At what point in a child's life do you think it's easiest for a mother to put it into care?' I asked.

She took a beat, squinting out through the bay window into the light. She could see how vulnerable I was; she must be trying to find the right answer for me. And then she said, 'I don't think there will ever be an easy time.'

But I didn't agree. Her tales had emboldened me. Surely it would be easier now. The longer we went on, the further we moved away from our pre-Immie version of life, the harder giving her up would become. Already, Jay couldn't countenance anything other than handing her over to professionals. I popped all the pills, yet still I couldn't get out of bed. Maybe my family had reached its breaking point. And Elinor? Ah – I found it very hard to think about her.

Ellie wanted to be a sister; I had longed for her to be one; Imogen gave her that identity. She did not yet know how different this sibling was from other people's. But the more Jay and I struggled, the more Elinor would become accustomed to our anguish, our rows and our tears; I couldn't do that to her. She was not yet three. Her experiences up until this point in her life were unlikely ever to become solid memories. If Immie were to go now, this brief period would fade, and she'd be left with only a vague sensation of her sisterhood.

My own childhood had taught me something about absent siblings. Long before I was told about my mother's dead first-born, I had fantasised about him. At primary school I invented tales about a big brother who played and fought and joked with me. When I was aged eleven, and my parents sat me down at the kitchen table and gave me their old news about him, I was not shocked – I knew it all already. I had always known that suffering babies died and went away, and still lived on in their healthy sisters.

I told Sheila that I thought Imogen was happy in hospital, that we were all happier with her there. She nodded. 'Well then, perhaps you should leave her to the doctors.' That felt right for Immie, safe in her hospital bed. It also felt right for me: me at her birth, on all fours on the living-room floor, abandoned. This time I would force them into caring for us.

Sheila thought that if the baby was seen as a medical case, then she might have access to the best funds. After all, Health receives by far the greatest share of public funding. I was immensely grateful for her reasoning, her ability to consider such practical-ities without my painful emotions getting in the way.

So this was the plan: I would tell the hospital I was leaving Imogen there. Sheila hadn't ever come across this scenario before. It sounded feasible, but we should consider one thing: if I chose to abandon Immie, would there be repercussions? Would they regard my unwillingness to mother her as evidence that I should not mother Elinor?

My God. Of course. The punishment. It made complete sense: I couldn't get away without punishment. Whatever the social worker had said, I had heard the stories – given half a chance, they took your children away from you. Your sparky, brainful children.

Sheila said she might be wrong; I should get in touch with a good lawyer to find out. The moment she left, I got out the Yellow Pages, in search of local family solicitors. One by one they listened to my tale and admitted they were unable to get involved with such a complex case. Eventually, someone put me in touch with a lawyer in London who specialised in such things. By the time I got through to her, it was evening, well past office hours. But there she was, all fired up and ready for action. I could feel the clarity of her mind, the breadth of her experience. She can cope with me, I thought.

What if I abandon my child in hospital? What exactly would happen? Could she stay there for ever? The answer was no. The local authority would take charge of her; care proceedings would be managed by Social Services.

Would they force me to have her fostered? No, they could not force me to do anything; I had parental responsibility. But fostering is much cheaper than a residential home. There is also an ethos that a domestic environment is the best place for any child to be cared for, however incapacitated.

Would our clinical negligence case alter if we abandoned her? No, the case was strictly hers, not her parents', so nothing would change.

Finally, the big one: will they penalise me by taking away my other child? No. The courts concentrate on the individual needs of the child; each case is seen totally independently.

Tuesday, 12 November

My deadline had arrived; there it was in my diary: 'Pick up Immie.' But instead I sat by the phone, waiting for the call from the hospital to summon me. Jay hovered about, convinced I was doing the right thing, but unconvinced I would carry it through. At around midday, even before the first ring completed, I picked up the receiver. A voice on the end tripped off the professional repartee – happy to report that Imogen was doing very well. I said nothing. Her bright tone shifted down a notch as she enquired politely what time I would be arriving.

I said, 'I shan't be coming in.'

'Is there anything . . .?'

'I can't.' Silence. I hoped she understood without my having to say anything else, because I would surely cry if I had to speak again.

'Let me have a word with Mr Randle. I'll phone you back.'

When she did it, was simply to say that the consultant understood we would not be coming to collect our child. Could we please attend a meeting next day in his office. I agreed.

I pictured Mr Randle at his desk with Immic's CT scan in front of him. He knew what was going on; he had seen my sort of situation before. I wondered what he thought about these empty heads and the way they destroyed eight out of ten families.

Then I rang my mother and told her what I had done. 'If you feel that's the right thing . . .' she said. I could hear the mixture of sadness and relief in her voice. I asked whether she would please get in touch with a retired paediatrician friend of hers who might advise me; I wanted to say the right thing at this meeting – to make my case absolutely credible and unequivocal. I wanted to know how common it was for parents to do this; how they tended to go about it; exactly what they said.

I waited for Mum to call back, motionless at my place by the phone. I hadn't moved from there all morning. The winter sun shone onto the white handset, making it glow. It made me feel strong and clear-headed, completely focused on carrying out my task. In no time at all, there she was with the information: in answer to my first question, roughly 16 per cent of very disabled babies were left in hospital, her friend had said. I wasn't sure whether the statistic was higher or lower than I expected. The main thing was the proof that other parents out there had done what I was about to do. As for my other questions: people left their children in all sorts of ways, but if that was truly my resolve, the paediatrician could suggest what to say. I said, yes, please, I wanted to say the right thing. Mum was finding it hard to speak.

'Then you must say, "I am not the right parent for Imogen."'

★

That afternoon, whilst Ellie was at the nursery, Jay and I threw out all the baby stuff. My mother once described to me her friends getting rid of a whole roomful before she returned from hospital after baby Martin's death. By removing all evidence of Imogen, I was proving to Jay that she was not coming back.

Together we had created this poor child, and together we excised her presence from our home. We emptied the shelves in the cupboard where the Babygros were stored, packing them into a case to take to hospital. I untacked the blackout lining from the curtains, gathered up the rattles. These things, and more, were chucked straight into the rubbish bin outside. I particularly remember a book titled *Baby Talk*, which I had used as Elinor's speech was developing, with a photo of a smiling toddler on the front. I didn't bother to take it to the charity shop in town; if my baby had no use for it, then it could slowly disintegrate in a landfill site. I did not mind some stranger salvaging other bits of Imogen's debris – the cot by my bed, the steriliser for her bottles, the high chair we had been keeping for when she could sit up. They all went into the back of the car, and Jay drove them to the dump.

When Elinor got home, all her sister's belongings had disappeared. She didn't say anything; she understood that Immie was in hospital and needed to stay there; she didn't have to know any more for now.

Wednesday, 13 November

Walking down the corridor towards the paediatric ward, I was surprised to see huge murals on either side. Through all the times I had passed by I had failed to spot them. They depicted a merry seaside scene, with boats and gulls and a Punch and Judy show. Sometimes utilitarian hospital elements had superimposed themselves onto the fun – a fire extinguisher sitting in the middle of the beach, a 'Swabs and Dressings' label floating on top of the steamship. On the door of the puppet booth was an advertisement for an upcoming lecture: 'Nutrition for the Cerebral Palsied Child'.

Jay and I were well armed for the meeting with our artillery of paperwork: he had his quotes from the internet, I my brochures. Immie's social worker was already in the ward, and she escorted us to the office. Mr Randle was sitting sideways at his desk, in the exact same position as when he took us through the CT scan. I chose a different seat this time, adjacent to the desk, from where I had a view of Oxford's spires soaring out of their valley.

The atmosphere felt solemn, careful, not at all what I had been expecting. Like waiting in a register office to register a birth, or a death, or both. Mr Randle asked me to confirm that I was not prepared to take Immie home. I used my 'not the right parent' line and then fell silent; there didn't seem anything more to say. He turned to Jay, who confirmed that he too could not look after her.

Then the doctor asked him, 'Have you ever thought of harming her?'

I thought the question must be to establish that our situation qualified for public funding. It was what the GP had said – they have to believe the child is in danger. Jay's head was down, but his answer came boldly enough:

'I can't say I haven't.'

'Then let us take the burden away from you.'

I got out my notebook and went through my arguments about residential care. I waved the brochure from the home whose facilities most impressed me, and said that, in my judgement, this would be the best place for my baby. I felt a bit like a student trying to justify a hopelessly insubstantial essay.

Mr Randle looked at the social worker and said, 'I don't think that is the right place for her at the moment.'

'Might you refer her there in the future?' I asked.

'Possibly, yes,' and he turned again to the social worker. I knew what she was going to say.

'Oxfordshire Social Services doesn't place any children under eight in residential homes.'

'But the Health Service might,' I challenged, sure of my grasp on tripartite funding.

'If you are not able to take Imogen home,' said Mr Randle, 'then she becomes the responsibility of Social Services.' I knew that was so; it was what the lawyer had said; I couldn't argue. I turned to Immie's social worker.

'What are you going to do?' I asked.

'I have been asking around and there is a very experienced foster carer in Abingdon. She is ready to take Imogen if that is what you want.'

'We need some space,' I said, looking towards Jay, but he didn't look back. 'How long will she stay there?'

'For now. Foster care is nearly always a temporary measure. Would you like to meet her?'

I nodded.

I suppose I felt defeated. After all that plotting and planning, the system had come up with its own solution: the foster care I didn't want. But I was no longer angry; we were being looked after, these people did care. Perhaps they were right about babies needing a domestic environment – what did I know?

The social worker accompanied me out into the ward and stood there as I lifted Immie from her bed and into my lap. Her eyes were open; she seemed so peaceful, so warm, firmer and chubbier than I remembered. I looked at the social worker and murmured, 'I do love her, you know.'

We were allocated a darkened side room to wait for the foster carer to arrive. Immie lay calmly in my lap. When the door opened it revealed a nurse and, behind her, a slim dark figure in a pinstriped suit. My first thought was that he must be a police agent. But, as he closed the door behind him, I realised it was the professor from the feeding clinic.

'I think we've met before,' he said, offering me his hand. Mine stayed tight around my baby's body. He beckoned to the nurse to take a seat and assumed a profile pose against the square window; it struck me as the most high-status position available. Was he about to launch into the nutrition lecture I had seen advertised in the corridor?

'Now, I'm told you're arranging for your baby to go into care.' He didn't wait for confirmation. 'We need to be realistic, don't we – assisted feeding is an inevitability. I recommend a gastrostomy. A professional carer will be quite familiar with the technology. A simple feeding tube is inserted into the stomach; nutrition is supplied by a pump. Imogen can have the operation whilst she's still here in hospital.'

Guilty me had been waiting for this. Here was my punishment – not from Social Services, but from the clinicians. A tube straight into her stomach, a pump . . . If her unnatural mother was not prepared to feed her, then she might as well be given a machine.

'But I've been feeding her,' I said.

'And how long does each feed take?'

'Maybe three, four hours – but I managed. The nurses haven't complained.'

The way he lifted his eyebrows suggested that perhaps they had.

'Why should a foster carer need this tube?' I continued.

'Because the baby will be much easier to manage.'

'But it's the one ability she has. Eating is what she can do . . .'

'Look, I've seen the scans and it has to be said: your daughter's not got a lot of brain left!'

My legs were trembling under my daughter. He was looking at me. This was my last chance to say what I thought, whilst I was still her mother. I leant forward in the chair, raised her body a little to expand my presence. I was not afraid. Very slowly, very pointedly, I said, 'I don't think her quality of life merits your intervention.' There – I had used the official language; I had met his bluntness with my own. Out of the corner of my eye, I saw the nurse wince.

'Ah,' said the professor. Head down, hands behind his back, he started to pace up and down in the couple of metres of floor available. He was calculating the best approach for his thesis. On elegant heels, he spun to face us.

'There are just two points I would like to make. Firstly, the technology is an entirely appropriate intervention for a child in her condition . . .'

'But it's unnatural,' I interjected.

'What do you mean, "unnatural"?' He wanted to run with this one.

'I mean that if you were to leave it to nature, she would die. That's what would happen if we lived in an Indian village.'

'But Imogen doesn't live in India! She's lucky enough to have been born in the First World, in the twenty-first century. We can't leave her eating problems unmanaged when we have the resources to do something. Do you know how long it takes a child to die of starvation?' He let his shocking word hang for a moment. 'Two weeks! Two weeks – and it's not a pretty sight! Every cell in the little one's body, straining for sustenance . . . Let's be honest: could you inflict that on your child?'

The professor knew I couldn't. But many doctors do, of course; it's called 'withdrawal of treatment' and it's how people with no hope of recovery have to die in my country. Where dogs are given a quick and painless injection to hasten their inevitable death, humans must die of starvation. That is the law. The Prof must have seen it many times. However, I wasn't up to debating such things. I had nothing left to say. All I could do was refuse to sign his consent form.

The foster carer arrived in his wake, a kind-looking young woman called Tania, her long straight hair melding with a dark dress, soft and velvety and reassuring. I couldn't meet her eye, didn't want to connect with her. I just wanted to get our meeting over and done with. I tried to pretend I was handing the baby over to Holly for just a few hours. Jay went with her to transfer the pram and baby seat from our car to hers.

The social worker escorted me downstairs to the canteen where we went through the pile of documents that needed signing. Across the tables I spotted a mum whose daughter had lain next to Immie in SCBU, waiting for the operation on her oesophagus. Now the baby was breastfeeding, with a girl Ellie's age sitting patiently on the chair next to them. The mother looked up; I willed her not to come over and ask how things were. She waved, and I waved back.

As Jay drove down the hill away from the hospital, I let out a howl. It was long and loud – as if my breath would carry it for ever. My abdomen felt as though the muscles were splitting, away from the *linea nigra* that had formed in pregnancy. I was being unzipped again, but this time there was no swollen womb between, just a gash, a searing hole. This was what it felt like to be torn apart.

The wail rose higher and higher in the echoing chamber of our car: 'I can't do it; I can't leave her, I can't.'

'But you decided . . .'

'You made me do it.'

'I didn't, Jules. It's what you wanted.'

'Aghh.' There were no more words. Words were meaningless compared to this monstrous feeling. Monster-mother-love.

As we hit the ring road I started to panic.

'We have to go back. I can't do it. You have to take me back. Turn around. Turn back, Jay.'

At that moment it was a practical impossibility, trapped as we were in the flow of traffic. At the roundabout Jay drew into a side road and turned to me.

'It's me or her, Jules.'

The hideous howl again. This was it – the choice. I had known it was there all the time, beneath all my reasoning, but I never thought Jay would dare to say it. I railed at him, accusing him of every kind of selfishness and cruelty. When at last I was spent, he asked me whether I still wanted to go back to the hospital. And I said no.

I had signed away my child. My reason had told me I needed to do it, and so I must see it through. I had to have time to myself again, to mourn her, and try to love the other people I loved. And once that time was past, maybe I could be with her again.

Next day I didn't get out of bed. I rang the social worker and asked whether Immie could come over just for a few hours. 'But you signed papers yesterday agreeing to no visits for two weeks, in order for her to settle in with her new carer.'

'What do you mean?'

'Well, you can imagine – it's very disconcerting for a child to come back to the birth family and then have to leave again. Imogen needs to understand that Tania's is her home for now.'

'But she can't understand – she doesn't have a brain!'

'I'm afraid the rules apply to Imogen as much as they do to any other child.'

'I need to see her. Please, just let me see her.'

'Oh dear. Perhaps we made the wrong decision. Foster care might not be the right thing for you . . .'

'I didn't know how it would feel . . .' And I wept.

'I'll see what we can do.'

I think they must have overridden the rules for me; I didn't ask. A couple of days later, Tania arrived with Immie and her other, teenage foster child in a wheelchair. Imogen was strapped to her in a brand-new, coffee-coloured sling. I don't remember holding her; I think I was a bit afraid I would crack if I got too close. Mainly, I was trying to put on a brave face for Elinor, pretending we were having a charmingly eccentric lunch party. I kept myself busy, serving home-made soup, mashing it with bread for the older child. She kept on laughing – a loud and jerky guffaw that soon became the focus of our gathering, compelling us all to laugh along. Whenever she took a break, her foster carer niftily spooned some soup mush into her mouth. The meal done, they recited 'The Three Billy Goats Gruff' together in staccato duet, Tania providing the ends of lines when the teenager's hollow voice failed to find the words. I watched her slender fingers dance up and down on the arms of her wheelchair, conducting her own performance, and wondered what had led her mother to give her up.

Though her charge was extrovert, Tania seemed a shy person, hiding behind long hair and glasses. At the same time, she had a dignity and strength about her that made me trust her completely. The way she kept smiling at Elinor, encouraging her not to be frightened of the crazy spectacle she had brought along, reassured me of her empathy with children. With me, she was warm and yet professional, feeling her way with how I wanted to be with Imogen, now that she was in her care. Maybe she picked up on my sense of failure in having handed over my baby to a more competent mother than myself; maybe she had seen it before. I did not feel humiliated in the way I had expected. Tania somehow made me feel that she respected me.

When it was time for them to leave, Tania (with Imogen still strapped to her) slid open the side of her van and launched the wheelchair up inside. I could see how strong and how determined this woman was. Once the van had swung out of sight, I cuddled Ellie and tried to explain that a foster carer was like the nurses – she was looking after Immie for us. Ellie couldn't understand why her sister had gone away again. She wanted to know who this older sister was in the wheelchair. I tried to fudge it all with 'It's not for long' or 'Let's wait and see', but her questions persisted and I could feel myself giving in.

'She'll probably come home soon,' I said.

Six, seven, eight, nine, ten,
Then I let it go again

December 2002

JAY, ELLIE AND I started visiting Imogen regularly soon after she
went to live with Tania. Her new home was about forty-five
minutes' drive away, a three-storey Victorian town house next
door to a stonemason's yard where fresh-hewn gravestones leant
against the walls. We rang the doorbell, and Tania came down the
narrow corridor holding Immie up high in front of her. As she
opened the door she declared 'Here she is!' as if Imogen had been
urgently demanding where Mummy was. I responded with
kisses and delight at how well she was looking, how beautifully
turned out. When I took her I could feel myself becoming calm,
the strain of surviving all this time without her dropping away. I
sat with her in my lap, feeling whole, my true mother-self again.

Tania answered all Elinor's questions, letting her explore her
sister's new home. She wanted to see where Immie slept and was
escorted up to a pretty bedroom under the eaves, with teddies
around the cot and Winnie the Pooh prints on the walls. When
they came down, Ellie sat on the sofa and watched in awe as the
big girl in her wheelchair descended through the trapdoor in the
ceiling, like a deus ex machina. The lift was just one of numer-

ous gadgets filling the house – hoists and standing machines in the bedrooms, a rubber shower bench over the bath, a big steel frame around the toilet. In the corner of the living room was a computer where Tania worked on her Master's thesis entitled 'Children with profound and multiple learning disabilities' – set aside now until she might have time again. The computer was also her access to support groups and chatlines for disability foster carers worldwide. Above it hung a dusty cross from some past Palm Sunday celebration, and a gingham collage of a red-roofed house embroidered with the words 'As for me and my house, we will serve the Lord'.

The bookshelves were packed with novels, many of them childhood collections – *The Chronicles of Narnia, Anne of Green Gables* and all of the *Chalet School* series. In the back room stood an upright piano with Mendelssohn's *Songs Without Words* open on the stand, and a tall bubble-tube with alternating coloured lights and fishes flitting up and down. Behind this hung a gallery of photos – fostering memorabilia, which interested Elinor immensely. She stood in front of the pictures, quizzing Tania about the dozen disabled children or more whom she had cared for over the years. There was a gleeful two-year-old girl clasping her hands, and a boy with a blank face standing at the front window, tapping. Most striking to me was a child being cuddled; she had wild woolly hair, dark eyes sinking behind great big lids and a tiny, emaciated body.

Our visits to Tania's home were surprisingly positive. It was the arriving and the leaving that were hard. Each time I parked the car, I sat for a moment wishing I did not have to go inside, to step into Immie's world again. And each time I left I felt the pull of my love for her, urging me to stay, to hold on to the invisible umbilical cord we still had. It tugged at me as I switched on the car engine; there was a yank as I turned onto the main road and up to the roundabout. Here the cord stretched taut, and I was straining against it; I had only to keep driving a full circle and the road would draw me back, back to my natural place with my baby. Resolutely, I steered off to the left and up the slip road into the conveyor belt of traffic. Forcing the car into the fast lane, I felt a final twang, like elastic snapping – I was free again.

Life at home began to resemble the pre-Immie one. We employed a local teenaged babysitter for the evening and went out. I cherished the freedom, once so taken for granted, to spend time with Jay watching a film, daring to enjoy a boozy evening together, without arguing. Whilst Ellie was at the nursery, I didn't have to rush home to my exploding household. I could do whatever I liked – wander round the shops without being stared at, go to the library without disturbing people.

I signed myself up to rehearse one evening a week for an Advent carol concert. I hadn't sung with the choir since early in my pregnancy, and most people in it didn't even know I'd had a baby. I arrived at the first rehearsal late enough not to have to exchange news, just launching straight into work. Only then did I realise my mistake: all the songs were of mothers and babies. Of course, that's what Advent was about. I just hadn't thought what torture the texts could be – tender lullabies, with the gentle mother cradling her babe to sleep, her little tiny child. I couldn't sing; I sat looking down into my lap and concentrated on not letting the tears burst out.

I should have realised. Singing had been such an important part of my mothering, particularly in those days with my face pressed to the porthole of Immie's incubator. I had always been able to perform the boisterous children's rhymes, but the lullabies had stopped very early on, once Immie started screaming. 'Summertime', for example. During the months leading up to her birth, Gershwin's hopeful melody had been a bit of a party piece for Jay and me (he on the keyboard, me singing). We had smiled together at '*your daddy's rich, and your mama's good-looking*'. Then, once Immie was home, when we were busy playing Mozart in an attempt to mend her scrambled brain, we had tried it again but kept on getting in a tizz. Jay was always the first to crumble; I would see his shoulders start to surge, and that was it

— we would blub together, hugging and reassuring one another that our trauma had passed. But, alas, it hadn't.

Once the first brain-damage news arrived, we stopped trying to make music together. And since Mr Randle's black scans I had even given up singing to Elinor. I just couldn't do it — that fundamental part of me had dried up.

A fellow singer in the choir prised it out of me, about Immie's being in care. Her response surprised me: 'A close friend of mine put her son into care thirty years ago — you should ring her.' The friend was away when I first called, in Calcutta, helping set up programmes for disabled children there, but she phoned as soon as she got my message. Although her experience had been long ago, it was vividly remembered: the years of trying to nurse her son, pretending she could cope as her marriage fell apart and her other children went astray. Then the messy business of finding a foster family. However, eventually that had happened and things settled down. Her severely disabled son now lived 100 miles away; she paid money towards his upkeep and visited a couple of times a year. The foster family were wonderful, loving people who adored him; they embraced his manifest needs in a way she knew she never could have done. Meanwhile, she was free to pursue her talents, helping hundreds of other people's disabled children in situations far, far worse than her own.

Ellie and Jay accompanied me to the counselling session I had booked whilst Immie was in hospital. The room was snuggled under the arches of a converted church. I sat in the chair next to the Kleenex and had a good cry. Jay did most of the talking. The counsellor brought out a box of toys and Elinor chose a couple of dolls, nearly life-size with pretty faces and floppy fabric bodies. She took ages dressing them and wrapping them in blankets.

When it was time to go, we looked around for our toddler and saw that she had crawled behind my seat with her dolls and was wrapping them in the thick drape of the curtain. She looked up at me.

'Can we leave the sisters here?'

'We need to put them back in the box for the other children.'

'It's no problem,' said the counsellor, 'you can leave them there.'

At home, Ellie's sister's presence was not entirely annulled. I had bought a big black box file in which to put all Immie's papers and stored it on the floor in the corner of the living room. Seated at my desk, I could see it jutting out from behind the nursing chair. Her life was now contained in that box. Behind it sat my work files; piled into a couple of cardboard boxes, they had been stashed there on our arrival at the cottage.

In the boxes were programmes and photos and reviews from theatre productions I had directed ten, fifteen years ago. There were journals and a couple of photo albums of my work in India over more than a decade. This was core material for the book I had taken up and so quickly abandoned in the autumn.

I opened an album and showed Ellie pictures of actors in colourful skirts and jewelled headdresses. There was me in a sari, backstage at a village show. 'Is that really you, Mummy?' she gasped. And I felt quite inspired – I wanted her to learn about such things and understand them. Back in September, I had realised how important it was for me to work. Now I could see ways in which my working on the book might positively benefit my child. Already she was inquisitive and imaginative about the world beyond her own, a world of which I had seen quite a bit. I wanted to engage that interest as she got older, not just through reminiscing, but by being actively out there, at work. I could see myself evolving from this stay-at-home baby period into a time when the adventurous person in the photo was also a mother. I was ready to go back to work.

However, Social Services were not going to make it easy. They had told me that fostering was usually temporary. If we weren't going to have Imogen back, her social worker came to tell me, then she would be have to be put up for adoption.

Adoption: give her up completely, sign away my parental responsibility, relinquish my ties with her. How could I possibly do it?

The only alternative, the social worker explained, was for Immie to return home. But that meant returning to the chaos, the mayhem of before. Jay would be sure to reject her again, leaving me to do the caring. For twenty years or more.

Jay and I were summoned to a meeting at Tania's house to talk with a group of social workers. They were tough, telling us that we needed to decide about adoption within a month. The sooner it was done, the better Imogen's chances of attaching well to her new parents. I pointed out that it was ridiculous to apply attachment theory to someone without a cerebral cortex. The social workers said they were carrying out the requirements of the fostering and adoption panel who always considered the baby's best interests. In my mind's eye, the absent, all-powerful panel became a row of nutrition professors in pinstriped suits.

I asked who exactly was this adoptive family? Kindly folk who saw a pretty cupid and desired her? Soon enough she would be unwieldy and dribbling, undergoing serious operations and suffering nasty medical conditions. What would they feel then? They might think they could cope and, when they found they couldn't, where would Immie be? Worse off than before. The social workers told us that they would be searching nationwide for a suitable adoptive family; the selection process was rigorous; everything would be done to support them. Yes, it might well mean Imogen's being taken far, far away from us. But I had to think of her, rather than myself. All children need stability.

I held my baby tight against me and let my tears fall.

'Can't you see?' I said. 'She has been in the world less time than she was inside me. I can't let her go.'

My fight with the system was on again. By the time we got home, I was resolved that we should go back to Plan A and pursue residential care. If stability was Social Services' priority, then a residential home would provide it. First of all, we needed to find the right place.

The special needs children's home in our local town was a large Georgian house set behind tall trees on the main road. The drive took us round the side of the building to a set of one-storey pre-fabs at the back. A teacher welcomed us and led us through carpeted bedrooms with their mighty gadgetry. Posters Blu-Tacked to the walls and cuddly toys lined up along the beds gave each room some sort of individuality, but it still felt more utilitarian than homely. It was far less luxurious than it had appeared in the brochure.

The tour took us across the yard to see the children. Our guide stopped at the door to ask whether we had seen children like this before. Clearly she feared we would be shocked. I said, 'Yes, in hospital. Imogen will be one soon!' and the door swung open. No desks, just a couple of tables; it was more like a shabby gym than a conventional classroom. A couple of children lay on their backs on mats, their carers gently stroking them and chatting cheerfully to one another. One boy of perhaps ten or eleven was strapped upright on a huge vertical step machine, with his head in some sort of vice. In the corner, a girl lay in a pool of coloured plastic balls, her lips stretched back over jagged, leering teeth. These children were much less pretty than my five-month-old, but I was neither repulsed nor afraid. I felt a great tenderness towards them.

In the headmaster's office we were given cups of tea and ginger biscuits. I wanted practical information: how much did the residential home cost? Well, they had recently been forced to increase the fees by 50 per cent, so it now cost £135,000 a year. Yes, it was a lot of money! The head explained that some families financed the placements through clinical negligence awards, but the majority had to get their local authority to pay; winning that battle often took years. In Imogen's case, in fact, we would not be eligible for a place for some time, as they did not take babies.

I said, 'We feel as though we don't know her.'

The head gave a snort of recognition.

'Parents often complain about that – they tell me their children don't recognise them.'

'When?'

'Whenever they give up and ask to send them here – when the child is five, or eight, or even later. Whenever they realise they aren't babies any more.'

'What are the parents like?' Jay asked.

'I have to be honest with you – all the parents I see are broken, really broken.'

I asked whether the school was open all the year round. No, it was closed over Christmas, when families were encouraged to have their children home. 'We introduced the holiday because we found that people were just not keeping in touch. It can take such a long time, it's such a big thing simply getting in here, that, once they have a place, parents just don't want to know. We call it "Dump and Run".'

Great, I thought, six years in the courts fighting for the money, and at the end of it what will be the result? We abandon her.

If we were going to put her into a home, we had to do it now, not once we hated her so much we never wanted to see her again. Jay agreed that he wanted to stay in contact with Immie, that her loved her, but he needed reassurance that she was safely in the care of professionals. We had to find a place that would take her whilst she was still a baby. I got out my list of charities and started phoning around. One head injury organisation, Cerebra, had an eager young volunteer at the end of the line who said he would research it for me. He soon rang back with the name of a baby hospice in Liverpool, the only place nation-wide that would take children under four full time. They were totally independent of the public service assessment process. Good.

Jay and I made the long drive to 'Zoe's Place' together, with me thinking, how am I going to stand her being three hours away? The hospice was small and peaceful, housed on an airy upper floor with rows of little cots and warm-hearted carers who reminded me of Mary, our health visitor. The first thing they said was, 'How can we help?' and I couldn't think what to say. I was already accustomed to the social workers' reticence, not this openness.

'Well, we were thinking of asking you to look after our daughter.'

'Of course. How long for?'

'Four years?'

'Fine!'

That got the tears going. I saw how entrenched I had become, how cynical and angry. In my fight with the gatekeepers, their rules and strictures, I had lost touch with the root cause of it all – my own vulnerability. In offering such generous support, these people were accepting my weakness. They were embracing me and my child.

And even as the tears fell, my neediness shifted. Maybe I don't need their help after all, I thought. Not this kind of help, anyway. I don't want Immie in an institution for years and years; I want to be her mother.

But I still wasn't certain I wanted her back.

Once Imogen was officially judged to have settled in with Tania, she was allowed to come and stay with us. Jay was keen to avoid such a backwards step; he said things had just started to settle down, and Imogen's return would be bound to throw us out of kilter. So I rang Nadine and asked whether I could bring the girls with me to Wales. She responded with her usual gruff good humour: 'Of course, come! Stay as long as you want!' I felt quite light-hearted as I drove into the Welsh hills with the sun behind me, my two babies safe together in the back of the car. So what if Immie screamed most of the way – I had begun to miss it. Ellie sat thoughtfully next to her and said, 'Immie's got a bad head, hasn't she, Mummy?'

Nadine walked down the hillside to meet us, flinging back the car doors and scooping up my brood. Lips smacked loudly on chubby cheeks, punctuating her words of love, '*Eres mi niña . . . preciosa . . . cariño mio . . . la más dulce . . . ángel de mi vida.*'

Our granny once more, Nadine held the baby and rocked her and fed her all weekend, as if perhaps she had been neglected in her absence. She strapped her into the papoose and led us up the mountain, with Ellie clinging to my back. There, bounding across the peat, I felt stronger than I had for a long time. In the evening, we filled a bath for the girls and whilst the running taps kept Immie from crying, Nadine swung her naked body back and forth in the water. Elinor laughed at the playfulness, sloshing her limbs. And I blinked back my tears because I had never managed this, just for Ellie to share a bath with her sister. At night I slept soundly under mounds of duvet, flanked by my daughters.

Nadine offered to accompany me home; she was right, if she held Immie in her arms then she would not scream. We sped southwards in the rain, three generations of females shouting 'Old MacDonald had a farm, *ee-i-ee-i-oh*!'

It was the first time I had sung in weeks.

Back at Tania's place, Nadine the professional carer strode about the living room, inspecting every nook and cranny, as if it were not quite up to the standards she would expect. I wondered whether I had not been critical enough of these fostering arrangements.

From this time on, I arranged to have Immie to stay one night a week. Jay just had to put up with it. 'Can't live with her, can't live without her. Like a bad love affair,' I told him. We would go together to fetch her on a Thursday morning and drive straight to the counselling session: Ellie seated on the floor with her toys, me in the corner with the paper hankies, and Jay on the other chair holding Immie and a bottle. I couldn't hold her because I felt it would confuse me, pulling my feelings inexorably into my flesh-and-blood dependency on her. I wanted to try to work out all my other feelings, as well as listen to Jay's. The counsellor was a trained child psychologist, and I trusted her perceptions about Elinor. Often she would halt us mid-discussion and try to interpret her play, or ask for her response. It was good for us all to share thoughts about Immie like this. I wanted to try to make decisions together.

The rest of the day was spent much as before – mostly seated in my nursing chair, feeding the baby. Tania had agreed to continue with the bottles; she understood my arguments against the gastrostomy, encouraging Immie's one obvious ability. But when a feed had continued all afternoon and into the evening, I marvelled that she could be so patient. The nutritionists were still waiting in the wings with their assisted feeding, for the inevitable future when she lost her ability to suck.

After a night with the syringes and the endless crying, and Ellie demanding, 'But *why* is she going to Tania's house?' my nerves were frazzled all over again. And then, once Imogen was safely deposited back in Abingdon, I came home to more trouble: the older sister digging in her heels and telling me, 'You don't look after her, Mummy, but I will.' One time I accidentally left Immie's seat in the back of the car when I dropped her off and spent the whole week being tortured by my own thoughts and Elinor's voicing of them. 'That's my sister's chair. She's our baby. Why does she keep going away?'

Ellie's third birthday was coming up and, a few days after that, Christmas. I needed to get on with happy family things. On the way home from nursery, we drove to the garden centre and chose the fattest spruce they had. Once it was squeezed through the door of the living room, Jay and I spent the evening shaving down the trunk so the Christmas fairy would just have room to fly at the top. When at last the tree was wedged in place, we swathed it with lights – Immie's fancy set, unwound from the playpen.

Next morning I got down the Christmas boxes. So many pretty, delicate pendants hidden away there; Ellie was now at the age to be trusted with them. She picked out one of the purple and green baubles Jay and I had bought just before her birth (and had hung that winter even as my contractions began). Dangling it from her fingertips, she stood in front of the window, watching the sequins flash. In one section of the box I rediscovered paper decorations that she and I had painted together last year. And here was the dodecahedron I made when I was twelve or so, intricately decorated in spirals of brown and gold. This year's tree would be more vibrant, more exotic than ever.

We arranged for Immie to come over on Christmas Eve and stay until Boxing Day. We would celebrate with the whole family in traditional fashion, with my two little girls, just as I had imagined when I was pregnant this time last year.

I decided to get in touch with our neighbour's friend who had won her clinical negligence case. I wanted to see what life might be like if we did manage to get compensation from the Health Trust. I also wanted to make contact with another CP mum, and for Jay to see her life. Rachel lived in an end-of-terrace house in West London. From the outside, on the dark evening we visited, you could see a solid garage door to the right-hand side of the property. Inside, it concealed a state-of-the-art, open-plan bedroom and therapy area for Rachel's eight-year-old daughter. This building conversion had been made last year when, after the statutory six years' legal battle, the NHS had coughed up. The money was now in trust for the child to receive the best care available for the rest of her life.

'Would you like a cuddle?' said Rachel, and a big wobbly girl was placed in my lap. I stroked her curly hair. The carer showed me the gastrostomy tube and the liquid food pumped into her: all very discreet. There was a standing machine in the corner, the special bed that enabled her to be turned at night. I thought how beautifully made it all was – expensive, for sure.

Jay and I sat with Rachel and her husband at the kitchen table, drinking red wine. We talked at length about the legal process, how hard they had found the court discussions, the invasion of their family's privacy. The case against the Health Trust should have been simple: there were printed records of the birth, formal admissions by doctors and midwives of their negligence. Rachel's husband was a solicitor; he had applied all his legal acumen to the case, as well as employing others. He said the money from the Legal Services Commission had not been enough and he had been forced to supplement it, especially towards the end. But sheer determination had paid off – look at the results. Their daughter had twenty-four-hour care and all the best therapies available.

The conversation divided, Jay talking to the father and me to Rachel. She described writing letters to MPs to try to keep her daughter's school open, the difficulty of finding carers even though they had the money. She mentioned a family she knew who had recently put their son up for adoption – how shocking it had been, and how he and the parents had suddenly disappeared from the community. I could see how important mothers with similar experiences must be to one another. I could see myself becoming Rachel.

In the car Jay and I came to blows. He was horrified at my enthusiasm for Rachel's life, appalled that I should want it. He had heard only negative things, seen only the huge stress the family was under. His conversation with the father had convinced him that we would never have any sort of relationship with Immie. We argued all the way home, one and a half hours' drive. Getting on for midnight, as we drove up into the Cotswolds, I remember the discussion turning suddenly to Immie's death. Though it hadn't been mentioned since she went to Tania's, Jay had been thinking about it a lot. He had come up with something from the play *A Day in the Death of Joe Egg*, where a father leaves his brain-damaged daughter out in the freezing night air so she will catch a chill and die. That's what he planned to do if I insisted on having Immie home.

I exploded.

'You're a murderer. You're a fucking murderer.'

I tried to grab his mobile phone from him, saying I was going to phone his parents and tell them of his crime. As far as I was concerned, the specificity of the plan made it well-nigh acted upon already. We grappled with that phone – thank God there was no one else on the dark and icy road. Jay managed to pull into a petrol station, still holding onto the mobile. He leapt out of the car whilst I strode over to a man who was innocently getting back into his.

'I have to borrow your phone,' I shouted into his face. 'It's an emergency. It's about my baby.' The guy rummaged about in his pockets and I rampaged away, tapping out Jay's parents' number.

It was engaged – he must be talking to them already, somewhere in the darkness beyond the station. No doubt he was telling them how bonkers I was. I chucked my borrowed phone back at its startled owner and charged across the yard, locating Jay and grabbing his from him. To his mother, I shouted: 'Your son's a murderer!' Over and over again, careless of her attempts to calm me.

God knows what the petrol station attendant thought, let alone his fleeing late-night customer. I calmed down enough at last to get back in the car and go home with Jay. But I wasn't going to let it pass.

Despite the cold nights, the birds had not yet started to strip the trees of fruit, and our holly was heavy with berries, plumper and brighter than they had been in the past couple of years. With gardening wire, I joined sections of holly together in a circle and twisted them with fronds of ivy, hanging my festive crown on the front door to welcome visitors.

Jay went over to the furniture-maker's workshop, and came back with a bag of sawdust to make a lucky dip for Ellie's birthday party. I had invited thirteen children – rather more than usual; most of them were from the nursery, they and their parents blissfully ignorant of our misfortunes. Anne came over to help me prepare a feast, bringing with her Ellie's favourite chocolate crispies in paper punnets. I bought strawberries and prepared a four-tiered strawberry cake with pink butter icing – a special request from Elinor that I might previously have vetoed as ludicrously unseasonal. By the Saturday afternoon there were mounds of sandwiches and sausages and cakes of all shapes and sizes, enough food for twice the number. I remember the party going off without a hitch, my trying to concentrate on the music and the games and the countless three-year-olds rampaging about. Someone brought their six-month-old baby whom they kept on tossing in the air, making it giggle. Despite all my evasion tactics, I could not help being drawn to it. Even without the giggles, I thought, having Immie here would be better than this hole in my life.

Friday, 20 December 2002

My darling Elinor,

This is for you to read when you are older. How old, I don't know. Maybe it will be lost by then. Daddy and I have argued again. We argue in the front of the car and you cry out behind – 'Don't fight, Mummy. Stop it. Stop fighting. You mustn't argue.' I am so sorry, my darling.

This has been the most difficult year of my life. Your little sister Imogen was born in such a terrible way. And somehow her fragile little life has come between us. I love you so much, I don't want you to lose out because of her. And yet, as time goes on, my love for her grows.

When you were born I fell in love with you: your liveliness, your laughter, your bravery. Your little sister has none of these things; her brain damage has closed her to the world, even to me. Yet I need to be with her; I need to look after her. I feel if I deny this part of me I will somehow diminish my ability to look after you. You came from the same place, I delivered you both into the world.

I know that you are strong. 'I will look after her,' you say, and I believe you, my beautiful little three-year-old. How will we manage – you and I? Will Daddy really leave us if we choose to be with Immie? It is the only way I can imagine being a mother. I love you so much, so much.

I wrote this on Ellie's birthday. Since my stay in Wales with Nadine, I had become increasingly convinced that Immie should come home. Jay was still convinced of the opposite. For me, things had become very simple: I needed my baby back, whatever it took, even if it meant leaving Jay. Elinor would have her sister, and I would feel whole again. I imagined my future single-parent self not so much a saint as some strident Amazon: powerful and independent, admired by all. Jay I imagined marginalised, vilified – the coward.

In my green file, I found a charity providing respite in my parents' area, but not in mine. I rang them and established that if we were living in Oxford, then one of their qualified nurses could come and babysit for us, possibly several times a month. There must be other advantages to living in the city – we had learnt to our cost that resources were meagre in the countryside. If I were to move into town, take a ground-floor flat with wheelchair access, things would be a lot easier. I was sure the SCOPE man had been right: friends and family were going to be the ones I depended on.

I have totally forgotten the event that is most central to this plan. It is one that haunts my mother, but I have wiped it clean from my memory.

One day just before Christmas, I turned up unexpectedly on Mum's doorstep, holding Imogen, saying I had decided to leave Jay and would she help me look after the children. She invited me in, sat me down and listened. Then she told me that she couldn't give me the help I needed. I don't think she said much more than this before my father came in. He was adamant that my leaving Jay would be wrong for all of us. I do remember one thing he said, probably on other occasions besides this one:'Don't smash it all up, Jules. Just because one thing is broken, don't destroy everything else in your life.'

Dad was correct: there was an element of vandalism about it –I did want to smash up all the cosy lives around me. Why not? They all still had brains, they could stand up for themselves; it was Immie who couldn't. She was the most vulnerable member of the family and yet they had turned against her. What did that say about them? Immie was something ugly that they had hoped to keep at bay, come to spoil their nice easy lives. They just could not bear the deformed daughter I had brought them.

The counsellor said Christmas would be hard. Christmas and birthdays are the hardest for mothers who have children in care. As planned, I picked Immie up on Christmas Eve and took her along for two days of family celebrations. At Midnight Mass, for the first time in my life I could not bring myself to sing a single carol. '*Where a mother laid her baby*' got me sobbing, and I did not stop. I just stood there, letting the grief rise and fall through me in its familiar waves. What I did not know then was that I would not sing again for a year and a half. Not a lullaby, not a carol, nothing.

On Christmas Day in London, Ellie was charming and joyful, just as I had hoped. The family tried to behave as normally as they could towards Immie, offering to take her from me so I could eat. At one point I remember her puking up a mighty cascade of milk and mucus, all over my cousin's sofa. As cloths and towels were sought, I declared, 'When your brain is as fucked as hers, this is what happens to your Christmas dinner!'

There were generous presents for both girls, though people had obviously had trouble finding something appropriate for the disabled one. She received an array of cute hats (Baby Gap was doing a great line in Peruvian ones with earflaps), all of them far too big; her head had stopped growing when she was a few weeks old, hadn't anyone told them? On the way home, I dropped the hats in a bag on the pavement outside the SCOPE shop.

Two days later I flew to Mumbai to research my book. It was the right thing to do – an experiment in not being with Immie, a trial time apart. I hadn't travelled to India since before I'd had Ellie; I would be entering a world I had only ever inhabited as a childless person. I agreed with Jay that I would keep my mind open for the two and a half weeks that I was away, and we would talk again on my return. It was horrid being away from the children, though I soon realised it was Elinor more than Imogen that I missed. For the first few days, Jay would phone and report how she was pining, off her food, not sleeping. The news really distressed me, so I told him to stop phoning. I had to cut myself off.

Much of the time I spent alone, travelling across arid terrain in buses and jeeps. In the cool of the night I sat for long hours in the street with my camera, filming the theatre. I was swept up in this world so different from my own – its crowds, its smells, its laughter; glad to be an insignificant dot in the huge mess of humanity.

By day, I wandered about the villages, taking photos to show Ellie when I got home – of children everywhere, perched on the back of bicycles, piled into a bullock cart or running barefoot through the dust. I wanted her to see their spotlessly pressed school uniforms, their school with its papier-mâché walls and rush matting to sit on.

There were babies all over the place, of course – bonny, beloved babies wearing eye make-up, and jangling anklets and all manner of decorations in celebration of their loveliness. On one occasion a woman dumped hers in my lap in order to take a photo of the two of us. I felt it mould to my body, fascinated by all the muscles holding its spine in place against my tummy – a soft strength Immie would never have. When an infant cried somewhere across the street, I longed to comfort it.

Every morning I woke with tears oozing between my eyelids. Crying in my sleep like this began to seem as normal as breathing. Once awake, I would lie there wishing I had died in the night; facing the fact that, despite what it had done, my body was determined to go on living.

I took to doing sit-ups on my bedroom floor, working my tummy muscles back to where they were before I'd had children. 'My body is a temple,' I chanted as I performed the exercises. A temple with an identity all its own, not from the lives that entered it. I recalled my dream about the balloon breasts and thought that perhaps at last I had let go of every baby-adoring part: my womb, my breasts, my face, my arms. My body was now mine again.

And Jay's, if I chose. From this distance, I easily recalled the early days of our love. I could not imagine ever finding such a thing again. I knew he was not the coward I imagined when I planned to leave him. His belief that we could not look after Immie was not cowardice; it was a deeply felt conviction that cohered with the evidence – that nursing our unconscious child for twenty years would surely destroy us, just as it destroyed other families.

And was I really such a tough Amazon? If I were to choose Immie over Jay, my life could only become tougher. It would be what Tussie Myerson and Gerald from SCOPE and even Rachel with all her funding had described – one long battle. Alone. Ellie would inevitably be caught up in it, without her daddy there to rescue her.

What was to be gained by keeping my baby? The only person I could see benefiting was myself, through feeling whole again. But was that feeling enough? I might think I was an Amazon, but what would everyone else see? An unemployed single mother with a profoundly disabled daughter; from my experience so far there was nothing to show that I would thrive in such a role. More likely, a life like that would make me angry, frustrated and lonely. To choose it was madness – a cruel, self-destructive madness.

I saw that Jay had confronted my madness with his own – his obsession with killing Immie. The consequence of infanticide was prison, but he had not cared. All he cared about was that he should become some sort of hero, sacrificing the daughter he loved in order to save us all from further suffering. The role suited him no better than that of Amazon warrior suited me.

One night I dream of Granny. She is wearing a bedjacket and pale lipstick, much as she did in her last weeks of life. But it is me rather than her lying in the bed – me as I am now, but also a child me, maybe eleven years old. Granny is sitting above me on the pillow, her long white hair floating loose over my face as she looks down. Her features are tender, almost smiling. As I gaze up at her, she places her hand on my forehead and begins stroking back my hair with firm, slow gestures. On and on she strokes, as if she is soothing away the ache in my brain.

When I awake, I am certain what the dream means: that Granny has forgiven me. Forgiven me for the terrible destruction that happened inside me, and for the suffering it wrought on my family. But most of all, through me she is forgiving her own mother for abandoning her.

Tuesday, 14 January 2003

Jay was there at the airport to meet me off the early-morning flight. We hugged for a long time, saying nothing, letting our bodies feed off one another. We kissed; we smiled; we noticed how one another's hair was beginning to go grey. What a mess it had all been. Stepping into his embrace after my enforced solitude, I was sure how much better life was together than apart. Elinor was proof of that – a shining celebration of our unity; her presence had always strengthened us. Imogen should have done the same, but instead she had broken our bond. We would never come together over her.

Now time had taken us out of 2002; we were getting further and further away from the birth. More than anything, I wanted to move on. The future offered Jay and me the chance to heal our relationship; perhaps not the wound of Immie's loss, but the other things that had been destroyed – love, creativity, idealism. And the child-grief might remain within our healed family, respected because each of us had felt it. We had been to the darkest place any pair of parents can go; we had seen one another at their most raw, most unhinged. That's an amazing kind of intimacy.

The main news Jay brought was that our landlords had given us a month's notice to quit the cottage – they were selling up. I was glad. It was an opportunity to leave all the Immie dramas behind, all the shadows of her birth and life with us that haunted the place. I looked forward to starting again somewhere people knew nothing about her, where we could just be a normal family again. So now we had to decide where: in the country, or back in the town again? A year ago I would have wanted to stay in the Cotswolds, or go even further away from London into the beautiful regions of Wales or the West Country. But my perspective had changed. Staying in the countryside now would be too much a grotesque parody of what we had once intended as our Good Life.

Now my priority was simply to be in a place where Ellie was safe, somewhere we would be within easy reach of a hospital, without need of ambulances. I could imagine the distractions of urban life being good for all of us – the mess and the crowd, the feeling that there were loads of other people around with similar confusions and pain. Let's go back to the busy city, where we met and fell in love not so long ago. And who knows, if things work out, we might have another, healthy baby.

I went to see the Professor of Obstetrics at the John Radcliffe specialist maternity unit. He took blood tests and asked me to research my family back three generations, to find out whether any of my forebears had had similar problems in pregnancy. It didn't take long to establish they had not, and the blood tests revealed nothing to explain why I'd had the abruption. The professor sent a letter stating as much and saying, 'If you were to go ahead with another pregnancy, there would be a 5 per cent likelihood of your suffering another abruption.' One in twenty. The risk seemed pretty low. Then again, with Immie's brain damage I had learnt what it felt like to be a low statistic. Once you have found yourself the exception to the rule, it's all too easy to imagine being it again. But if we were living near a hospital, if I was signed up with the specialist unit, then my next child would have the best chance of a safe arrival.

I had to take the risk. As the successor to my mother's babyloss myself, I knew that one child cannot replace another. Nevertheless, my having another, healthy baby would be a great source of joy for many people, well beyond our nuclear family. The compulsion in me to create a new life was a vital part of my healing process.

My New Year's resolution was to wean myself off the 2002 dependencies – drugs and Immie. I needed to come off the antidepressants because I wanted to get pregnant, but also because I wanted to feel my emotions again. I had had enough of the glass barrier between me and the world, me and my feelings. I reduced my dose by breaking the capsule and discarding half the powder. I checked on the internet and found that (as I suspected) it was the period of coming off the drug where people reported that their minds went haywire. Luckily for me, I took things slowly and suffered none of the horrors described on the websites. Within a month I was back in a drug-free world, which I now knew to be a luxury.

As far as Immie went, I used the counselling sessions to explore this perverse notion of weaning myself off my baby. We still went along to our Thursday sessions as a family: Ellie playing with her dolls, Jay holding Immie and me talking. I went back over the birth, the anxiety and the mourning. On we talked, about mothers thinking they were indispensable, mothers needing their babies, mothers feeling guilty. And gradually I accepted what I had told Mr Randle when I left her in hospital: that I was not the right parent for Imogen.

But her foster carer was. Tania's was a true vocation. She had found it more than a decade before, as a teenager visiting respite centres with her social worker mother. After working in nursing homes and residential schools, she dared to try what she really wanted to do – fostering profoundly disabled children. In the schools she had met other single foster carers and had become increasingly confident in her own ability to do such a job. She researched the local authorities, and chose Oxfordshire because it was known to support foster carers better than other regions; also because her very practical mum was there to lend a hand.

I could understand that caring for a severely brain-damaged child was something she chose to do, knowing how important her work was. I could even imagine doing this job myself in another life, were the disabled child not my own. I once confided that I had been oppressed by my loss, and Tania responded: 'Yes, for you Immie is what she might have been; for me she's just Immie.'

Tania received a bundle of tax-free allowances for every child in her care, plus all the benefits for which they were eligible – a typically messy bit of British bureaucracy. It was not big money, but enough to live on. She was planning to buy a three-bedroom, ground-floor flat. Her care package for Immie was more generous than we could ever have hoped for as the birth family. So now we had to persuade the social workers that it was in Immie's best interests to stay with Tania.

'But foster care is unstable,' came the anticipated response.

'Not in this house, it isn't,' said Tania.

I went to see the family lawyer who a month previously had given me the facts about leaving my baby in hospital, and spent an expensive hour discovering all about the Children Act and the way the fostering and adoption panel was likely to behave. She reassured me again that my parental responsibility gave me the right to ask for what I wanted, and advised me not to be bamboozled by the bureaucrats. Then I wrote a statement declaring why I could not look after Immie, and why I didn't want her adopted:

> In the future, I would like to have as much input as possible in her life, providing her with whatever financial and emotional support is feasible. I feel very strongly that her sister Elinor should be given the opportunity to form a relationship with Imogen. Elinor is at present too young to understand the problems Imogen is going to have, but I think it would be a destructive act to deny her her sister.

Imogen's social worker filled out her enormous form, detailing all sorts of aspects of our lives and emphasising the success of Imogen's placement with Tania. The panel could mull that over for a while.

We decided to move to Oxford. I didn't have the energy to start over again in a totally fresh place. The city's familiarity was comforting; my parents lived there, with Immie and Tania only a few minutes down the road. I had never lived in Oxford as an adult and looked forward to uncovering new aspects of the community. Aware of so many writers living and working there, I would be in good company whilst working on the Indian theatre book. I would cycle to the comfort of the university library and pore over obscure texts, immersing myself in distant times and places. The solitariness suited me; I didn't want to do small talk, or chat about the family. Quietly, diligently, I planned to create something new to send out into the world. My mother had been right: being creative was one kind of compensation for what had happened.

Mark the vicar came round with a farewell gift from everyone in the parish – a beautiful painting of the church tower, framed in gold.

In February, we moved our array of country clobber into a little Victorian terraced house in the centre of town. Anne said she would take the freezer and other big things we left behind. Our new garden was an urban postage stamp. Good – gardening had been such an important part of my nurturing self, especially through my pregnancy with Imogen. Now I needed to forget it, be clean and cerebral and out of touch with the seasons. The big diesel lawnmower and plenty of tools would have to go to the dump. But the double swing we had erected at Immie's birth was still in good nick. London cousins moving to a bigger place said they would take it, but I was not prepared for Ellie's reaction. On the day the removal men came to pick it up, she was out in the garden. 'Why are they taking our swing? Why, Mummy? You can't let them take it – it's Immie's and mine.' Throughout the laborious dismantling and loading up, she cried. Even after it had disappeared down the lane, she would not be consoled.

In every room of our new home, boxes were piled from floor to ceiling. As we unpacked, Elinor kept on saying we had left her favourite dolls behind. 'Let me unpack everything first', I said, then we'll be able to see.' It took a good few weeks to complete the job, but she was still complaining.

'My Lissy dolls, where are my Lissy dolls?' I had never heard the name. She didn't have many dolls anyhow.

'What do they look like?'

'They're pretty. Little, with dresses . . .'

'What colour hair?'

'Blonde.'

'How many were there?'

'Lots. They have a house with a swing you can play on.'

It took her a good year to stop asking for them. Meanwhile, I went on the internet and discovered that Lissy dolls do in fact exist – rigid plastic dolls with heart-shaped faces and big, dark, empty eyes. Just like Immie.

Once we were settled in our new home, we kept having Immie over each Thursday, but stopped having her to stay for the night; it was less upsetting that way. Often when I was alone with her for the day, I felt angry – angry that she had brought such grief to the family, that she would never return my love, that she had survived when she should have died.

'Why can't you just say you don't want to see her?' said Jay.

I couldn't really explain. Maybe it was because of my great-grandmother that I needed to prove I did 'give a damn'. Maybe it was the visceral part of me that needed to be close to my baby whatever the emotions she generated, feeling complete even as I felt angry.

I reasoned that I was giving Tania regular respite. Though I never saw any evidence, her nerves must be racked once in a while, surely. A day off from screaming was important; it might even ensure that she kept going in the long run.

We continued taking Immie and Ellie to the weekly counselling sessions. Jay and I took the opportunity to talk over what had happened, to try to understand one another's perspective. We needed to link the destructive elements of our recent past to a creative future together. The counsellor helped us build our confidence again, as loving people who could enjoy and support one another. She was careful to insist that each of us was not a bad parent; that grief had perverted love. I began to accept that Jay's standing firm about not being able to care for Immie had enabled me to travel my more rocky journey to the same conclusion.

After the counselling, we spent the day together. If I became impatient with Immie's screaming and retching, Jay was there, bundling her tight and taking her away. Now that things were settled with Tania, he dared to be close to Immie again, nursing her for all the hours she needed. He had kept to his conviction that he would love her once more as long as she was with a professional carer – now that she no longer threatened to destroy our family.

Often Jay took Immie to the piano, clutching her to his stomach with one hand whilst the other traced its way across the keyboard. With the pedal down, one note might resonate around the room for half a minute before the next came to land upon it. His slow serenade was made of surprising and intriguing patterns, stretching from the deepest to the highest and back again. And in response, Immie would cease her yelling and raise her heavy head as if she were concentrating on the sound, eyes wide and mouth opening in an expression that you might call awe. Her hearing must still be intact, buried deep in the core of her brain. Somehow these sounds had meaning for her, they gave her some sort of pleasure. Now I understood why Mr Randle had been so interested in the importance of music in our family.

Jay's making a fuss of Imogen like this meant a lot to me. It revealed his warmth, his sensitivity towards our baby. This was the gentle, generous man I had fallen in love with, and with whom I had chosen to have a family. His being tender with little Im made me more tender towards him. And myself.

Immie's birth had brought love enough to our family for two children; her weekly return allowed that love to find its natural balance. The rest of the time, I feared Jay and I might stifle Ellie with the excess. I could imagine myself becoming a pushy mum, wanting Elinor to achieve maximum potential because her sister couldn't, or a fussy mum, excessively anxious about her. Once, when I caught her clambering on a kitchen chair, I wrenched her down with 'I don't want another brain-damaged daughter.' And immediately I regretted it – I wanted Elinor to be free of my loss.

During Immie's visits, she would kiss and cuddle her and say she loved her.

'When will she come back?' she would ask.

'She's not coming back,' I replied, gently. 'We can't look after her, even though we love her.'

'Immie *is* part of our family.'

'I know, but she's too poorly. She's not going to get better, Ells.'

'Other people get better.'

'Yes, but not Immie.'

'Then we must get another baby . . .'

'Yes, darling. But it's not so simple.'

'. . . Two babies, one for me and one for you, Mummy.'

Getting pregnant can be quite a slog for a woman fast approaching forty; I knew that. The ovulation tests, the carefully planned lovemaking, the forbidden foods and the all-important folic acid. If one doesn't watch out, there's little fun to be had in middle-aged procreation.

And then there are the false alarms (particularly if, like me, you have been pregnant several times before). Perhaps this morning's tiredness is a sign, or maybe this sudden surge of energy . . . My constant empty feeling, my bloated feeling; the lack of appetite, then the appetite. I'm sure I can feel twinges in my boobs, the milk glands starting up. My sense of smell is weird today; melting cheese smells like baked apple, and mushrooms reek of ammonia. Or maybe the empty window in the pregnancy test is correct and my period is just delayed by a day again.

I tried to balance all the serious planning with a shrug of carelessness. To concentrate on work and family and the fulfilment they gave me.

In March, when I flew out to India to continue my book research, Jay and Elinor joined me for a couple of weeks. We booked into a series of glamorous hotels, and spent a lot of time lounging by swimming pools and in shady gardens. Jay and I recalled a similar holiday a year before Ellie's birth. My conservative Indian friends had kept on referring to him as my husband, and to the trip as our honeymoon. This time, with our pretty three-year-old riding on her daddy's shoulders, they were shocked that we were still unmarried. Even we ourselves started wondering why. In a fortress town on the edge of the desert we commissioned a jeweller to make two gold rings for us. And in the back of a noisily speeding jeep, with sand billowing up around us, Jay shouted, 'Will you marry me?' and I shouted back the same. As we kissed, I saw Ellie's face beaming with satisfaction.

How I wonder what you are

IMOGEN'S FIRST BIRTHDAY. I was pregnant again – only a few weeks, but already frightened of another abruption. I awoke sweating at three-thirty and escaped back into fretful sleep until six, when Ellie clambered into bed. Now I could dare to wake properly, because those terrible, destructive hours had passed. Jay had stomach cramps, insisting it must have been something he ate last night. I couldn't tease him out of it – his writhing was too grotesquely close to the way I must have been a year and a couple of hours ago. He staggered downstairs and ran himself a hot bath. I plonked Ellie in front of the TV and curled up in bed alone; I needed a cuddle. At last Jay came and joined me, folding his body tight behind mine, our legs entwined. We lay there for a long time, hardly breathing, paralysed in our sadness.

I had promised Elinor we would make a chocolate cake for Immie's birthday; she was looking forward to seeing her. She always loved going to Tania's house. So we set to work: the best cooking chocolate thrashed to rubble; cream carefully heated. My little girl placed the bowl on a stool, both hands bravely restraining the electric mixer as it pitched about. Luscious icing, not yet set, slid down the sides of the cake as I handed the plate to her, strapped into her car seat. Then we veered down the motorway, the big sister asking, hopefully, 'Mummy, if I get brain damage, can I go and live with Tania as well?'

The cake was our birthday present to Immie – we planned to mash it with some milk for her. Tania had said chocolate was Immie's absolute favourite; on a recent trip with the Brownies to Cadbury World, she had developed a serious penchant for it. I was grateful to have some idea of what to give her on her birthday, but suspected Tania had made up Immie's love of chocolate. How could someone without cognisance have a penchant for anything? Then I realised that I myself was not free from such delusions. Immie's birthday celebration imposed a convention on a child who could never possibly comprehend it. It was doubly absurd considering Immie's birthday had been such a traumatic, destructive event for us.

Tania made things easier by informing me that chocolate is thought to stimulate the chewing reflex in brain-damaged children. This clinical language, free of emotion, was easier to take. I could understand Imogen's body needing the chocolate to help her with a basic survival mechanism. That must be a good enough reason for giving it to her.

As usual, Tania brought Immie to the door and led us up the corridor, chatting away about their week. She described taking Immie for hydrotherapy at the local baby pool – how much fun they'd had. My response was perhaps too reserved, but she could handle it. Hell, she had fostered children whose mothers never came to see them, let alone on their birthdays.

Tania's mother was there on the sofa with presents for Ellie. Imogen lay in my lap, giving me that calmness again; I imagined this feeling would never go away. Her hair was growing fast and Tania had pulled it into fluffy bunches on either side of her head (they masked the microcephaly). Her hands were open at her sides, no longer clenched and digging into themselves. Sensitive, generous hands, just like her dad's. I took the left one and kissed the mottled bruise from the piercing of so many needles a year ago. A whole year from that terrible day: I was grateful for the simple passage of time that makes things bearable. And there were other things to celebrate. I looked at her lying there, peacefully staring towards the window. It was only over the past couple of weeks that she had been able to do that. Her crying had died right down. Maybe it was due to the new anticonvulsants, or simply some settling in her head. I calculated that Tania had put up with as many months of screaming as I had. Now we could both toast their ending.

But just as that notion occurred to me, my charge started fretting, arching her back and snorting. 'Imogen,' warned Tania, taking her off me, 'don't you get up to your tricks again. Stiff legs – oi! You behave!' and she bent the legs at the knee, pushing the little torso forward so the muscles relaxed. She was using the vocabulary you'd use for someone with consciousness, someone who can control her behaviour. It's hard not to. In speaking to Immie, Tania has to use everyday language, brimful as it is with ideas and feelings. The only way to avoid them would be to shut up entirely.

I watched Imogen, as objectively as I could. I didn't want to fall into the trap and start pretending she understood. But now that she had stopped screaming, she did have the opportunity to hear things outside her bubble of anguish. I could see that her eyes were open, moving about as she caught the bright inflections of Tania's voice. Yes, she was definitely listening.

Did she ever listen to my voice? I wondered. Did she remember my intonation from all those months of nursing her? I could not recall when last I had talked to her, but it must have been well before the black scan. I had been silent in her company for many months. Now I was thinking that my voice should be the one she was most familiar with – she had heard it from inside my womb even before her birth, before her cortex got zapped. Perhaps the residue of those memories was still stored somewhere in the frayed bits. So I followed Tania's example, emulating her tone. 'Happy Birthday, little Im. My Sleeping Beauty. We made you some chocolate cake.' It felt strange, but good, like talking to animals. Mary the health visitor would be shocked all over again at my comparing Imogen with an animal, but it's the closest equation I can find. There are those who scoff at people talking to dumb animals, but I am not one. I am certain of the reassuring effect it has, both on them and on me. And often, though an animal cannot speak, it does understand.

Ellie found a talking pad belonging to Tania's older foster child, a shiny yellow dome that spoke when hit. She wanted to know whether Immie could have one, and Tania assured her she already played with this. I flicked the record-switch at the back and Ellie held the pad up close.

'*Twinkle, twinkle little star, How I wonder what you are.*' Now every time Immie biffed her yellow dome, that would be her statement.

Off went Elinor on one of her tours, inspecting her sister's home. She was fascinated by the Palm Sunday crucifix on the wall, and wanted to know about the church it came from. A committed Anglican, Tania takes Immie there every Sunday. She says much of her strength comes from her 'dialogue with God'. When she puts her sick foster children to bed at night, she believes she is leaving them 'on God's doorstep'. And if they were to die, she says, she doesn't believe that's the end.

Christianity is the religion I was brought up in, where I was baptised and where I baptised my children. During the darkest times with Immie, my own dialogue with God helped – the railing especially. Mark the vicar and the rest of the church community supported me enormously, with their great compassion. Now Tania and her God have taken on my unbearable Immie burden. Through receiving such love, my respect for Christian faith has deepened, my trust in its potential for goodness expanded manifoldly. I am not sure whether my own commitment to God has intensified, but it hasn't weakened either.

'*God so loved the world that he gave his only son . . .*' Funny that. Christianity is based on the abandoning of a child. I look at Tania's crucifix and think of Christ in agony on the cross, asking why His father has forsaken him. And God does not respond. I suppose Christians must accept that, in the moment of our redemption, God abandoned His child.

Mark the vicar was the first to suggest it might not be my destiny to care for Immie, that it could be someone else's. From his experience in the children's hospital, perhaps he understood my suffering in the face of my child's. Perhaps he knew that giving her up would ultimately be the way to heal me, to heal all of us.

Looking back at those dark days after the major problems prognosis, with Immie's drugs lined up in the living room, I see that I had already reached my limit as her mother. I knew the medicines were not going to make her better; they were simply to 'manage' her. I felt such an aversion to them because they confirmed the impotence of my mother-love, my inability to kiss my baby's head better.

I suppose this begs Ellie's question: what would I do if she became brain-damaged like her sister? It is an agonising thought, but let me try to imagine it. Surely I would hold on in there for twenty years or more, because I had known her in a way I never knew her sister. Or I would do so simply because I could not bear to go through the same thing twice. But I know the MENCAP statistic: eight out of ten parents nursing a child like Immie say they are at breaking point. Knowing this, I have to accept that I might well hand Elinor over, if Tania would take her, of course. Well, at least Ellie thinks it's a good idea.

Tania cut a little slice of birthday cake and mashed it to a gruel with milk from the bottle. She spooned it against Immie's hard palate, and because she was not screaming any more there was an opportunity for her to react. She opened her mouth wide, noisily tasting the sweetness. Her head tipped back a little, her tongue curled upwards, making an effort to swallow. At last the mush was gone, and she opened her mouth again in that 'O' shape that used to threaten a shot of vomit. It could well be the same now – get ready for nasty brown gunge on the carpet. But no, I was wrong. Her mouth was broadening, her head was tilting back, eyes wide. I could see her two brand-new top teeth as her lip stretched back. Yes, this was what we'd given up waiting for, the milestone that cancelled all the others: Immie was smiling.

It was not the smile she might have had, that reflection of a parent's pleasure, soon developing into the ability to charm. No, this smile was for no one but herself. But it still signalled happiness – the single most important emotion we wish for in our children. At last, Immie had discovered happiness.

Of course, Tania took the whole thing for granted. She was already convinced that Immie loved chocolate. Tania has decades of experience with children like her, developing a separate level of communication that never compares them to 'normal' children. Through her eyes, I can appreciate that Immie defies the world of milestones and targets, the framework of modern life, and possesses her own time and space. In accepting her as she is, we acknowledge the value of stillness; we escape the tyranny of goals and achievements in our own lives. Without any sentimentality, Tania really does see this as 'special'.

'Where's the booze?' Tania cracks open a bottle of French Merlot, and we knock it back with the cake. 'Cheers.'

Two days later I miscarried. 'If you would like to see a counsellor . . .' said one of the nurses in the gynae clinic, looking at my records. But I wasn't so distressed; after letting go of a five-month-old baby, a foetus was nothing. Besides, I might not yet be ready to carry another child. I needed more time before taking on the responsibility of someone else's brain inside me. Even the possibility of a baby's safe arrival rather freaked me out – what might I do if it screamed?

I tried to concentrate on happy things, things not to do with babies. Work was a good antidote. I enrolled in evening classes, made a major shopping trip or two to London. Immie had introduced me to the real value of escapism. Jay and I started avoiding the documentaries and the serious movies; instead, we were in perpetual pursuit of a really good comedy. And when we found it, we were the ones laughing loudest and longest.

I was learning to ward off painful feelings, to defend myself against the destructive power of loss. Sometimes I would sense a grief wave approaching and somehow, through sheer concentration, I could push it back before it socked me. As I'd anticipated,

I had to be careful to protect my Immie wound. There were plenty of things to avoid – any kind of child loss, for starters. In the old days, I would have stopped to look at the messages pinned to bouquets left beside the road where a child had been killed; in the newsagents, I would glance beneath a 'Family Tragedy' head-line in the local paper. But now, if I was tempted to enter other people's sorrows like this, the grief would overwhelm me, perhaps not immediately but soon after. Next time I must just keep away.

Of course, some grief-inducers were harder to dodge. My world seemed to be full of perfectly symmetrical families – two little siblings, close in age. Meeting friends of Elinor or going to a family party, I steeled myself; I got through. Sometimes I felt a mixture of fascination and love for those able-bodied children who should have been Immie's playmates. But I couldn't engage with them fully; I knew I had to keep a distance.

Tania thought Imogen needed a wheelchair – that definitive mark of disability that I had imagined when Virginia Nicholas first revealed the brain damage. The NHS bureaucracy (which paid) could not understand why such a young child should require one. But Tania and Immie's physiotherapist argued it would support her back, help correct the skewed development of her limbs. Through their great persistence, it arrived a few weeks after her first birthday.

The frame (£1,000) was an amazing chrome contraption that could tip up and back and round, with the best suspension in the world. A big shopping basket underneath and red springs over the wheels were the most striking aspects of its state-of-the-art design. A specially moulded seat (£3,000) sat inside the outer frame, forward or rear facing. The upholstering was bright green with jungle animals leaping across the fabric. There were straps to keep her legs and torso in the right position; a curved and padded headrest, a removable tray in front. Because she was growing, she would need another seat within a few months; the frame might last just over a year before it needed replacing.

On Immie's visits to us, we would dismantle the wheelchair

and fold it into our modest car boot. I knew that, as time went on, it would become too big to fit; then we would be dependent on Tania driving her back and forth in her van. We also had to find room for two more seats: the conventional child's car seat, and an orthopaedic foam chair to use at home (donated by Social Services; she needs a new one annually). Apart from the plastic feeding bottles, nappies (provided via an NHS 'continence' supervisor for the rest of her life) and a change or two of clothes, there were all sorts of extra paraphernalia. First the leg splints: pieces of hard plastic moulded to a right angle, to be strapped to the lower part of her legs for as long as she can bear (an NHS orthotist fits them; she needs about two pairs a year as she grows). Then the collection of individual glass bottles containing high-voltage feed prescribed by her nutritionists, plus powdered thickener to make the liquid easier for her to suck. Plus essential daytime medication and emergency drugs, with syringes for their administration. And to think I once found it a hassle loading up the baby basics.

At last Immie and her belongings were dumped in our front room. As I became accustomed to her visits, and she stopped screaming all the time, I was less likely to get angry and frustrated. Ellie was less inclined to endless kissing and cuddling. In fact, now that our baby did not need constant nursing, we were in danger of ignoring her altogether.

It's hard to find a way in: ease a toy into her grip and soon enough it drops out; flutter a piece of aluminium foil in front of her eyes but can you be sure she sees it? Chatter away and maybe she's listening, or maybe she's not. Her responses are so subtle, so inconsistent, that you would have be with her more than once a week to be sure they exist.

I knew we should make more effort, do something together with Imogen. But what? The playground, the dinosaur museum, the children's library – none of Elinor's new-found city entertainments were relevant to her sister. Go and see some friends?

One Thursday I knocked on the door of a neighbour with young children, heaved the wheelchair over the doorstep and through the narrow hallway into the front room. It felt very odd, revealing this double life of mine in such an overt fashion. There sat Immie, filling up most of the floor space, seemingly oblivious to Ellie and her friends bustling around her. I did not have the confidence or conviction to speak for her as Tania might have done. And I could see the sadness in my host's eyes as she repeated the old refrain, 'She looks just like you!'

I gradually got back in touch with my friends. Some (especially the childless ones) seemed to understand straight off that I could not care for a profoundly disabled child. Others found it really hard hearing my tale, trying to engage with my inability to mother my lovely babe. One day when Immie was over, I took her to lunch with a school friend (a confident mother of three) who offered to cuddle her whilst I went to the loo. When I returned, she was sitting bolt upright, arms straight out in front with Immie's body arched fearsomely across them. I was quietly pleased – now she had an inkling of what I had been unable to bear.

I feared that some people would be critical. One came straight out and said, 'I could never give up a child of mine!' And I wept – I knew what she meant. I badly wanted to preserve the bit of me that felt the same. So with this friend, as with many others, I kept mention of Imogen to a minimum and never took her to see them. That way, I could pretend I was just a normal mum like them.

I had compartmentalised my life, as Nadine had suggested all those months ago – rather more than she had intended. I suspected that she disapproved of my giving up my baby. I imagined she thought I had failed in the most fundamental aspect of mothering – doing my duty to the person I had brought into the world. But I'd made my decision; I had to live with it. With Nadine now settled in Wales, I took the cowardly option and lost contact with her.

In September 2003, Elinor started morning school in Oxford. Often, I would pick her up at lunchtime and drive her to the Cotswolds to visit Mark the vicar or Anne at the farm, or simply to retrace our old walks across the fields. I wanted to keep in touch with the countryside in this way, planning holidays and weekends where we could spend even longer there. But the thought of returning permanently was too stressful. Even the one local ambulance – absent on the night of Immie's birth – had been taken out of service; the possibility of Elinor needing one and not getting it terrified me. Perhaps when she left home Jay and I would return to country life, but until then these excursions would have to suffice.

Ellie remembered our mushroom hunts and wanted to repeat them. So down to the meadow we strode, lightly through the spinney. Behind the chicken wire hid this year's generation of pheasants, busily pecking out their final days before the shooting season. When one of them spotted us, there was a flurry and a rasping as they hurried out of sight.

Ellie went ahead through the gate – head down, scanning the ground. But I held back, taking in the broad expanse of pasture. This was where I had come all those months ago, to stand against the oak tree and pray for my baby not to be brain-damaged. How vain that prayer had proved. Coming towards me was the mare, skittish and proud, with her yearling at her side, all gangly and fluffy and charcoal grey. But behind them the architecture of the field had changed; the big old oak was lying on its side, blown down in a storm.

I walked out into the open space, towards the prostrate tree. As I approached its sad, inert form, I recalled how confident I once was of its strength, how sure of its permanence in this landscape. The roots that should have held it fast were ripped clean from the surface of the earth. Like the sturdy mother I once hoped to be, this tree had given in to weakness.

Elinor was hopping across the tussocks towards me.

'Look, Mummy, look!'

In her fists were the fattest, whitest field mushrooms you've ever seen.

'How many children do you have?'

The amount of times that question gets asked, as you wait at the school gate, or stand around in the chilly playground. On moving house, I had intended to avoid talking about Imogen. But faced with having to lie, it was a different matter. I felt I owed it to her to be truthful, to acknowledge her presence in our family. So I tried.

'Two. The other one lives with a carer in Abingdon; she's badly brain-damaged.'

The mums got all het up; they didn't know where to put themselves. Their innocent bit of chit-chat had become a big embarrassment. I must be their nightmare – the thing that kept them awake at night when they were pregnant. Maybe they were pregnant now. They were flustered; I could see they wanted to run away, and some of them did. Truly, they turned on their heels and fled.

I tried lying: 'Just the one' kept life simple. But if Ellie was within earshot, I was in trouble. 'No, Mummy,' she interjected, 'you've got two children – me and Immie. She's nearly one and a half.' Oh dear, yes, silly me, I'd plain forgotten.

When she went on a play date, I got in a bit of a panic – some-how I had to let the parents know before she did. Otherwise, next time I saw them, they would take me aside, tactfully confidential: 'We weren't sure whether to believe her or not, but . . .'

One day at the playground, I was sitting on a bench, gossiping away, when little Isaac came running round the side of the climb-ing frame. 'Mummy,' he shouted, 'what's brain damage?' Ellie appeared behind him, sheepish. I told our tale as economically as I could, aware that I had been chatting to this woman for weeks without revealing any of it. The boy asked a few more questions, but the atmosphere was decidedly cool. I sensed the barrier of difference that had risen between us.

On the way home, Ellie was pensive.

'I think I'm going to stop telling people about Immie,' she said.

As time goes on, I become more practised in anticipating people's reactions and fielding them. Sometimes when they hear my story there is some association in their own lives – a difficult birth, a sick child, disabilities borne. On rare occasions, I find myself talking to a woman whose baby is elsewhere: who does not see her child because of money difficulties, mental problems, a divorce; the refugee who left her children in Zimbabwe. I am glad to find her – we know one another's fragility, the wound we hide. There are tears in our eyes as we listen to the other woman's story; there is silence. We remind each other that our children are probably better off like this, whatever its effect has been on us.

I imagine how lonely it must have been for my great-grandmother. I search for information about her, but she has left no letters, no diary, nothing to tell us why she abandoned her daughter. Perhaps there was a good reason; perhaps she feared that she would fail her, one day smash her head against the wall. And having abandoned her, maybe she felt that cutting all ties with her daughter was the only way to survive. For both of them.

Whatever her reasons, my experience with Immie has taught me about connections between mothers and daughters, how feelings pass from one to the other, even through generations. I feel very fortunate that the social workers, the counsellor and others have engaged with my emotions and, without judgement, helped me. In turn, I want to halt the legacy of 'She just didn't give a damn', as I imagine that abandoning her daughter left my great-grandmother with a deep wound. I now believe that she felt the torment of her abandoned child in herself, but for her stiff-upper-lip generation there was nowhere to express it.

In November 2003 I became pregnant again – it was five months after the miscarriage, exactly a year after putting Immie into care. Within a few weeks, I was visiting the JR's specialist maternity unit, watching my second heartbeat flash on and off the radiologist's screen. They said it was strong, that the tiny new life inside me looked unlikely to miscarry. But I felt strangely removed; I did not sing or talk to it, or lie in the bath and wait for the growing foetus's movements as I had done previously. No, this time I couldn't afford to bond with the baby inside me, just in case . . . That would have to happen later, once I knew it was safely outside my womb.

The pregnancy coincided with my getting to the top of the waiting list for NHS counselling. Imogen's neurologist had referred me to the counselling centre several months before, at my request. The weekly family counselling with Jay had run its course; the charity had its own waiting list of desperate mothers needing our slot. But I wanted to continue my regular bouts of Immie-mourning. Everyone around me assumed that after a year I had got over the worst; indeed, I dearly wanted to move on. But I had discovered the second year of bereavement to be lonelier and more erratic than the first. I still needed somewhere to go and blub.

Once a week, cared for by my thoughtful counsellor, I could value my tears. I saw them as my safety valve, releasing the loss and the anxiety before they could overwhelm me. The oestrogen pumping through my pregnant veins heightened such emotions; as my belly swelled, the terror of Immie's birth and its consequences were constantly on my mind. Weeping in front of the counsellor, an NHS employee, was one way to cope. Her very presence proved that the Health Service did care about me and my baby. And once I had got through this next birth, I looked forward to having no more need of her.

A more habitual coping mechanism was to keep busy. The new child's arrival was a natural deadline for work on the Indian theatre book, and I strove to complete it in time. Though I still did not sing, I found myself hungry for live music, organising a raft of babysitters so Jay and I could spend evenings in concert halls and clubs. Jay got a commission to write a new opera for a London company about the recent *Columbia* space shuttle disaster, when the whole crew had perished on their return to earth. The emotional focus of his interpretation was a female astronaut who had received a Good Luck card from her son with a picture of an angel falling through the sky. Her story was all about risk taking, of needing but leaving her child. I agreed to direct the show and was soon caught up in its evolution, spending long hours in Jay's studio, poring over word-settings and dramatic structure. These activities harked back to our pre-baby days, and we relished their revival.

Imogen was settled with Tania; all of us felt secure in our novel extended family. Now I could begin searching for positive, practical outlets for my feelings about her. With the rejuvenation of my theatre-directing skills came the potential of making them useful to her world. I got in touch with the Oxford Playhouse and asked for a meeting with the Director. By the time I left, she had committed to staging fund-raising events in her venue. First off, she would take a collection for my counselling charity after each performance of that season's panto. In February 2004, Ellie and I went along to the theatre for a photo call with the local newspaper. We stood on the pavement outside, holding between us an outsized cheque with the takings emblazoned on it – £2,000.

The pregnancy seemed to alter my attitude to Immie, releasing me from some of the inertia that had grown up around her visits. Though I still restricted them to one day a week, I determined to enter her world more fully. Tania put me in touch with a local charity that held workshops for disabled children and their families, and I booked the whole family in for a 'fun day'. It was a half-hour drive out of town, in the middle of sweeping arable fields. The playground had swings with huge red plastic seats in which Immie's body could be supported. The brand-new roundabout was big enough for her wheelchair to enter and be fixed in place. Jay took hold of the bars and pushed, round and round on its smooth axis, watching Immie lean her head back into the wind and the 'O'-shaped mouth widen into her grin.

Indoors, a group of profoundly disabled children and their families were sitting around drinking coffee. There were a couple of girls in wheelchairs in the corner with their mothers; they looked older than Immie, but just as incapacitated. I went over to join them. The conversation was about drugs. On the mums chattered about which anticonvulsant cocktail worked the best, how often they had to administer the emergency mega-dose – a technical language like no other. They didn't make it sound particularly highfaluting; their conversation was totally relaxed – the equivalent of other mothers' chats about school studies, or

friendships. The trouble for me was that I was not knowledge-
able enough about my daughter to join in. I just sat there,
stroking Immie's cheek, smiling inanely. I thought of Rachel
with her daughter in London and my once imagining being part
of their world. Instead, mine is a secret community – mums who
give their children up. Sixteen per cent, according to the paediatrician who advised me. I got in contact with one of them, the
woman who did it thirty years ago. But where are all the rest?

In the hall, the workshop leaders spread out a parachute silk,
familiar to Elinor and me from toddler groups. Some adults and
able-bodied siblings lifted up the edges, and the disabled children
were laid on crash-mats beneath, the colourful dome gently waft-
ing above their heads. I lay next to Immie, holding her hand,
wondering whether she could see anything. She seemed to sense
the movement of the air around her, and the sound of our voices.
There was a set of tubular bells to the side, and someone began
hitting them. As the resonance reached us, she smiled.

Another mother was crouched on all fours, straddling her
prostrate daughter. She was supporting her own weight in one
arm, but with the other she pulled a floppy little hand up around
her neck. Once it was in place, she leant down to get the other
one. But she had let go of the original, and it thudded onto the
mat. Now that she had the second hand at her neck, she tried to
hook up the first one, but she was not fast enough. Again and
again she failed in her Sisyphean task. And all she wanted was a
cuddle.

I wondered whether this was one of those families in the
MENCAP survey who say they are at breaking point. Although
the mother put a brave face on it here, back home things might
be very different.

Later on that day, the music therapists welcomed us to their
workshop with guitars and microphones. Having collaborated
with musicians every day of our working lives, Jay and I were in
our element. A couple of families were sitting round in a circle
with disabled kids in their mothers' laps; I took Immie out of her
chair and joined them. Jay sat next to us with Ellie.

The guitarist was going from one disabled child to the next, singing. He leant in towards Immie and improvised a little song: 'Imogen, I-mo-gen, the lovely I-mo-gen.' Sentimental tears pricked at my ducts – it was such a lovely name. But its bearer couldn't care less; her head was lolling down onto her chest. They arranged a microphone on a stand in front of us and retreated to one side of the room behind a mixing desk. It didn't look as though Immie was going to take up the opportunity to sing, but Ellie was game. She leant forward and called, 'I-mee,' and the speakers echoed back at us with added reverb. Then in a more sing-song intonation, 'I-mee, where *are* you?'

I tilted myself back in the chair and placed my palm against Imogen's forehead, drawing her up against me. Her eyes were open, blinking. She heard her sister's call, as if from far off across the hills. I could feel the muscles in her back tensing, and saw her lips begin to part.

'Agh,' she went.

A burst of noise, a straining sound; she pushes deep from her diaphragm. Her legs push out as she does so, but her arms are surprisingly relaxed. Her chin is tilted upwards, as if there is some urge to communicate.

'Agh.' It is definitely not crying, the only noise she ever had cause to make before. No, there is no distress at all. This is a very deliberate exclamation, it is Immie's voice.

'I–mee,' sings Elinor.

'Agh.'

'I–mee,' again.

'Agh.'

She doesn't leave any silence between the end of Elinor's call and her response. She is absolutely on the beat of a regular four-time rhythm. And now I can hear tonality too: if Ellie's voice is high, then so is hers, if it is low, then she adjusts down. Sometimes her sound is bang on the note, again and again.

When Ellie gets bored, the musicians at their sound desk take over, mixing in an echo of Immie's voice with the calls they have recorded: 'Imee – Agh – where are you? Agh – Imee.' The layered sisters' voices on the sound loop are the orchestra, whilst Imogen performs her live solo above it.

The clinical negligence case rambled on. Our lawyers got the records from the JR at last, and began their research employing expert witnesses. The Legal Services Commission coughed up tens of thousands of pounds to fund it. The midwifery expert came up with a string of criticisms of the way the professionals had behaved on the night of Imogen's birth, compiling copious notes to support her judgement. The obstetrics consultant had a more difficult job assessing whether Immie's brain damage had been caused by any negligence. His hypothetical best-case scenario concluded that, had I been taken to the JR in an ambulance, it would have taken a good half-hour or more to check me in and diagnose what was going on. A Caesarean section would eventually have brought my baby into the world between five and ten minutes earlier than her actual birth had done. It was going to be difficult, though not impossible, to prove that the brain damage had happened in those few minutes.

I might have pursued the case. I might have employed another expert witness to come up with more favourable hypothetical timings. Now that I no longer had to nurse my sick child, I could imagine driving myself through five or six years of legal battle for her, and at the end of it receiving millions of pounds from the NHS coffers. But how would the compensation money actually improve things?

Public services already pay out vast sums for her care, without the courts forcing them to do so. Having suffered an economy birth, Imogen is now getting first-class recompense. Her equipment, drugs and foster care I estimate to cost well over £30,000 a year. She sees countless specialists: she attends regular clinics with the nutritionist, the neurologist, the orthopaedic surgeon and others; there are specialists to keep an eye on her incontinence, her wonky teeth (disintegrating fast because of a mixture of medication and stomach acid), her dodgy digestion, her seriously limited eyesight, her erratic respiratory system . . . And so on. At home, she has visits from physiotherapists, occupational therapists, wheelchair experts, all sorts of educational experts, nurses and social workers.

But central to her life is her foster carer. Tania is in touch with all these people and knows better than any of them what she needs. I could not imagine some fancy set-up with streams of expensive carers being an improvement. With Imogen's profound inability to communicate, she is better off with one person who can connect and intuit what is best for her. That Social Services have found her someone with Tania's humour, practicality and intelligence seems nothing short of a miracle.

How could I ever have thought that a foster carer might mistreat my baby? It's not just that from the start I judged Tania totally trustworthy. I know now how rigorously she is scrutinised. Her social worker visits a minimum of once a month; Immie's social worker comes every three months, and there is an unannounced visit every twelve months. Each time, the house is inspected: are there poisonous plants in the garden or dangerous additions to the decor? Tania has to keep a diary of Imogen's health and welfare, reporting any accidents or exceptional occurrences to her Social Service overseers.

In return for all this external control, Tania is provided with the support she needs. When Imogen first came to live with her, the local authority employed an extra helper for three evenings a week and one morning. It was not an enormous amount, but still more than twice what I would have received as her (unscrutinised) birth parent. And because Tania is a single mum and a recipient of state allowances, they cannot deny her need. If there is a shortage of carers (as is often the case), she is prioritised. If she demanded more help, they would have to provide it. Social Services understand how important it is that the fostering placement does not break down.

The fostering and adoption panel looked at our paperwork and decided that Imogen should stay put. I thought that perhaps Tania should adopt Imogen in order to ensure stability in the long term. It now seemed academic to me whether she should adopt or foster – it was no longer a case of giving up my baby, simply of making the law work for us all. But then I realised that Tania's fostering status ensured the best care package for Immie; it would be madness for her to adopt and thereby lose the support.

For a long while I just couldn't believe my luck. I kept on thanking Tania: when we talked on the phone, when I went to her house or delivered Immie back after her Thursday visits. Thank you. Thank you. But she would look awkward, seldom responding even with the expected 'No problem' or 'That's OK'. She obviously didn't like being thanked. Perhaps she was pointing out that she worked not for my sake, but for Immie's; as a rule, fosterers save unmothered children. But I wanted her to know that she had managed to save a whole family.

In May 2004, Jay's opera went on in London – as colourful and uncompromising as any of our previous productions. And on the very same weekend, at my instigation, the Oxford Playhouse hosted a major fund-raising enterprise for Helen House, the local children's hospice. I had known the hospice since long before Immie; when I was at school in the 1980s, its charismatic founder came to talk to us about her work. She explained how she had created a place for children with a 'life-shortening condition' to come and have fun, be adored, for their families to get a break. A charitable foundation, it received no funding from public services. I remember pledging all the income from our school fête to Sister Frances' sick children.

The hospice is the only place where Tania can get respite: fourteen nights a year, divided up as she chooses. As I discovered when searching for help after Immie's diagnosis, the local authority resource centres (recently radically reduced in number) offer families respite only once the child is seven. In Imogen's case, she may never be eligible for that help because she is too needy; their staff lack sufficient nursing skills. As in many residential centres (including the full-time ones), if a 'special' child like mine becomes sick whilst staying there, she has to be sent home. But at the hospice it is the opposite – children there really are given special care.

Helen House is hidden on a side street behind one of the busiest, shabbiest roads in Oxford. Grocers, cycle shops and cafés spill out onto its pavements. Buses chase one another to the next crowded stop, vying for space with cyclists and cars and people doing dodgy deals. Taxis rush past the hospice on their complicated short cut to the next job. But behind its bright-red front door and white picket fence, all is loving and tranquil. Along the corridors, bright atria send shafts of sunlight down in welcome. The floors are clad in sea-blue carpet, the fire doors guarded by handsome black and white rocking horses. There is the smell of home cooking, and in the play area are more glamorous Barbie toys than Ellie has ever set eyes on. When you reach your child's bedroom (named after a tree), her first name is written up on the noticeboard in bold, colourful letters.

During Immie's stays at Helen House, she gets seriously pampered. Her carer files and paints her fingernails as immaculately as any beautician. She has her hair washed, which includes a scalp massage; then it is plaited up with glittery ribbons. She is taken for a float or two in the hydrotherapy pool, lounges on the lawn or in the sensory room, takes part in as many music therapy sessions as possible. And she is certain to receive lots of cuddles (something absolutely forbidden in the resource centres). Doctors and nurses are available round the clock, with careful attention given to specific medical problems. They offer support and advice to Tania every day of the year, even when Imogen is not resident. And if she is recovering from a hospital stay or becomes suddenly extremely ill, an emergency bed is always available.

There is also the room where she can die. During my introductory tour, my guide said I needn't go in there. But I wanted to; I wanted to feel its peace, the spirit of all the children who had died there. I know that Helen House provides all sorts of bereavement counselling and support for siblings and parents. I have met the chaplain – as gentle and concerned as all the other carers there. But these days, the idea of Immie's dying is less significant than the fun we can all have getting there. When I first heard this philosophy – that the hospice was a place to get the most out of children's shortened lives, it was a huge watershed for me. I understood for the first time that envisaging her death, longing for it even, did not prohibit me from joy in Imogen's life.

Hence a fund-raising evening of comedy and music called *Childish Things*. My brother is a successful actor; he wanted to do something to help his niece. So I badgered him about creating a lucrative gig, and he managed to cajole his famous friends into performing on the Oxford Playhouse stage. Their hilarious show could have packed out the auditorium several times over; it raised more than £40,000 for our cause. And Helen House decided to continue staging the event every year, creating a growing body of publicity, cash and many, many laughs.

Friday, 18 June 2004

On the day before Immie's second birthday I was admitted to the JR Women's Centre, eight months' pregnant. A small bleed had convinced the obstetrics professor that I should stay in hospital under close supervision until the birth. He escorted me to the ward desk and introduced me to the midwives: 'This is our VIP patient,' he said, firmly.

I was escorted to my own room by the woman who had been the midwifery representative at Imogen's internal inquiry meeting. I didn't ask why she had chosen to leave officialdom and take up nursing again. She asked after Imogen and I gave my usual response: 'She's as well as someone with her condition can be – beautifully cared for.'

My room was a floor below where I had stayed after Immie's birth. I lay on the bed, looking up at the stained ceiling tiles and thought of those poor sods on the level above – Level Seven, the tragedy level.

When the Professor of Obstetrics turned up, he said, 'You're lucky to be here this month; once the school holidays begin, this special care unit will be closed.'

'Why?'

'Because the Trust saves money by employing midwives on flexible contracts and they all want to take their holidays at the same time.'

'And what about the patients?'

'During July and August they just have to join everyone else on the open ward downstairs.'

Level Five – the place Virginia Nicholas used to refer to when she boasted of how much better her special care babies fared. I crossed my fingers that Level Six was indeed the lucky one.

'So now I'm here, what do you want me to do?' I asked.

'There's nothing you can do, I'm afraid. But having you here means we can deal with an emergency. If the same thing were to occur again, we could get you into surgery in five minutes.'

'And the symptoms?'

'You know what they were last time; you can let us know immediately anything like that happens. But some women with recurrent ante-partum haemorrhage have no symptoms at all.'

Forget solo travels in faraway places, forget reckless driving or kamikaze cycle rides: this pregnancy was the biggest risk I had ever taken. As the baby asserted herself, wriggling and kicking at my womb, I was increasingly burdened by this hazarding of someone else's life inside me. For the last seven weeks of the pregnancy, I made regular Tuesday morning visits to the hospital, queuing up with the diabetics and the red-faced women with soaring blood pressure to present my urine sample at a little booth. There must have been hundreds of us, great big fat worried mums, sitting for hours in the same waiting room where I had so recently waited for meetings with Virginia Nicholas. Some of my fellow baby-bearers sat calmly knitting or sewing; we were all a bit drunk on excess oestrogen. I tended to grab *Hello!* magazine and disappear into its folds.

I was reconciled to joining the hospital machine again. I was as patient as could be, waiting my turn to see the blood pressure nurse, the phlebotomist, the consultant, the professor, the radiologist, the second radiologist . . . I couldn't afford to indulge worries I might once have had about exposing my baby to too much ultrasound. I knew I was getting the best possible care. The whole exercise might take until lunchtime, but I always came away from the clinic less anxious, more able to get through the week ahead without panicking. I parked the car as close to the house as possible, facing in the direction of the hospital so that we might speed there at any time.

They offered to induce labour at thirty-seven weeks, one week before the point at which my abruption had happened last time. I understood that it would be safer to have the baby early, but I couldn't face going through labour again. It wasn't the pain, it was the responsibility of keeping my child safe on the way out – the same journey that had done for Immie. No: better to hand over to the clinicians. Now that I was subject to the best possible care, I wanted to trust them all the way. With an elective Caesarean I relinquished any possibility of control; I was simply a passive patient. And thinking tactically, as the clinical negligence case had taught me, anything that went wrong could be proven incontrovertibly as the Health Authority's fault.

Thursday, 1 July 2004

The morning of my operation arrived, clear and calm. It was a different month from Imogen's birth; that was good. I rather regretted that this pregnancy was to end, or maybe I was just nervous about the op. Jay arrived early and I posed naked, but for my white surgical stockings, for him to take final photos of baby-bearing me. We had decided not to have any music on the sound system during the birth – we had none during Ellie's or Immie's. What I had not considered was how quiet things could be through the laborious preparatory process. When the anaesthetist admitted that the silence was making him nervous, I suggested we turn on the radio.

Once the surgeon and her team arrived, I asked for silence again – I was intent on hearing only the baby's arrival. Blue surgical gowns, chrome machines all around, silver-blue light filling the room, a circle of bright overhead spotlights: they couldn't have created a more sci-fi environment for a twenty-first-century birth. And the noise – a suction machine like a dentist's, sucking away my bodily fluids. At least I couldn't hear the slicing.

Then suddenly the baby – a girl – was flying silently over the puppet-theatre curtain that masked my lower body. The paediatrician at the resuscitation table behind me must have taken her. Why? What was wrong? And then the voice – thank God, my child mewled, or rather she clucked, just like a hen. Face down, there she was on the patch of skin between my breasts. I could feel a greasy mop of hair, and her limbs sliding about on top of me. She seemed to be trying to dig her way back in, poor thing. And I cried. Of course I cried, despite all the emotion-deadening drugs they had pumped into me. I turned to Jay and moaned, 'This is what Immie should have had.'

I don't remember exactly how it happened, but by the time my bed had been wheeled to its place on the ward, the baby was gone again. 'We've had to take her to SCBU,' said the midwife, 'for observation. Your husband is with her.'

'Why?'

'I think she might be having breathing difficulties. What have you decided to call her?'

'Beatrice.'

'Are you OK?'

'I'm alone.' And I wept again. It was that terrible emptiness of Immie's birth, this time with tears. This time, surely my heart would break. The midwife scurried off in search of my records. Someone else came and asked whether I would I like to see a photo of baby Beatrice. I shook my head. It felt as dead as the fat white legs spread out on the bed in front of me.

And then, round the corner of the curtains, the sudden entrance of a doctor. Through my morphine haze, it takes a moment to place the familiar, smiling figure. Despite the morphine, I feel a tightening in my gut. Can it really be her? Immie's neonatal paediatrician, Virginia Nicholas.

'How long will she be in SCBU?' I ask, feebly.

'I'm afraid only Beatrice knows the answer to that,' is her answer, before she exits swiftly back to her baby factory.

Jay arrives to hold my hand and say there is nothing we can do, just wait. She is on a drip, in an incubator . . . But my mother has called: Elinor wants to come and see the new baby. I promised that she could.

When Ellie turns up, Jay lifts me into a wheelchair and she walks alongside, grave and protective, as we make our way to SCBU. The same wooden half-door, the same etiquette, the same washing ritual – everything exactly as it was two years before. We round the corner into the corridor ward and there in front of us, in the very same position as Immie's, is our incubator. The nurse brings out her charge, wrapped tight in a blanket, her left hand all wired up and strapped to a splint, and she places her in my lap.

Slowly I lift the bundle upwards and tilt the screwed–up little face towards the light. I draw the folds of the blanket away from her skin. Such frailty. The cool of the air disturbs her, and slowly her eyes open – first one and then the other, squinting up at me. It's a grumpy look, as if to say, 'Who are you, disturbing me?' And then I begin to sing; it has been such a long time. Gently, easily, the melody is flowing through me: '*Twinkle, twinkle little star . . .*'

Easter 2007

WE ARE GETTING MARRIED, at last. After so many years of being too independent, too busy or too hassled for a wedding, I am doing the traditional thing. I am going to walk down the aisle of the local church with my man, our three little girls close behind. Ellie has chosen the bridesmaids' frocks: three identical handkerchief dresses in duck-egg blue with sequins twinkling around the skirts. I have no idea what I shall wear, nor Jay, but we are planning a glorious love party. I want to create an invitation using a picture of our three girls.

Immie has been with her foster carer for more than four years now. We still have her over every couple of weeks, often on a Friday when I am home with two-year-old Beatrice. Tania delivers her to the door, enthroned in her wheelchair, chest held high by the moulding. Her hair is tied up with pretty velvet bows; she is wearing the frilly skirt they bought on a recent trip to Disneyland (even a long-haul flight to Florida can't faze Tania). Beatrice and Ellie are delighted to receive identical skirts to match their lovely sister's.

I am always struck by Imogen's beauty; maybe it is because she has no complicated thoughts to spoil her features. As Tania points out, her being a beautiful child is a great asset in a life of complete dependency. Surely such prettiness inspires her carers to be especially caring. And with any luck it prevents complete strangers from being frightened off. We forget how frightening disability can be for people who have no experience of it.

As I lay Imogen on the sofa, Beatrice is clambering on top of her.

'*My* sister!' she cries, determined to win the competition no one else is having. She wraps her arms around Immie's torso and kisses her demonstratively. 'My little big sister,' she says.

Ellie hangs back. Is she just a dreamy seven-year-old, or is she feeling sad? I often wonder whether the trauma she went through during Immie's first months has left its mark. She says she can't remember anything about it, not even the crying. She used to insist that she never intended to have children, and I imagined it was because she feared the 'terrible accident' happening to her baby. But since Beatrice's birth she has changed her mind and now says she wants eight. Maybe that means the impact of Immie's birth has subsided, and she can accept her for what she is, not for what she might have been. That has been everyone's journey. Except for Beatrice, of course, who simply arrived in the world with a 'little big sister'.

'Do laughing! Do laughing!' pleads Bea. Jay takes Imogen in his lap and lifts up her shirt, tickling her hard across the ribs and under her arms. Immie goes floppy as a rag doll, starts to smile and then launches into full-blown laughter. It is irregular, chesty, rather like a dirty chuckle. We all find it hilarious.

We are taking Immie to Helen House, where she is to stay the weekend. It's a short walk away. Maybe we will find somewhere there to take the photo for the wedding invitation. Jay escorts Ellie on her scooter. Beatrice squeezes between me and the wheelchair, stretching up to the handles and trying to push it along the pavements. I feel proud that having a dependent sibling brings out such determined protectiveness in our youngest, just as it has always done in Elinor. A couple of lads outside the pub gaze at us as we pass. 'Cool buggy!' one of them calls out, and I grin.

We're not the perfectly symmetrical family, I think. We are obviously imperfect and flawed. That's real life. I'm proud to have such a disabled daughter. Her complete vulnerability, her total inability, is shouting to the world: *aren't you all like this? All of you fragile people? Underneath that toughness, this is what it's really like to be human!*

But the street is narrow. Ten paces on, there is a row of cars parked on the pavement, and I have to force the wheelchair off the kerb into the middle of the road. Now I am pushing Immie in the street, up and down the speed bumps, using her well-sprung chair as a shield for my able-bodied child. A people carrier honks at us. What does the woman at the wheel expect me to do? The pavement is totally blocked. She is the strong one, whose children have abilities; can't she make a bit of space for children who don't? The horn honks again.

'Fuck off!' I spit. And remind myself that my able-bodied children's lives must be spent standing up for themselves in that woman's world.

We approach Helen House through the gardens. The sun is shining, the birds are twittering, the herbaceous borders are immaculately tended: this place always manages to hold its own, exuding love and protectiveness even when the rest of the world seems not to care. For this weekend's stay, Immie's tree-named room is 'Lime'; her carer is waiting there with huge Easter eggs for Ellie and Bea. Taking Immie's hand in welcome, she tells me she feels more rigid than usual – her fist so tight it will not open. Perhaps she should be getting a higher dose of muscle relaxant. I have no idea, but doubtless the Helen House doctor will. In the meantime, the nurse inserts rolls of surgical gauze under her fingers to prevent her nails from cutting into the palms.

As Imogen grows older, there are more and more problems like this to deal with. Now nearly five, she needs more than a dozen medicines a day, most of them administered both morning and night: drugs to stop her muscles seizing up; drugs to stop her fitting; drugs to stop her dribbling; drugs to stop her vomiting; drugs to make her poo; drugs to make her sleep.

I don't have to administer them, but as the sole person with parental responsibility I am still in the front line for Imogen's medical care. Every operation she has, I must sign forms and listen to specialists explaining the risks. When she was three, the nutrition prof was proved correct and she lost her ability to suck. The gastrostomy and another, associated surgical process followed, with all sorts of nasty side effects. But now the tube is doing its work – drugs and liquid feed are pumped straight into her stomach.

A year or so ago, the orthopaedic consultant became concerned about her hips. Her arms and legs in spasm are continually pulling against the joints. At night, she lies in a sleeping system, a board with moulded sections from which her limbs cannot escape. By day, Tania is constantly massaging her in order to relax the muscles, trying to prevent her lengthening body from becoming too deformed. She had a minor operation last year, freezing the muscles in her thigh to try to prevent the hip from popping out. But now the specialist says she needs four hours of major surgery, if her epilepsy allows for the general anaesthetic . . . Oh God. I can't take it in. I try to pretend it's nothing to do with me; were it not for my legal responsibility, I would leave it all to Tania. She's cool-headed; she knows so much better than I do what Imogen requires.

This is one major, practical reason why Tania should have parental responsibility. On my marrying Jay, it is something he will automatically attain (at last). But it is Tania who really needs it. She should be able to get on with caring for Imogen without having to ask my permission all the time. With the new Adoption Act of 2004, we now have the opportunity to grant Tania legal status. We are planning to use the newly invented 'Special Guardianship Order' in order to give her parental responsibility alongside Jay and me. If she can negotiate with the local authority to retain her fosterer's care package, then she will become Immie's legal guardian. The order will provide Immie with security and Tania with the power to make major decisions about her upbringing. Our daughter will then have three legal parents – an officially extended family.

I want to stay in touch; I want Imogen to gain all that she can from her birth family. But I know that Tania's is her first home. Some time ago, a neurologist's report came in the post, stating that when Tania left the room during a consultation Immie seemed to show 'stranger anxiety'. In other words, the doctor judged that she had attached uniquely to her. I think this might well be so. I often feel it when I take her back to Tania's place – how she seems to become calmer, more contented. And for a couple of years now Tania has been performing her whistle. It is a three-note call, to the rhythm of 'I-mo-gen', two high notes and then one a third lower. When Immie hears it she leans back, her feet kicking outwards, and smiles. Tania laughs and repeats the tune, and Immie's mouth gapes even wider with joy.

I am not jealous. For me, these little things would never be sufficient; I would be forever longing for more. The emotional connection I had with Immie in my womb will never come to fruition in her life. And this loss is what I come back to every time people ask why I cannot care for her, why I gave her up. I tell them that I cannot look after my daughter because I cannot have a meaningful enough relationship with her.

The ties are still loosening. In the past few months I have started talking about Imogen 'going home' to Tania's house. When I talk about Tania, I call her Immie's 'foster mum' rather than 'foster carer'. Sometimes I think of myself not as Immie's mother at all, but as an aunt or even a more distant relation. I could simply be the means by which Tania's child came into the world – a surrogate mum.

Ellie is calling: 'Come and see the snow tree, we've found a snow tree!' I follow her into the meadow beyond the hospice building, in time to see Beatrice remove her last bit of clothing. She is standing naked on a white carpet beneath the spreading branches of a flowering cherry tree. Petals drift about her on the breeze, just like a light shower of snow. Now she is scooping up the petals from the ground and rubbing them onto her tummy; maybe she likes the smell.

I show Ellie how to make a snow angel by lying on my back and moving my arms up and down, my legs in and out. She joins me on the grass and we each sweep away the petals, creating the shadows of wings and skirts out of the whiteness. Gingerly we curl up and away to see what we have done. There they lie, side by side, our angel selves.

Where's Immie? We must bring her to our bower and take that photo for the wedding invitation. The petals look like confetti in our hair. Here she comes – Jay is carrying her through the garden towards us.

Acknowledgements

I WOULD LIKE to thank everyone who appears in this memoir for making it possible. There are many others who do not feature, but whose influence was essential – special thanks to Jo and Esther, Lizzie and Penny, Annie and Gitte, Rob and Jenny.

In the publishing world, I owe a great debt of thanks to my agent, Victoria Hobbs at A. M. Heath, and to Sara Fisher for covering for her during her maternity leave. You have both been impeccable in your support and efficiency. Thanks, too, to Anya Serota at John Murray for launching me on this journey, and to Eleanor Birne and Helen Hawksfield for guiding me so dexterously to its conclusion.

Finally, a big thank you to Lisa for her conviction, and to Jay for being there every step of the way.

The author and the publisher would like to thank the following for permission to reproduce copyright material: extract from 'You're' by Sylvia Plath, from *Sylvia Plath Collected Poems*, published by Faber & Faber Ltd, © the Estate of Sylvia Plath (1981); lyrics from 'Baby I Love You', words and music by Ronnie Shannon, (1967), © Fourteenth Hour Music Corp/Pundit Music Inc, USA, reproduced by permission of EMI Songs Ltd, London WC2H OQP.